PITT LATIN AMERICAN SERIES

PITT LATIN AMERICAN SERIES
Cole Blasier, Editor

ARGENTINA IN THE TWENTIETH CENTURY
David Rock, Editor

BARRIOS IN ARMS: REVOLUTION IN SANTO DOMINGO
José A. Moreno

BEYOND THE REVOLUTION: BOLIVIA SINCE 1952
James M. Malloy and Richard S. Thorn, Editors

BOLIVIA: THE UNCOMPLETED REVOLUTION
James M. Malloy

CONSTRUCTIVE CHANGE IN LATIN AMERICA
Cole Blasier, Editor

CUBA, CASTRO, AND THE UNITED STATES
Philip W. Bonsal

FEMALE AND MALE IN LATIN AMERICA: ESSAYS
Ann Pescatello, Editor

PANAJACHEL: A GUATEMALAN TOWN IN THIRTY-YEAR
PERSPECTIVE
Robert E. Hinshaw

PUERTO RICO AND THE UNITED STATES, 1917-1933
Truman R. Clark

REVOLUTIONARY CHANGE IN CUBA
Carmelo Mesa-Lago, Editor

SAN BERNARDINO CONTLA: MARRIAGE AND FAMILY
STRUCTURE IN A TLAXCALAN MUNICIPIO
Hugo G. Nutini

SELECTED LATIN AMERICAN ONE-ACT PLAYS
Francesca Colecchia and Julio Matas, Editors and Translators

SOCIETY AND EDUCATION IN BRAZIL
Robert J. Havighurst and J. Roberto Moreira

PUERTO RICO

and the

UNITED STATES,

1917–1933

PUERTO RICO

and the

UNITED STATES,

1917-1933

Truman R. Clark

UNIVERSITY OF PITTSBURGH PRESS

Library of Congress Cataloging in Publication Data

Clark, Truman R.   birth date
   Puerto Rico and the United States, 1917–1933.

   (Pitt Latin American series)
Bibliography: p. 219
   Includes index.
   1. Puerto Rico—Politics and government—1898–1952.
2. Puerto Rico—Relations (general) with the United
States. 3. United States—Relations (general) with
Puerto Rico. 4. Puerto Rico—Economic conditions.
I. Title.
F1975.C54   320.9′7295′05   74-26019
ISBN 0-8229-3299-7

Grateful acknowledgment is made to the following, who have granted the
author permission to quote material that appears in this book:

Merritt Lane, Jr., for a letter from Lindley M. Garrison.

John S. Holmes, of Holmes & Holmes, Attorneys and Counsellors of Law,
for a letter from John Sharp Williams.

Warren G. and George T. Harding, nephews of President Warren G. Harding,
for letters from the president.

For my parents, Harold and Lanore Clark

. . . Before the people of Porto Rico can be fully intrusted with self-government they must first learn the lesson of self-control and respect for the principles of constitutional government, which require acceptance of its peaceful decisions. This lesson will necessarily be slowly learned, because it is a matter not of intellectual apprehension, but of character and of acquired habits of thought and feeling. It would be of no use to present to the people of Porto Rico now a written constitution or frame of laws, however perfect, and tell them to live under it. They would inevitably fail without a course of tuition under a strong and guiding hand.

—Elihu Root, Secretary of War
Annual Report for 1899

Porto Rico and the Philippines are ours to have and to hold and to dispose of as Congress in its wisdom may see fit. If we retain them, a period of pupilage—a time for education—must be theirs, so that they may be fitted to understand and have the capacity to enjoy the rights of American citizenship.

—Senator George C. Perkins,
April 2, 1900

About the Author

Truman R. Clark has received degrees from Abilene Christian College, the University of Oregon, and Bryn Mawr College. After teaching at several junior colleges and the University of Pennsylvania (summer sessions), he joined the Department of History at Pepperdine University, where he is now Associate Professor and Chairman of the department.

He has read papers at the 1972 national meeting of the Organization of American Historians and the 1974 annual meeting of the Pacific Coast branch of the American Historical Association. Articles by him have appeared in *The Americas, Caribbean Studies,* and the *Pacific Historical Review.*

Dr. Clark lives in Los Angeles with his wife, Sally, and five children, Terry, Susie, Sherry, Timmy, and Sandy.

Contents

Figure

Preface

Little research and writing have been done concerning the relationship between Puerto Rico and the United States in this century. In part, this is because it has been a colonial relationship of one sort or another, and Puerto Rican historians have seemed to shy away from it in preference of the pre-1898 period of the island's history. This paucity of historical work on Puerto Rico as an American possession also reflects the high degree of specialization among United States historians: Latin Americanists have looked on the topic as not within their purview, while historians of twentieth-century America see it as Latin-American history. Historians in the United States have overlooked this area also because they accept—at least unconsciously—Samuel Flagg Bemis's concept of a "great aberration," and see anything about an overseas empire as belonging only to the turn of the century.

Puerto Rico's colonial status vis-à-vis the United States did not end in 1900 or 1917; Puerto Ricans often raise the very good question as to whether that status has yet ended. Certainly if one reads William Appleman Williams or Gordon K. Lewis,[1] one becomes aware of an enduring, although changing, nature of United States imperialism.

The period covered by this study, 1917 to 1933, should have been one of measured steps away from an imperial relationship. The Jones Act of 1917 theoretically changed the status of the island and its people from colony and colonial subjects to something else (it was never stated *what*). In fact, however, the period saw the opposite pattern develop—a careful structuring of the relationship between island and mainland so as to keep the *substance* of government in Yanqui hands.[2]

Just as the history of Puerto Rico in this century revolves around Washington and not San Juan, so the materials to document that history are now to be found primarily in the United States. This is not to say that there are no documents of great importance in Puerto Rico, for there are. But many of those materials are not available to historians, and possibly never will be. Perhaps the imperial relationship is largely at fault in this; perhaps a slightly paranoid fear of being hurt by the documents has made Puerto Rican political figures and their descendants reluctant to open the materials they have for general use by scholars.

Throughout this book, the name of the island has been spelled "Puerto" Rico, even though Americans were using the term "Porto" Rico until 1932 (see chapter 7 for a discussion of the problem). The exceptions to this usage are the instances when I have quoted a person who called it "Porto" Rico and have reproduced the names of documents, committees, companies, and the like.

Acknowledgments

Many people have helped to bring this book to completion, and I wish to thank them. I hope that the book is equal to their individual efforts. The personnel of several libraries and archives were invaluable, particularly Mr. James Howard and Mrs. Maria Joy of the National Archives, Miss Mary Wolfskill of the Manuscript Division of the Library of Congress, and Miss Andrea Durham of the Ohio State Historical Society. My research in Puerto Rico was greatly aided by Professor Henry Wells of the University of Pennsylvania and Professors Thomas Mathews and Aída Montilla de Negrón of the University of Puerto Rico. My thanks go to Mr. and Mrs. Lionel Epstein of Washington for their hospitality. Professors Arthur P. Dudden, Mary Maples Dunn, and Elizabeth Foster, all of Bryn Mawr College, played major roles in different ways during the dissertation phase of this study—and Arthur Dudden has contributed much since that time. I am grateful to the Women's Christian Temperance Union of Southern California for providing me with some research funds. Louise Craft of the University of Pittsburgh Press has greatly impressed me with the expertise she has applied to the production and editing of this book. Mrs. Mary Barton and Miss Mary Lou Knight were so competent as typists that I had absolutely no worries in that area of the work. My wife has played a greater role in the task of writing this book than she realizes.

PUERTO RICO

and the

UNITED STATES,

1917–1933

1 | From Spanish to United States Citizenship

During the years 1898 to 1917 Puerto Rico changed from a Spanish to an American colony. At the beginning of 1898 Puerto Ricans were Spanish citizens; the Puerto Rican governmental system was Spanish in its structures and practices; the insular economy was tied closely to Spain. In 1917 the Puerto Ricans became American citizens; the Puerto Rican government was American in form and function; and the United States had replaced Spain as the dominant force in the Puerto Rican economy. In only one area—the Hispanic-American culture of Puerto Rico—had Spain not been shoved aside by the brash yanquis as they entered into worldwide empire.

When the Spanish-American War brought Puerto Rico into the hands of the United States in 1898, the people of that island were interrupted in the first year of their only opportunity for self-government during four centuries of Spanish rule. In 1896 the Autonomist Party of Puerto Rico had sent a commission to Spain, where an alliance was made with Spanish liberals led by Práxedes Sagasta. When an assassination the next year suddenly brought Sagasta to power as prime minister of Spain, the bargain was consummated; in return for the support of the Puerto Rican Autonomists, Spain granted an autonomous constitution—or so it was called—to the island. (Spain was having enough troubles in Cuba, and wished to see Puerto Rico remain quiet and loyal.) It will never be known how much actual self-government would have been allowed the Puerto Ricans under the new arrangement, for hardly had elections been held early in 1898 when the United States went to war with Spain, and Puerto Rico was returned to military rule under General Manuel Macías.[1]

The "splendid little war" did not amount to much in Puerto Rico. American troops landed at Guánica on July 25, 1898, and on Au-

3

gust 14, General Nelson Miles left the island under the command of General John A. Brooke. During his short stay in Puerto Rico, General Miles did one thing that was long remembered and was the subject of bitter controversy. On July 28 he had "published generally" a letter or proclamation "To the Inhabitants of Puerto Rico," which stated that American forces came "bearing the banner of freedom" and desiring only to crush "the enemies of our country and yours." This proclamation also told the Puerto Ricans:

> We have not come to make war upon the people of a country that for centuries has been oppressed, but, on the contrary, to bring you protection, not only to yourselves but to your property, to promote your prosperity, and to bestow upon you the immunities and blessings of the liberal institutions of our Government.[2]

Over the years, these words by General Miles have been recalled as an example of the hypocritical nature of U.S. imperialism, as insincere rhetoric promising liberal treatment and governmental autonomy beyond what the United States really intended to grant the island.[3]

Until May 1, 1900, Puerto Rico was controlled by American military governors. In this period public sanitation, education, defense of law and order against roving bands of robbers, and relief work (after a destructive hurricane) added to the governors' problems. On the whole they did an excellent job, considering that they were military men, not trained civil administrators, and that they had no guidelines or precedents, no knowledge of Puerto Rican culture or politics, and very little knowledge of the Spanish language. On the negative side the military governors changed the governmental and judicial processes and personnel so often that Puerto Ricans were confused—perhaps in part because the governors themselves were confused. One of the governors, General Guy V. Henry, carried on a running battle with the Puerto Rican press which resulted in some very un-American suppression of newspapers.[4]

By 1900, the debate among Americans over imperialism had begun to wane, and the election of that year was *not* decided by the issue of imperialism.[5] By this time, the question concerning Puerto Rico was not—and perhaps never had been—whether or not to keep the island, but what kind of government to give it. What made this question important was the fact that the type of government provided for Puerto Rico would set a precedent for the other new possessions of the United States. The Philippine Islands, for example, where Americans were then fighting the people they had freed from Spanish control, were not yet ready for civil government. Puerto Rico was to lead the way; its civil government would be, in the phrase of Lyman Jay Gould, "the roots of American colonial policy."[6]

To provide a civil government for Puerto Rico, Congress needed information about the new possession. There were several sources available: the official reports of the three American military governors; the report of Henry K. Carroll, whom President McKinley had sent to Puerto Rico in 1898 to investigate conditions and make recommendations; and the report of the "Insular Commission," which carried on an investigation in 1899 for Secretary of War Russell Alger.[7] In December 1899 a new committee was formed in the Senate, the Committee on Pacific Islands and Porto Rico, with Joseph Benson Foraker as its chairman; this committee immediately began hearings to gather additional information on Puerto Rico.

From Senator Foraker's committee came two bills to give civil government to Puerto Rico, on January 3 and January 9, 1900, but neither of these bills moved very rapidly through the Senate. Meanwhile, Sereno Payne, chairman of the House Committee on Ways and Means, had introduced a bill labeled "a bill temporarily to provide revenues for relief of the Island of Puerto Rico, and for other purposes." This bill passed in the House of Representatives on February 28, and on March 1, Senator Foraker reported it to the Senate, where it was handed to his Committee on Pacific Islands and Porto Rico. When the bill was returned to the Senate for debate, it was a far more extensive measure than a simple revenue bill; Foraker's committee, with guidelines laid out by the McKinley administration, had transformed it into a bill for a civil government for Puerto Rico. Foraker never indicated who in the administration was responsible for molding the measure into a civil government bill, but Sereno Payne said many years later that it was Secretary of War Elihu Root who formulated the "Foraker Act."[8] On April 12, 1900, President McKinley signed it into law—a "temporary" civil government for Puerto Rico.

On only one basic point was the Foraker Act similar to the civil governments of the western territories of the continental United States from 1861 to 1912: these governments, like the new one for Puerto Rico, were formed by "organic acts" passed by Congress, not by constitutions written by the residents. In other fundamental ways Puerto Rico was accorded different treatment. According to Earl Pomeroy, the unique aspect of the American territories was their transitional nature—the fact that territorial governments were considered a step toward equal statehood in the Union.[9] This was the thing most obviously left out of the organic act for Puerto Rico.

Under the Foraker Act, the president of the United States appointed the governor of Puerto Rico and an eleven-man Executive Council. The act specified that five members of the council be Puerto Ricans, although there was no reason why all eleven of its members could not be natives. In practice, it was not until 1914 that more than five Puerto Ricans sat in this executive body. The Executive Council served both as the upper house of the Puerto Rican legislature and as the governor's cabinet, since six of its members were heads of executive departments. Until 1914 the six Americans in the council were always given these administrative posts, and the five Puerto Ricans held positions "without portfolio." The lower house of the legislature, the House of Delegates, was composed of thirty-five men popularly elected. The governor could veto any legislation; and if by a two-thirds vote in both houses a bill was passed over the governor's veto, the Congress of the United States could still nullify it. Thus, the United States controlled the legislative process of the Puerto Rican government. Because the majority of the men in the upper house were Americans (until 1914), there was never an occasion in which Congress found it necessary to rule on any bill passed in Puerto Rico.

Puerto Ricans were not made American citizens by the Foraker Act, although Senator Foraker had tried to have this done in the organic act.[10] They were instead given the rather vague status of "citizens of Porto Rico, and as such entitled to the protection of the United States." Even the name applied to their island was meaningless; "Porto Rico" was a non-Spanish name which became official by virtue of its use in the Treaty of Paris and in the final draft (but not the first) of the Foraker Act. It supplanted the ancient, and correct, "Puerto Rico" ("Rich Port") until 1932. Puerto Ricans were represented in the United States House of Representatives by a biennially elected resident commissioner, who could speak and propose bills, but not vote.

The Foraker Act provided that the insular government be financed at first by an application of 15 percent of the United States tariff rates to all goods entering Puerto Rico or shipped from the island to the United States (the Dingley Tariff of 1897 was then in force).[11] This was to be in effect only until March 1, 1902, or until a permanent plan for financing the Puerto Rican government could be devised. After the insular government prepared a revenue system sufficient to meet its operational needs (the so-called "Hollander plan" devised by Professor Jacob Hollander, who also reorganized the finances of the Dominican Republic in 1905), free trade was begun between the United States and Puerto Rico in 1901.

Political parties and issues were a major difference between the western continental territories of the United States and twentieth-century Puerto Rico. Whereas politics in the former were within the framework of the national parties and national issues, Puerto Rican politics were always strictly insular. They were dominated by the questions of Puerto Rico's status (with independence and statehood the original extremes of this issue), the related issue of autonomy, political patronage, and—under the Foraker Act—the problem of citizenship.

Status was the major political issue in Puerto Rico from 1900. American congressmen and presidents frequently said that it was an empty question stirred up by self-seeking politicians on the island.

This did not satisfy the Puerto Ricans. There were deep feelings on the island that the United States had promised the island either independence or statehood when it took Puerto Rico from Spain and when General Miles made his proclamation. The Foraker Act did not define Puerto Rico's status in regard to the United States; it did not call Puerto Rico a possession, a territory, or anything else (although it did say that the governor and the attorney general should each "have all the powers" of their respective offices in "the Territories of the United States").[12] This was no accidental oversight; Henry G. Curtis, one of the members of the Insular Commission, wrote in 1899: "Time alone can demonstrate whether we shall ever want to make them States. If we are not certain as to this, we should not make them Territories; for statehood follows Territorial conditions."[13] The so-called "insular cases" decided by the Supreme Court in 1901 (*DeLima* v. *Bidwell, Downes* v. *Bidwell, Dooley* v. *United States*) emphasized this lack of definition in Puerto Rico's status: the island was not "foreign," but neither was it a part of the United States.

Puerto Rican political parties appealed to their voters by taking stands on the ultimate settlement of Puerto Rico's status. The first two major parties were the Republicans and the Federalists. In general, the Republicans (who had no real connection with the Republican Party of the United States, although they often tried to claim such ties) were cooperative with American officials and policies, and looked toward statehood for Puerto Rico. From 1900 to 1904 insular politics were largely in the hands of the Republicans, because the Federalists boycotted the elections of 1900. They did this to protest Governor Charles H. Allen's arrangement of electoral districts, which they felt favored the Republicans. After 1904 insular political power was dominated increasingly by the party known as the Union of Puerto Rico, which was a rebaptized Federalist Party. The Unionists were led by Luis Muñoz Rivera, newspaper editor, poet, and political figure of importance from the early 1890s. Most of their native backers considered them the party of independence.

In spite of the independence plank in his party's platform, Muñoz Rivera was too realistic to believe that he should stake all his hopes on that ultimate solution. Americans had too frequently stated, as did Congressman Finis J. Garrett, that ". . . no one in the United States, no matter what his political affiliations may be, would for one moment consider giving up Porto Rico or permitting her to pass from under the sovereignty of the United States."[14] Above all, Muñoz Rivera wanted more autonomy for Puerto Rico, and anything which furthered this was agreeable to him. In 1912 he wrote: "The Union Party asks for citizenship. Why? Because nothing is lost to ask something that will look good. . . . If it is necessary to choose between self-government and American citizenship, the choice will be . . . self-government without citizenship before citizenship without self-government."[15] As Puerto Rico's resident commissioner in Washington from 1910 to his death in 1916, Muñoz Rivera worked with American congressmen for passage of a new organic act to replace the Foraker Act and give more self-government to Puerto Rico.

A third political force to emerge after 1901 was the Socialist Worker's Party (*Partido Socialista Obrera*), which was virtually identical with the largest labor union of the island, the Free Federation of Laborers (*Federación Libre de los Trabajadores*). Santiago Iglesias Pantín, who had founded the organizations, led them both. Iglesias' party did not make status or autonomy the major issues, but claimed that both independence and statehood were political tricks, mere smoke screens hiding the real problems of Puerto Rico.[16] The Free Federation of Laborers was considered a branch of the American Federation of Labor, and Samuel Gompers not only kept up an active correspondence with Iglesias, but also came to Puerto Rico on at least two occasions, 1904 and 1914, to investigate personally labor conditions.[17]

The Republicans, Unionists, and Socialists battled over many issues, but three problems were predominant in the era of the Foraker Act: autonomy, United States citizenship, and the Puerto Rican economy. The Foraker Act and the practices of the first few American administrations in Puerto Rico narrowly limited the amount of self-government the Puerto Ricans could exercise. As we have seen, the executive branch of the insular government was appointed, predominantly American in personnel, and was also, in the Executive Council, blended with the legislative branch of the Puerto Rican government. Therefore, only one house of the legislature was popularly elected and composed of Puerto Ricans. The governor's veto power and the nullification prerogative of Congress completed American control over the legislative branch of Puerto Rico.

Americans also controlled the Puerto Rican judiciary: the president of the United States appointed the justices and the marshal of the Puerto Rican Supreme Court, and the governor appointed the judges of the district courts. Puerto Rico was also made a federal judicial district, with a district judge, district attorney, and marshal for the district all appointed by the president of the United States. Lindley Garrison, Woodrow Wilson's first secretary of war, wrote of the "all-American" aspects of this federal court.

> The Foraker Act and its amendments give an unusually wide jurisdiction to the United States District Court. This court was thrown open to any litigant who was a citizen of any place other than Porto Rico, for the trial of all important cases. This jurisdiction is unnecessary. American citizens have ample protection in litigating in the local courts, which have always stood well, and which are more or less directly amenable to the supervision of an American Governor and an American Attorney General. The Federal Judges have the idea that they are the protectors of American citizens in Porto Rico—an idea which they have frequently not failed to express, and which has tended, as much as any other single circumstance, to agitate whatever underlying basis of race prejudice there might be.[18]

There was little self-government for the Puerto Ricans under the Foraker Act even on the local level. William F. Willoughby, who was for several years a member of the Executive Council, told an American audience in 1909 that the secretary of Porto Rico—who was more or less a lieutenant governor and was always an American —originally had the legal right "to veto any municipal ordinance or annul any act of a municipal officer." This was, according to Willoughby, a conscious policy of making local government "rigidly controlled from above," to teach proper governmental processes to the Puerto Ricans.[19]

American authority over local government in Puerto Rico included control of the police. Unlike the states of the Union, Puerto Rico had no local police. The insular police force, normally 625 men, took care of all matters of law and order and crime detection. In 1908 the force was divided into sixty-six police districts, one for each municipality, each headed by a district police chief. The district chiefs were usually Puerto Ricans; but their immediate superior was the chief of police in San Juan, who was usually an American and directly responsible to the governor. The insular police were also used for hurricane-relief work and epidemic control (there was a bubonic-plague epidemic in 1912 and an influenza epidemic in 1918 that together took ten thousand lives). They were usually increased in number just prior to elections, to assure calm.[20]

The third facet of American control over the municipalities was the appointive power of the governors. In a typical fiscal year, 1912–13, Governor George R. Colton appointed, besides judges, secretaries, and marshals of courts, ninety municipal councilmen and nine mayors (*alcaldes*).[21] These were appointments to vacancies occurring in elective offices.

It was this appointive power of the governor that brought on the "appropriations crisis" of 1909. Because the majority party in any election usually used its victory to entrench its position against the losing party, the early governors tried to spread out patronage by using their appointive power for the minority party. Governor Charles H. Allen said in 1902:

> In order to secure minority representation and to check the abuse of political power in municipal administration it has been found helpful when vacancies occur in the municipal councils to appoint councilmen of the political party opposite to that of the majority to fill such vacancies until the next municipal elec-

tion. At first, this was very distasteful to the majority, but we kept the plan up and it has accomplished the greatest good.[22]

Governor Allen had noted that the Republicans, who were in the majority in the years of his administration (1900–02), had found this practice "distasteful"; the more nationalistic Unionists, when they became the victorious party after 1904, saw it as tyranny.

In the early months of 1909, Governor Regis H. Post refused to accept Unionist recommendations for some judicial vacancies in Puerto Rico, and he and the Executive Council blocked several bills passed by the House of Delegates. The entirely Unionist House of Delegates, after passing some fiery resolutions, retaliated with a weapon used by the American colonial assemblies against the British governors in the eighteenth century: it refused to pass any appropriations measures to enable government to continue to function in Puerto Rico. President Taft asked Congress for emergency legislation, and at the same time petulantly complained that Puerto Ricans had "forgotten the generosity of the United States." He fumed that since "we have gone somewhat too fast in the extension of political power to them for their own good," the power of appropriation should be taken away "from those who have shown themselves too irresponsible to enjoy it."[23] Congress quickly responded with the "Olmsted Amendment" to the Foraker Act, which stipulated that whenever the Puerto Rican legislature should terminate its session without providing appropriations for the next year of governmental operations, its executive branch could proceed to appropriate the same amount as in the previous year. The Olmsted Amendment also ended the doubt about which department of the United States government had authority over Puerto Rico, by placing it officially in the hands of whatever department the president should designate; as expected, Taft chose the War Department, with its Bureau of Insular Affairs.[24] The Bureau of Insular Affairs has been described as the nearest thing the United States ever had to a colonial office;[25] and in the affairs of Puerto Rico, from 1909 until 1934, it held more power than any other agency of the United States.

Yet this power, as we shall see, was not used positively, but negatively; in this the BIA was not different in its approach to Puerto Rico from Congress, presidents, and colonial officials. The question of Puerto Rican autonomy was closely related in American minds to the feeling that the United States, as a superior civilization, should be the keeper of its "little brown brothers"—in other words, the typical turn-of-the-century imperial justification. This was often stated in openly racist terms. Senator Albert B. Fall of New Mexico told his colleagues that he knew "the people of Spanish descent" such as Puerto Ricans well, and though he felt "kindly" toward them, he also knew that "they must be led."[26] Speaker of the House Joseph ("Uncle Joe") Cannon on several occasions told the House that the Puerto Ricans were not "competent to exercise sovereign power" because they were people of mixed race and because they suffered the "enervating effects" of living in the tropics.[27] Dr. Samuel McCune Lindsay, the second commissioner of education under the civil government, presented this supposed inferiority of Puerto Ricans in "scientific" terms:

> You need not expect the Latin American to be contented. Biologically that is easily explained. It is a process of selection by which all his history for centuries past has been a protest against existing conditions. He will always find fault, but beneath his fault-finding there is a genuine human heart, and there is a kindly spirit, and an earnest purpose to strive for the best things.[28]

William Willoughby expressed some common stereotypes of Puerto Ricans when he said that the island was "inhabited by persons having none of the traditions of self-government behind them, with temperaments more excitable, with the custom of valuing immediate rather than ultimate results, and with the characteristic firmly ingrained in them of emphasizing personal, family and other considerations at the expense of public interests."[29] District Judge Peter J. Hamilton advised President Wilson to go slowly in granting autonomy to Puerto Ricans since they were "of the Latin American excitability," and, worse, he claimed that "the mixture of black and white in Porto Rico threatens to create a race of mongrels of no use to anyone, a race of Spanish American talkers."[30] Hamilton was among the few Americans who couched their arrogance in hostile words; more often, as with Speaker Cannon and Dr. Lindsay, the American view of Puerto Rican inferiority came out in condescending "sympathy," such as that of President Theodore Roosevelt, writing during his visit to Puerto Rico in 1906 to his son Kermit: "The towns are dirty, but they are not nearly as dirty and offensive as those of Italy, and there is something pathetic and childlike about the people."[31]

This belief that Puerto Ricans were unfit for self-government was tied to the question of their American citizenship. Individually Puerto Ricans could go through the normal naturalization process for aliens, but a mass grant of United States citizenship was a different matter. There was overt opposition to a grant of American citizenship to Puerto Ricans, and this opposition fell into four categories. First there was the argument of Puerto Rican racial inferiority. Senator James K. Vardaman of Mississippi, whose political career was virtually synonymous with white supremacy in his home state, fought citizenship for Puerto Ricans with these remarks:

> I really think it is a misfortune for the United States to take that class of people into the body politic. They will never, no, not in a thousand years, understand the genius of our government or share our ideals of government. . . . I think we have enough of that element in the body politic already to menace the Nation with mongrelization.[32]

Vardaman's fellow senator, Albert Fall of New Mexico, also voiced fear of "mongrelization" by Puerto Ricans; he declared that "the trouble with this great United States today is the fact that we have among our members alien citizenship, not true American citizens. You say we are a melting pot for all the nations of the earth. Yes sir; and we have had an overdose of it. We have not been able to digest it."[33]

A second argument against American citizenship for Puerto Ricans was that they did not need it, that the status of "citizens of Porto Rico" gave them all the rights and protections of American citizens. Martín Travieso (who himself was a naturalized citizen of the United States) complained, "Whenever we make a plea for citizenship, the usual answer of those opposed . . . is, that the question of citizenship is a purely sentimental question."[34]

The third idea in opposition to American citizenship for the people of the island was the belief that "the next step inevitably would be a demand for statehood."[35] General George W. Davis, who had been one of the military governors before the Foraker Act, told an American audience in 1909 that "before making Porto Ricans full citizens of the United States, which means ultimate statehood, it was desired to observe the use they would make of qualified citizenship."[36]

Fourth was the conviction that any Puerto Ricans worthy of American citizenship would individually become naturalized under the present laws, without the granting of mass citizenship. It is true that some Puerto Ricans were naturalized during the 1898–1917 period (most, if not all, were Puerto Ricans residing at least for a few years in the United States). But this naturalization procedure contained one useless and anachronistic aspect: that of renouncing allegiance to the king of Spain, an allegiance legally terminated at the conclusion of the Spanish-American War.[37]

Many Americans were not against extending United States citizenship to Puerto Ricans. They felt, as did President Roosevelt, that it was a matter "of right and justice to the people of Porto Rico."[38] But talk was cheap, and usually these people did not actively work for such a citizenship law. Roosevelt, for instance, mentioned the need for granting American citizenship to Puerto Rico in at least four messages to Congress, yet had no qualms about saying of the Puerto Rican troops at his inauguration, "I am proud to call them . . . my fellow Americans."[39] In 1912 President Taft stated that he was "heartily" in favor of a bill for Puerto Rican citizenship; his heartiness was tempered, however, by a warning that it must be "entirely disassociated from any thought of statehood."[40] The first president who actively sought American citizenship for Puerto Ricans was Woodrow Wilson; from 1914 he worked with Senator John Shafroth of Colorado, Representative William Atkinson Jones of Virginia, Resident Commissioner Luis Muñoz Rivera, and Governor Arthur Yager to change this and other aspects of the Puerto Rican organic act.

An additional problem entering into the citizenship issue was that of what *type* of American citizenship: individual or collective. Collective, or blanket, citizenship would be given to all citizens of Puerto Rico except those refusing it. Many Americans believed, as did Governor Yager, that to do this would be to force American citizenship upon the people, and that citizenship should be a matter of the individual's right to go before a judge or through some other legal process to claim it personally.[41] The abortive Olmsted bill of 1910 (introduced by the same Marlin Olmsted whose amendment to the Foraker Act had ended the "appropriations crisis") was originally designed to give Puerto Ricans individual citizenship, and so was the first draft of the Jones bill of 1914; neither, consequently, aroused much interest among Puerto Ricans.

Status, autonomy, and citizenship were the basic issues of Puerto Rican politics; the Unionists and the Republicans ignored another problem—the insular economy. Before 1898, coffee rivaled sugar as the leading product of the island. After American occupation the economy of Puerto Rico was tied increasingly to sugar production alone. Between 1899 and 1909 lands planted in sugar in Puerto Rico rose from 72,146 to 145,433 acres.[42] Free trade with the United States was a boon to the sugar industry of Puerto Rico, but it did not help several other facets of the insular economy: (1) The United States, with its high standard of living and relatively expensive food items, replaced Spain and other European countries as supplier of many of the staples of daily life for Puerto Ricans. (2) The United States did not replace Europe as buyer and consumer of Puerto Rican coffee (American palates were accustomed to coffee from South America), and this industry sagged after 1898. (3) Since American industry was able to ship freely into Puerto Rico, it stifled any possibilities of nonagricultural industries in the island.[43] (4) Spanish capital had never come into Puerto Rico in large amounts; American capital did, with the result that even before 1900 sugar production was falling into the hands of just a few large, corporation-owned plantations. These large *centrales*, as they were known, ignored or found loopholes in the amendment to the Foraker Act which had been designed to prevent such non–Puerto Rican exploitation of the insular economy. This amendment, known as the "500-acre" law, limited to that amount of acreage the holdings of corporate land-holdings; however, it included no provision for enforcement. Further, it had no way to prevent a corporation from purchasing and using land in the name of an individual. Until the 1930s the "500-acre" law was a dead letter.

The great mass of workers in Puerto Rico were agricultural laborers, and the wretchedness of their lives—their low wages, the long periods of unemployment they suffered, their lack of accident compensation or other benefits, and the success of the *centrales* in fighting labor unionization—contributed to a great deal of labor unrest. Strikes frequently involved the burning of the fields of sugar cane. They also usually involved the insular police, jail sentences for leaders of the Free Federation of Laborers, and the forcible breakup of labor rallies or parades. During the period of the Foraker Act, the most widespread strikes and violent clashes between strikers and police were during the administration of Governor Yager. Samuel Gompers, who claimed to have met all the governors of the island, said Yager was the only one he did not like.[44] Yager had no more affection for Gompers's friends in Puerto Rico, telling President Wilson that "the so-called labor leaders and agitators of the strike in Arecibo are in reality political leaders of a recently organized socialist party and are playing a game for political control of the municipality."[45] Labor gains in Puerto Rico were difficult, and the great lack of contact between the two major parties of the island and the labor movement there did not help.

Even with tariff protection, Puerto Rican sugar had barely been holding its own in the American market against sugar from Cuba and elsewhere when the Underwood-Simmons Tariff of 1914 put sugar on the free list. Fears ran high in Puerto Rico that this would ruin the insular sugar industry and cause massive unemployment. Through the efforts of Governor Yager and Puerto Rican political leaders, Congress was persuaded first to hold off the sugar-tariff change until 1916 and then, a few weeks before it was to go into effect, to rescind the free-sugar clause altogether.

Aiding in the development of the Puerto Rican economy was the progress made in public health and education. American efforts in these areas were little short of revolutionary during the seventeen years of government under the Foraker Act. The galloping statistics in public health, education, and construction of roads and public buildings were standard topics in speeches and writings justifying American colonial expansion. Each governor gave such statistics a prominent place in his reports to the federal government.

The American civil governors of Puerto Rico under the Foraker Act—Charles H. Allen (1900–02), William H. Hunt (1902–04), Beekman Winthrop (1904–07), Regis H. Post (1907–09), George R. Colton (1909–13), and Arthur Yager (1913–21)—were honest administrators who tried to do a good job. On the whole they were well educated: their number included graduates of Amherst, Harvard, and Johns Hopkins, and Allen and Yager held Ph.D. degrees. Most of the governors had experience in colonial administration or at least in government service: Allen was an assistant secretary of the Navy under President McKinley; Hunt was secretary of Puerto Rico under Governor Allen and had earlier served in the territorial governments of Idaho and Montana; Winthrop had been in the insular administration of Governor General Taft in the Philippine Islands for three years; Post had been auditor of Puerto Rico and later secretary, for a total of four years; and Colton had been in charge of the customs services of the Dominican Republic and the Philippine Islands.

Various factors influenced the selection of these men for the governorship of Puerto Rico: previous administrative work under the President (Allen and Winthrop), personal friendship with the President (Yager), and a reputation as a firm colonial administrator (Colton). But never were the wishes of any Puerto Ricans—political leaders, legislators, or the public—involved in the choice. The governors were outsiders in every way. None of them knew sufficient Spanish to communicate with the Puerto Ricans without interpreters. None had any connections with any of the political parties on the island. The terms of the first four governors averaged less than three years per man, and only Colton and Yager were in office long enough to get to know their jobs well. None of these men developed enough love for Puerto Rico to remain on the island after his official duties had terminated; they all came to administer a colony, did their jobs, and left. The only Puerto Ricans they knew were those who were wealthy and educated and most often only those who spoke English and were strongly pro-American.

All of these flaws were even more commonly found in the other American administrators in the Puerto Rican government—the members of the Executive Council, the judges, the police chiefs, and others. The manner of their selections was sometimes totally unrelated to the specifics of working and living in Puerto Rico. An example is found in a note from President Taft to General Frank D. McIntyre of the Bureau of Insular Affairs:

> When Ward is promoted to be Secretary I will make a personal appointment of my own—pure personal patronage—in the appointment of one Alphonso P. Sawyer, of Seattle, Washington. He is a man with good business sense, a graduate of Yale, and I believe would get along as well as any Yankee could get on in Porto Rico. He doesn't know the language, but I presume that ultimately he would pick up some.[46]

Such standards as these for the selection of the men who would oversee America's colonial populations might well have been avoided had the organic laws for those colonies been designed to make the colonial governments more responsive to native needs and desires. The Foraker Act reflected little confidence in Puerto Ricans as responsible citizens.

From 1910 on, there were frequent efforts in the United States Congress to reform or replace the Foraker Act. The bill introduced in 1910 by Representative Marlin Olmsted of Pennsylvania was designed to be a new organic act for Puerto Rico. It would have made Puerto Ricans citizens of the United States (individually, not en masse), separated the Executive Council from the upper house of the Puerto Rican legislature, made that upper house progressively elective,[47] created departments of agriculture, commerce, and labor in the Puerto Rican government, and more strictly enforced the legal-acreage law. (The amount of legal acreage for agricultural corporations was to have been increased from 500 to a more realistic 3,000 acres.[48])

Congressman William A. Jones and other critics of the Olmsted bill found one fault in it beyond all others: it was designed to lodge even more areas of the Puerto Rican government in the Bureau of Insular Affairs. Jones saw "all through" the Olmsted bill "a set purpose" to bring Puerto Rico under the control of the BIA. Agreeing with him was Congressman James R. Mann of Illinois, who caustically stated that the bill left little reason to bother pretending to have a Puerto Rican legislature, for everything would be run by Americans. Tulio Larrinaga, the resident commissioner from Puerto Rico, when asked in debate if he would prefer to see the island continue under the Foraker Act, bluntly replied: "I would; most decidedly. Leave the citizenship provision there and do not touch the Foraker Act. There is more legislative power under the Foraker Act left to the people of Porto Rico than in this act."[49]

Within the Olmsted bill there were four avenues of increased authority over Puerto Rico for the chief of the Bureau of Insular Affairs. He would have authority over the civil service of Puerto Rico. He would be the direct superior of the new "executive secretary" who would replace the position of secretary of Puerto Rico. He would have the power to approve or disapprove the choice of banks for deposit of insular treasury funds. Without his permission American members of the Puerto Rican government would not be allowed to return to the United States on temporary business or personal matters. (This could have prevented a governor from going to Washington to lobby for some congressional action regarding Puerto Rico which the BIA opposed.)

The Olmsted bill also would have made the sixty-six municipal judgeships appointive rather than elective. The worst part of the bill, thought Finis J. Garrett of the House Committee on Insular Affairs, was that which turned over control of Puerto Rican elections to a three-man commission appointed by the governor. The bill did not even require that the commission be bipartisan. This, as well as the change in municipal judgeships, was, Garrett believed, "an effort to legislate out one party [the Unionists] and legislate another in [the Republicans] and keep it in."[50] The bill had been described by Olmsted as a measure of the Taft administration. It is possible that President Taft was still thinking of the "appropriations crisis" of the previous year and intended through the Olmsted bill to replace the troublesome Unionists with the more tractable Republicans as the major party in insular politics.

The Olmsted bill passed through the House of Representatives (with some amendments, such as one making American citizenship collective). The measure was never brought up for discussion in the Senate, and died on the calendar there in February 1911, almost a year after Marlin Olmsted had first proposed it to the House of Representatives. One factor in its demise was the firm, yet quiet, opposition of Senator Elihu Root, who believed that American citizenship for Puerto Ricans would "dilute our electorate."[51]

In 1912 Congressman William A. Jones tried to push a bill through Congress that would do nothing more than make Puerto Ricans citizens of the United States. Being a simple bill, not aimed at revamping the whole Foraker Act, it had no trouble passing through the House of Representatives. Jones's citizenship bill, however, remained in committee in the Senate for almost a year, and when it was reported back to the Senate, it was merely kept on the calendar until its death at the end of the Sixty-second Congress.

The 1912 Democratic victory in the United States made a liberal reform of the Puerto Rican government seem more likely. The Democrats had often deplored the imperialistic policies of the Republicans, and through the years they had declared that they would give more autonomy to the American overseas possessions.[52]

President Woodrow Wilson decided in 1913 to make a former Johns Hopkins University classmate, Arthur Yager, the new governor of Puerto Rico. Yager became the first governor to make a real effort to work with the Unionists and their leader, Muñoz Rivera. In his first year of office, Yager appointed three Puerto Ricans to the Executive Council, two of them to executive posts; for the first time Puerto Ricans outnumbered Americans on the council.

In 1914 Governor Yager, President Wilson, Resident Commissioner Muñoz Rivera, Congressman William A. Jones, and Senator John Shafroth of Colorado began the most concentrated effort yet to replace the Foraker Act.[53] They put their hopes on a bill which Jones whisked through his Committee on Insular Affairs and reported back to the House of Representatives within a week, by March 26, 1914. (This bill was the first of three known as a "Jones bill"—two dealing with Puerto Rico and one with the Philippines.) Then for seven months these five men carried on an anxious correspondence as they waited for the House to consider it.

In June, Yager wrote to Jones, urging him to try to get the bill passed in that session of Congress so that the regularly scheduled November elections in Puerto Rico could proceed under the new organic act.[54] President Wilson was by this time wondering what the status and prospects of the bill were.[55] The prospects were not good. In July, Muñoz Rivera wrote Governor Yager that he did not believe Congress would in that session get around to the Jones bill without "the supreme influence of the President."[56]

President Wilson, the advocate of strong executive leadership, was not ready to exercise the necessary "supreme influence." When, in August, John Sharp Williams asked Wilson whether "it is about time we were recognizing the fact that Porto Rico ought not to be governed by the War Department as if there were still a military occupation of it," Wilson replied: "I entirely agree with you about the status of Porto Rico. There is a bill pending which would do them full justice. I wish with all my heart it might be brought out and passed, but other things are for the present crowding it to the wall."[57]

The Jones bill of 1914 was never discussed in the House of Representatives. Many American political leaders had talked of "doing the right thing" for Puerto Rico by making its people citizens of the United States and by reforming its constitution, and one or another of the early efforts to do these things had been backed by every person or group relevant to the issue. But those bills failed to become law.

Early in 1916, Congressman Jones presented yet another bill in the House of Representatives to replace the Foraker Act. This bill passed the House on May 23, 1916, and—in a fairly different version—the Senate on February 20, 1917. The two houses had a conference of the managers of the bill to iron out the differences, and both houses accepted their agreements by February 23. President Wilson signed the Jones bill into law as Puerto Rico's new organic act on March 2, 1917.

How is it that this Jones bill succeeded in becoming law, whereas other bills with no more apparent opposition had failed? There were several things in its favor which those bills had not possessed. The bill came in the wake of another Jones Act—that of 1916—which granted more self-government (and the promise of future independence) to the Philippine Islands. This legislation set the example for the Puerto Rican bill. Also, President Wilson worked more actively and spoke more strongly for a new organic act for Puerto Rico than had any previous president.[58] Besides speaking out for the Jones bill, Wilson made its passage more necessary by agreeing to a suggestion by Luis Muñoz Rivera that the insular elections of 1916 be delayed until they could be held under the new organic act. Thus, after November 1916, there was a general feeling that things in Puerto Rico were at a standstill which could be relieved only by turning the Jones bill into a law. (In addition, Muñoz Rivera died that autumn, and the Jones bill seemed to be an appropriate memorial to him.[59]) Backers of the Jones bill also emphasized that this legislation could end the sentiment for independence on the island, and remove the "uneasiness" and "suspicion" that Puerto Ricans were feeling after seeing that the Philippine Islands had not been given any specific date for independence in their Jones Act.[60] Another reason for the passage of the new Puerto Rican organic act was that in early 1917 involvement in the European war appeared imminent; a happy, loyal Puerto Rico populated entirely by American citizens seemed more important than usual.[61] As Congressman William Green of Iowa pointed out: "While we hold it, it is an outpost for defense of the Panama Canal; held by any other nation it becomes a point of attack in war and danger in peace."[62]

The Jones Act of 1917 is best remembered for granting collective citizenship to the Puerto Ricans. Those who wished to refuse this status had six months in which to go before a court and state their desire not to be Americans. The new organic law also separated the Executive Council from the upper legislative house, and unlike the Olmsted bill made that Senate immediately elective. It made minority-party representation in the Puerto Rican legislature more likely by increasing the electoral districts for the lower house from seven to thirty-five, and by providing that one member of each house be elected from no specific district but rather as a member "at large."[63] The law gave to the Puerto Ricans several "bill-of-rights" guarantees. However, it failed to tighten enforcement of the "500-acre" corporate land limitation, although continuing it; two more decades were to go by before the "500-acre" law was more than lines on paper.

Nearly all discussion in Congress over the Jones bill had centered upon three topics: American citizenship for Puerto Ricans, suffrage requirements (finally settled very liberally by leaving requirements up to the Puerto Rican legislature and specifying that no property requirement could ever be added), and prohibition of alcoholic beverages. This last point was highly controversial, coming even before the Eighteenth Amendment had been added to the U.S. Constitution. Prohibition for Puerto Rico was the special legislative project of Senator Asle Gronna of New Jersey. It came not as a result of any demand from Puerto Rico; Puerto Rico had a major rum industry, and excise taxes upon liquors provided a considerable amount of the yearly revenues of the insular government.[64] The memorials and petitions which Gronna read to bolster his case were like those he mentioned on February 12, 1917: "I have here hundreds of letters from patriotic women who have gone down to Porto Rico to make an investigation of the conditions there."[65]

Governor Yager recognized the artificiality of prohibition for Puerto Rico, and saw in Senator Gronna's project several dangers. It could ruin the chances for passage of the entire Jones bill. If put into effect in Puerto Rico, prohibition could seriously upset insular governmental revenue, and its enforcement might over a period of time be very damaging to Puerto Rican–American relationships.[66] President Wilson agreed with Yager that a prohibition amendment to the bill would be inopportune and tried to keep it out.[67] But Yager and Wilson were not successful in stopping the Gronna amendment. Fortunately, prohibition did not doom the Jones bill, mainly because Senator Henry Cabot Lodge introduced an addition to the prohibition amendment which required a referendum to be held in Puerto Rico along with the general elections to be held July 16, 1917. There was little evidence to suggest to any member of Congress who was opposed to adding prohibition to the Puerto Rican organic act that the people of the island would actually return a majority vote for prohibition.

The occasion of President Wilson's formal signature was marked by a small ceremony in the presence of Secretary of War Newton D. Baker, Senator Shafroth, Congressman Jones, Samuel Gompers, General Frank McIntyre (Chief of the Bureau of Insular Affairs), and Gonzales Llamas (a Unionist representative, in the place of the late Luis Muñoz Rivera).[68] After seventeen years, less two months, the law "temporarily to provide revenues and civil government for Porto Rico" ceased to be the organic act for Puerto Rico.

In the United States the opposition to the Jones Act faded away after it became law, even though there were a few Americans who continued to feel, as did former Secretary of War Elihu Root, that giving citizenship to the Puerto Ricans had been a "stupid chuckle-headed performance on the part of a Congress."[69] On the whole, Americans believed that the problem of Puerto Rico was settled, that the Jones Act gave Puerto Rico autonomy and full territorial status as well as American citizenship.[70] In a decision in 1917 Judge Peter J. Hamilton of the United States District Court in Puerto Rico held that the island was now a "territory incorporated into the United States," and that all congressional legislation applicable to the continental territories was now effective for Puerto Rico.[71] When Governor Yager informed the Bureau of Insular Affairs of Hamilton's position, General McIntyre commented:

> I am, of course, sorry that Judge Hamilton has placed himself with reference to the Government of Porto Rico in direct opposition to what was the plan of the executive department of the government and, as I have always understood, of Congress, as to the matter of making it an incorporated territory. I believe that . . . the two errors we made in our Porto Rican bill were in not abolishing the District Court and in not providing that the statutory laws of the United States should not apply to Porto Rico except where Congress specifically so provided.[72]

The United States Supreme Court, in the cases of the *People of Porto Rico* v. *Carlos Tapia* and the *People of Porto Rico* v. *José Muratti,* in January 1918 reversed Judge Hamilton's stand, and left the position of Puerto Rico as it had been before the Jones Act.[73] For this reason, from 1917 to 1933 much of the activity of Félix Córdova Dávila (Puerto Rican resident commissioner in the U.S. House of Representatives) and several members of Congress who were interested in Puerto Rico was concerned with attempts to have United States laws extended to Puerto Rico.[74]

Luis Muñoz Rivera, in his last major speech before his death in 1916, had predicted that most Puerto Ricans would reject the Jones Act because its American citizenship was not accompanied by sufficient self-government.[75] He far overestimated the number who would go before a court within six months to refuse American citizenship, as provided for in the Jones Act. Six days after President Wilson signed the new organic law, Vicente Balbas, one of the longtime leaders of the independence party in Puerto Rico and editor of the newspaper *Herald de las Antilles,* declined United States citizenship before a district court. In all, only 287 other people took the same step. Some of these people claimed Spanish or other foreign citizenship, while others asked to retain their former status as simply "citizens of Porto Rico." By July 1917, however, over eight hundred people on the island had done the opposite: they had taken advantage of a clause of the Jones Act which allowed anyone born on the island of "alien" (non–Puerto Rican) parentage to claim American citizenship by taking an oath of allegiance to the U.S. Constitution before the Federal District Court in Puerto Rico.[76]

A bill was introduced in the Puerto Rican House of Delegates to express to the president and Congress of the United States the gratitude of Puerto Rico for the new organic act, but it failed for lack of a quorum on March 14, 1917.[77] The great leader of the Republicans, José Celso Barbosa, was quoted as saying of the Jones Act, "At last we have won."[78] But the Unionists also called it a "legitimate triumph" for their party, since it granted more autonomy and American citizenship "without prejudicing the definitive determination of our status."[79] That is, it did not set Puerto Rico on a definite road toward statehood.

Supporters of the Jones Act stated that it gave Puerto Rico a new form of government and insular autonomy, but there were some things about it which definitely were not new and many things that fell short of autonomy. Nothing unique was achieved when President Wilson on March 21, 1917, signed an executive order placing Puerto Rico under the jurisdiction of the Department of War and assigning it specifiically to the Bureau of Insular Affairs. The Bureau of Insular Affairs already had eight years' experience as the sole authority over the Puerto Rican government and several years' experience before that sharing this responsibility with other federal departments. And it had Major General Frank D. McIntyre. When a congressional committee was holding hearings on the reorganization of the army in 1920, one suggestion was to transfer the duties of the Bureau of Insular Affairs out of the War Department. Against this idea Secretary of War Newton D. Baker told the committee, "I think it unwise, because I can not conceive of any better organized bureau than the Bureau of Insular Affairs, as long as Gen. McIntyre is permitted to live and be the head of it." Baker went on to say that while a major general was not necessary to that post, and a colonel or even a civilian might do a good job at it, "Gen. McIntyre's extraordinary knowledge of these people, his understanding of them, is a thing which at least during his active career we ought not to part with."[80]

Even though both the Unionists and the Republicans praised the additional features of self-government which the Jones Act brought Puerto Rico, neither party was satisfied. The Unionists reaffirmed their struggle for "the establishment of a completely democratic regime which would give to our people the ability to pass laws, without restrictions, dealing with all the matters that affect their life and their rights, and to elect all the functionaries of the public administration."[81] The Republicans called for an elective governor, elective heads of executive departments, the status of an incorporated territory, and full statehood when the illiteracy rate should fall to 29 percent. They also protested the use of terms like "our new possessions" in reference to Puerto Rico and the Philippine Islands.[82] Puerto Rican leaders appealed to President Wilson's famous "Fourteen Points" and emphasis upon "self-determination" for nations in seeking autonomy.[83]

Governor Arthur Yager also believed that the Jones Act was imperfect. But he did not feel that its imperfection was a matter of too *little* self-government for the islanders. He was "quite sure that the intention of Congress was to proceed with due caution . . . and to reserve to the national government for a considerable period all of the checks and restrictions upon the local administration" until Puerto Ricans "should have demonstrated their capacity to manage safely their own government thru native officials."[84] Yager advised the Bureau of Insular Affairs against a Puerto Rican governor or a governor elected by the Puerto Ricans.[85] The major flaw in the Jones Act, Yager believed, was that it lacked a literacy requirement for voting.[86]

The first election held under the new organic act was set for July 16, 1917, and each of the three parties wanted its people to be in command. At stake were four new positions in the lower house of the legislature (now called the House of Representatives) and all nineteen places in the insular Senate. The Unionists continued their preeminence in Puerto Rican politics, winning thirteen of the seats in the Senate and twenty-three of the thirty-nine places in the House of Representatives. The Republicans took all the other seats in the two houses, except for two in the lower house that went to the Socialists. Santiago Iglesias was defeated for senator-at-large, a rather surprising loss since he had the whole island from which to draw working-class votes.

Governor Yager attributed Iglesias' defeat to the large number of ballots which were incorrectly marked by illiterates. He noted with satisfaction that it was Iglesias and Gompers who were largely responsible for not placing literacy restrictions upon suffrage in the Jones Act, and gloated that "the Federation of Labor is reaping the harvest of its own sowing."[87] Iglesias petitioned the Puerto Rican courts for a writ of mandamus for the Executive Council to recount the ballots, but on August 1, 1917, the Puerto Rican Supreme Court denied his petition.[88] There was no more sympathy for Iglesias or his labor union from the insular courts than from Governor Yager. But the largely Unionist Senate was more receptive to Iglesias' appeals, and recounted the ballots of the senator-at-large contest. Iglesias was declared by the Senate the winner over Santiago Veve Calzada, a Republican.[89] In a later chapter it will be seen how this belated (and possibly fraudulent) victory by Santiago Iglesias was a turning point in the history of the Puerto Rican labor movement as well as in Puerto Rican politics. It had implications far beyond the fact that for the first time the Socialists had a voice in the upper house of the insular legislature.

Puerto Ricans had accepted the many changes of the period between 1900 and 1917 with a minimum of difficulty. They had readily accepted United States citizenship; they recognized in many ways the fact that their island's economic welfare was dependent upon U.S. markets and industries; and in government they had adapted to a host of American-style innovations and American political values.[90] In the next fifteen years, Puerto Ricans would prove anxious to accept some other changes which were brought by the new organic law. These were not changes providing increased autonomy for the island or decreasing its economic dependence upon the United States, but innovations making Puerto Rico more like the United States.

2 | Prohibition, War, and Woman Suffrage

Prior to American occupation of Puerto Rico in 1898, Spanish domination of the island had been so complete that Puerto Ricans repeatedly affirmed Spanish attitudes toward international affairs and civic life. These assertions were basically loyalty professions, designed to make the best of colonial status. Gordon K. Lewis sharply criticizes the United States for making necessary a new set of such fawning declarations of loyalty by squelching native hopes and cultural patterns beneath an imported "Americanism." One such "profession of loyalty," says Lewis, was centered around the prohibition of alcoholic beverages.[1] This chapter considers Puerto Rican prohibition in the light of Lewis's charge, as well as two other aspects of Puerto Rico's relationship with the United States in the period between 1917 and 1933 which could be seen in the same way: Puerto Rican involvement in the First World War and the advent of woman suffrage in 1929. Were the activities in these three areas merely Puerto Rican efforts to please their new masters? Or is it possible that they were indications of a successful grafting of the American experience upon Puerto Rico?

Besides electing officials in the new government, there was a second issue of importance at stake in the election of July 16, 1917—the question of prohibition. The Jones Act had left the final decision on the application of prohibition in Puerto Rico to the voters of the island. In congressional debate over prohibition, it had become obvious that the major demands for it came from people who were not Puerto Ricans, and that the only requests for it from the island were from some of the Protestant religious groups.[2] But on an island where Protestants were only a tiny percentage of the religious total, and where a major liquor industry provided the livelihood of many

31

workers as well as a large part of the governmental revenues, a victory for the "dry" forces seemed to be unlikely in that referendum.

Prohibition won, however, by a vote of 102,423 to 64,227. Part of the reason for this upset is that neither the Unionists nor Republicans bound their followers to vote either way on the issue, but the Socialists, with their large working-class vote, strongly supported prohibition.[3] Part of the victory might also have been in the use on the ballots of the symbols of a bottle for legal liquor and a coconut for prohibition. To a Puerto Rican voter (particularly one of the many who could not read), the coconut symbolized prosperity, as a wheat stalk would mean prosperity to a Kansas farmer.[4] But the major factor in the referendum seemed to be a powerful wave of patriotism which tied prohibition with United States citizenship. This popular sentiment swept up whole towns through emotional prohibition meetings, parades, petition drives, speeches, and advertising. It included in each community a thorough cross section of the population: Republicans, Unionists, Socialists, Protestant ministers and Catholic priests, society matrons and working women, labor organizers and Chamber of Commerce leaders. Some antiprohibition leaders ostentatiously switched sides and supported prohibition.[5] Against all this frenzy of activity, the "wet" forces really had little chance. Some liquor companies placed clever little ads in the newspapers,[6] but there was little other public notice of opposition to prohibition. The final vote should not have surprised anyone, after the popular excitement of the spring of 1917 which celebrated prohibition as an affirmation of United States citizenship. Lewis's phrase "profession of loyalty" would appear to be quite correct in regard to the coming of prohibition to Puerto Rico.

According to the Jones Act, after the referendum on prohibition, the actual law was to go into effect throughout the island on March 2, 1918. This was well before the Eighteenth Amendment to the U.S. Constitution was ratified (January 29, 1919) and almost two years before national prohibition officially began in the United States. Thus, until the beginning of 1920, prohibition in Puerto Rico was strictly a local matter. The Puerto Rican legislature passed a law in December 1917 defining illegal liquor by alcoholic content,[7] and in April 1918, President Wilson assigned the enforcement of prohibition in Puerto Rico to the insular treasurer.[8] When national prohibition went into effect, a federal prohibition director was assigned to Puerto Rico; but for one reason or another, the U.S. government continued to leave prohibition enforcement in local hands much more often in Puerto Rico than was the case in the states of the Union. (This may have been simply to avoid the whole burden of enforcement under difficult circumstances.) In 1922 Congress passed an act giving Puerto Rican courts concurrent jurisdiction over prohibition cases with the Federal District Court in San Juan.[9] In that same year the judge advocate general's office advised the Puerto Rican attorney general that he was to prosecute violations of the Federal Prohibition Act, in the name of "The People of Porto Rico."[10]

An effect of prohibition which Governor Yager foresaw was the subsequent need for new sources of income for the insular government, to replace the excise duties on liquors, which had provided up to one quarter of the revenue.[11] In February 1918, Yager called a special session of the legislature to deal with this problem, and several laws were passed to take up the slack; these laws provided for an additional tax on incomes and on several luxury items such as automobiles, diamonds, and pianos, and for the laying of fees on public documents executed before notaries and on the registration of land titles.[12] By 1923, the Puerto Rican excise taxes had been extended to include such items as matches, chewing gum, soap, carpets, neckties, hand fans, glass show counters, dancing capes, shoes, hats, cash registers, barber chairs, dynamite, and "bombons."[13]

Prohibition was even less successful in Puerto Rico than in the United States. It was almost impossible to enforce on the island. Homemade stills were as easy to construct there as in the United States, and mash for brewing was far more easily obtained, thanks to the sugar-cane industry which made molasses for fermentation readily available.[14] Each year the insular government announced the number of homemade stills captured and destroyed, and each year the figure was approximately that of 1923—1,067 stills.[15] In 1921 Antonio R. Barceló claimed that there were 10,000 illegal stills in Puerto Rico, and he may well have been correct.[16] Wealthy Puerto Ricans and Americans residing in Puerto Rico did not need to build stills, for they bought smuggled Scotch or other liquor. Nearly all the foreign ships which tied up in San Juan harbor played a cat-and-mouse game with insular prohibition authorities, as they attempted to send ashore illegal liquor.[17] The proximity of Puerto Rico to other islands where liquor was legal brought about a bustling rum-running trade which had almost every stretch of beach in Puerto Rico as a potential landing spot.

John T. Barrett, who was federal prohibition director from 1923 on, discussed in a report the difficulties of prohibition enforcement in Puerto Rico. His staff was too small for an island even of Puerto Rico's size: eight agents, four clerks, one chemist, and the shared use of a Coast Guard patrol boat which had a crew of eight men. He also had the official cooperation of the insular police and the ninety men employed by the customs service in Puerto Rico. He complained, however, that many of the police had already been "trained" to leave smuggling alone, for smuggled liquor went to the rich and important men of the island, men who could have a policeman fired or transferred. The police in one section of Puerto Rico, he believed, were "almost entirely subsidized by the smugglers." Barrett's men were forced to operate under irritating ground rules: they could not put up a roadblock across any Puerto Rican road or highway, they could not shoot at automobiles, and they were given no automobiles for their own use. Whenever they wanted to make a raid, they had to look for taxis or automobiles for hire; neither was always available when needed. The final straw was that the smugglers knew too much about the operations of Barrett's force; they had an "unbeatable" espionage system, headed (Barrett believed) by the former chief prohibition officer in Puerto Rico, Charles E. Berry.[18]

Another indication that prohibition was unsuccessful in Puerto Rico is the paucity of reference to it in the correspondence between the four governors who served during those years and their superiors in Washington. The only mention of prohibition by these men was usually in their annual reports to the president, in which they told how many arrests had been made, how many convictions had been obtained in the courts, and how many stills had been destroyed. There were two exceptions. One was the stern vow made by Governor E. Mont. Reily in his inaugural speech that he would really begin to enforce prohibition.[19] The other was a short period of anxious correspondence in 1922 between Governor Reily, the War Department, and a coal company that sold coal to ships docking in San Juan over the prospect that prohibition might cut off the lucrative position of San Juan as a port of call for foreign steamers. Reily, the coal company, and the San Juan Chamber of Commerce petitioned the War Department to get Congress to exempt Puerto Rico from the prohibition of liquor brought into American waters.[20] The worry was in vain; Congress did not make Puerto Rico an exception, and foreign ships did not stop docking at San Juan.[21]

Prohibition in Puerto Rico apparently generated no local enthusiasm equal to that of those who had originally voted for it. When insular newspapers began to argue for the removal of prohibition in 1931, a petitioning campaign was set in motion to convince the War Department that it should be retained and enforced more strongly. Dozens of letters and resolutions were sent to the War Department—but almost without exception they were signed by representatives or whole congregations of Protestant churches on the island.[22] The insular Socialist Party had long since dropped its advocacy of prohibition.

Just as prohibition had accompanied the Jones Act, so, in a sense, had the United States' participation in the First World War. Within a month after the passage of the new organic act, the nation that had recently claimed Puerto Ricans as citizens was at war with Germany. A few days before war was declared, Governor Arthur Yager, certain it was imminent, urged the War Department not to forget that Puerto Rico needed merchant ships for its normal economic life, and stated that San Juan was "exposed and defenseless" against enemy warships. He also asked General Frank McIntyre, Chief of the Bureau of Insular Affairs, what to do about any German merchant vessels in Puerto Rican harbors if war should be declared, and what the policy of the insular government should be toward the Germans living in Puerto Rico.[23] General McIntyre, replying one day before President Wilson signed the congressional resolution of war against Germany, soothed the governor's fears. He assured Yager that Puerto Rico was protected by the United States Navy, just as the rest of the American coast, and that the freighters then involved in the trade between Puerto Rico and the United States would not be diverted elsewhere. The governor need not worry about impounding the three German merchant ships then in San Juan harbor, for orders had already been sent to federal customs and immigration officials in Puerto Rico to intern the vessels and their crews. His advice to Yager in regard to German citizens residing in Puerto Rico was to treat them with consideration, as individuals, not as a class. They should not be interned or molested in any way unless they broke specific laws, and then only those individuals who were guilty should be dealt with.[24]

The people of Puerto Rico had always prided themselves on being peaceful, but the response of the Puerto Ricans toward American entry into the European war was positive. During the month after war between the United States and Germany had become official, each of the Puerto Rican political leaders sent to the federal government expressions of patriotism like that of Barceló to President Wilson: "Unionist Party assembled in Convention in San Juan pledges unqualified support to American nation and its illustrious President in the present conflict, expecting Porto Rico shall be assigned with its full quota of sacrifice and suffering to obtain victory."[25]

Puerto Rican participation in the First World War did not mean suffering in battle, except for a few Puerto Ricans who either went to the United States and joined the army there or who were already residing in the States and were drafted. The first Puerto Ricans to be involved in the war effort were the 640 men of the Porto Rican Regiment of the United States Army, who were sent to guard the

Panama Canal in June 1917. During the war, several training camps were set up in Puerto Rico, among them two or three for officers' training, which produced 425 Puerto Rican officers in the Reserve Corps. A total of 236,853 men were registered for draft purposes, 17,855 of whom were actually inducted into the army. Many of these were volunteers. Only 139 draftees failed to report for army duty. Before the end of the war, over four thousand Puerto Rican troops were stationed at the Panama Canal; the remainder—nearly fourteen thousand men—continued training in Puerto Rico.[26] The army units of Puerto Rico, like other American military groups at that time, were racially segregated; for most Puerto Ricans, this was the first formal racial segregation they had ever experienced.[27]

Besides military service, there were two other ways in which Puerto Rico contributed to the American war effort. First, the insular government helped to push the "Liberty Loan" drives on the island, and three of these raised a total of $5,271,500 for the war effort. Second, many Puerto Rican women and American women living in Puerto Rico made bandages and did other work for the Red Cross. Henry Dooley, a prominent businessman of Puerto Rico, headed the insular Red Cross organization. When one of the ships of the New York–San Juan route, the *Carolina,* was torpedoed and sent to the bottom by a German submarine in 1918, among the $500,000 in cargo lost were some sixty-three thousand Red Cross bandages made in Puerto Rico.[28]

The war created a manpower shortage. One of the laws which Governor Yager asked the insular legislature to pass in 1918 was an authorization for the commissioner of education to issue temporary teaching licenses to people qualified to fill in for schoolteachers who had resigned to join the army. Yager also worried about the noticeable loss of men from the insular police to the army.[29]

Another important impact of the war upon Puerto Rico was that of food shortage. Governor Yager, who always kept the positive aspects of a situation more prominent than the negative, never mentioned an actual shortage of foodstuffs on the island. Certainly the Bureau of Insular Affairs and the Wilson administration were not anxious to publicize any pinch felt in Puerto Rico either. But there are some facts that show that food was scarce. For one, Yager admitted that the number of ships entering Puerto Rican ports in the fiscal year 1918–19 was the lowest in ten years, having dropped 15.7 percent from the year before (tonnage dropped 17.4 percent, indicating either smaller ships were involved in the Puerto Rican trade or vessels were partially empty).[30] Puerto Rican food was to a great degree imported (see chapter 5), and a one-sixth drop in imports was bound to mean a food shortage, especially for the lower socioeconomic groups. Another hint of the gravity of the food situation was the power and publicity given to a six-man Food Commission in Puerto Rico. The first president of this commission was Antonio R. Barceló, the president of the Puerto Rican Senate and head of the Unionist Party, but he soon resigned, to be replaced by Albert Lee, "Porto Rico's own Hoover, the benevolent despot of Uncle Sam's island citizens."[31] It is a good guess that Barceló resigned because he saw how many enemies the Food Commission was going to make, a fact that would not have helped his political career.

The Food Commission carried on several activities. It worked toward price control (which would discourage hoarding and speculation) by requiring local police chiefs throughout the island to send lists of prices of sixty-four basic consumer items to the commission each week. The commission put pressure on the police chiefs to force merchants to lower prices that it declared exorbitant. With the help of the police, the commission instituted legal proceedings against price violators. In its first year of operation the Food Commission reported a total of 205 cases taken into the insular courts, 160 of which resulted in convictions. The punishments ranged from one to ten days in jail or alternatives of one to ten dollars in fines.[32] Another part of the work of the Food Commission was a publicity campaign for subsistence farming on the island. Puerto Ricans were urged to grow beans, rice, corn, bananas, and sweet potatoes. From the autumn of 1917 to April 1918, the land planted with these crops increased from 137,000 to 335,000 acres.[33] This important change toward food rather than cash crops was a temporary result of the work of the Food Commission and wartime shortages, not a permanent trend.

The war also generated patriotic fervor on the island. Puerto Ricans spoke of their part in the conflict many times over the subsequent decade, usually as proof that, as Félix Córdova Dávila said in 1918, "no more patriotic nor devoted people exist beneath the flag than the citizens of Porto Rico," who longed to "take their places side by side with their brothers from the States on the far-flung battle line in France."[34] This was flowery oratory, but there is good indication that Puerto Rico's involvement in the war was more than patriotic words. More than talk were the outbursts of stoning of homes of Germans in Puerto Rico after the sinking of the *Carolina*. Perhaps even more significant was the noticeable bitterness toward Spaniards as neutral friends of Germany,[35] for Spain and Spaniards had always held a warm place in the hearts of Puerto Ricans.

The European war would never have involved Puerto Rico had the island not been an American possession. Even the belligerent fervor of the Puerto Ricans could not diminish the awareness that it was the United States' war. Prohibition, in like manner, was the United States' social reform. And the idea of giving the vote to women was even more purely an import from the United States. In a culture such as that of Puerto Rico, which has had as one of its chief characteristics the ideal of masculine superiority, the concept of a woman as a member of the body politic was almost nonexistent.[36] As a part of Spain's empire, Puerto Rico had never dreamt of such a novelty as woman suffrage. Neither was the idea brought forward by any of the island's governors during the first twenty-three years of American rule. But in June 1919, the United States Congress passed the Nineteenth Amendment, giving American women the right to vote (many states had already done so). The consequences for Puerto Rico of the passage of this amendment were unclear. The amendment could be interpreted to include the women of Puerto Rico. Or if Puerto Rican women did not receive suffrage with the Nineteenth Amendment, at least it would be easier to work toward a local law to achieve the same end.

There were two organizations in Puerto Rico working for woman suffrage early in the 1920s—the Suffragist Social League of Puerto Rico (*Liga Social Sufragista de Puerto Rico*) and the Democratic Suffragist League (*Liga Sufragista Democrática*). The former was founded in 1917 and claimed to represent "the most intellectual feminine element of Porto Rico"; the latter prided itself in representing the island's large number of working women.[37] The Suffragist Social League was led by Mrs. Milagros Benet de Mewton, who by 1924 had assumed the presidency of an organization which represented her suffrage group in the United States and other countries, the Pan American Association of Women of Porto Rico.[38] In propagandizing the cause of Puerto Rican woman suffrage in the United States, this organization seemed to have been the most effective. However, the most powerful suffragette group in regard to insular politics came to be the Puerto Rican Association of Suffragettes (*Asociación Puertorriqueña de Mujeres Sufragistas*), which began organizing in late 1926, and was led by Mrs. Ana Roqué de Duprey, the grand dame of Puerto Rican feminism.[39]

The activities of these suffrage groups were copied in part from the methods of United States feminist organizations and in part were novel programs designed to fit the peculiar situation of Puerto Rico.[40] They held mass meetings, they sent petitions to legislators in the insular and federal governments, and they published feminist magazines such as *La Mujer del Siglo XX* (*The Twentieth-Century Woman*) and newspapers such as *Nosotras* (the feminine-gender *We*). When General McIntyre visited Puerto Rico late in 1920, some of the suffrage leaders unsuccessfully tried to arrange an appointment with him.[41] The women sometimes held well-planned *manifestaciones* or demonstrations.

Like the nineteenth-century feminist associations in the United States, the Puerto Rican suffrage groups encountered stubborn opposition and heart-rending difficulties. The dues of the organization led by Ana Roqué de Duprey were only five dollars a year, but even this amount was large to many women in Puerto Rico. It was reason to talk of sacrifice: "The men sacrifice monetarily for their ideals. I don't see why women have to be less."[42] There was never enough money for the leaders of the organization to rent an office or hire a stenographer.[43] And even the most ardent suffragettes admitted that it was "asking too much of women to give themselves fully to the duties of the home and to those of civic life at the same time," and suggested that a woman with children should hold group meetings in her home "and thus not have to leave her children unattended."[44]

The opposition the feminists received from Puerto Rican men was less vicious than that which the United States women had encountered.[45] Perhaps it was Latin politeness that caused the men of Puerto Rico to use arguments not so harsh as the one that women have weaker brains (even though Latin American men were more confident than those from North America that women were weaker intellectually and morally). Perhaps it was their Roman Catholic religion, which placed less emphasis upon "proving" one's point from Scripture, that kept Puerto Rican men from arguing that the New Testament forbade women to leave their domestic "place." But Puerto Rican men did have arguments against woman suffrage. The most common was that by indulging in voting and other civic activities, the Puerto Rican woman would run a great risk of losing her grace, spirituality, and sweetness—the things which attracted men to her. The "first day of her civil emancipation is also the first of her social slavery."[46] A second reason frequently given for not granting the Puerto Rican woman the franchise was that she was too pure and virtuous, and politics was yet dirty. This was used often with a reference to the war (clearly a "man's business") during the 1917–18 period.

No, Puerto Rican women, wait a while, until the environment is favorable and healthy so that you who always have given a high tone to our society, will not come to soil the purity of your actions and be made faint by the things which go on in an insane war, since you are not forward and bold like the American woman; neither are you like the European woman, a daughter of adventure.[47]

The third argument against woman suffrage was that most of the women did not want it.[48] This was probably true, for it is doubtful that the average Puerto Rican housewife, struggling to raise a family on the small wages made by her husband, was very alarmed at not being allowed to vote. Even though the suffragettes replied that their many activities showed the great demand for suffrage among women of the island, they acknowledged that theirs was an upper-class movement by repeated assurances that they were not asking for the vote for illiterate women, but only for those who could read and write. These women, given the vote, would not lose the respect of "cultured and educated" men.[49]

This emphasis upon literacy worked against the women who used it. The last thing an illiterate Puerto Rican man wanted was to have women who were literate equal to him in the right to vote. And no political party cared to see the voting laws changed to allow only people—of both sexes—who could read and write to have the franchise. Besides arousing opposition among men, the emphasis upon literacy as a part of female suffrage split the ranks of women fighting for the vote. When a woman suffrage bill was in the Puerto Rican Senate in 1919, one of the telegrams received by that body pointed this out: "Eight hundred working women of Loiza met in assembly demand the female vote without restriction. Our motto [is] all [of us] free or all [of us] slaves."[50]

Bills to grant suffrage to Puerto Rican women were introduced in the insular legislature in 1919, 1921, 1923, and 1927 unsuccessfully. The first of these originated in the Senate and died there. The leaders of all three of the Puerto Rican political parties voted in favor of this bill and also for the 1923 bill, which also failed to pass in the Senate. After the vote on the 1923 bill, José Tous Soto, the Republican Party chieftan, suggested that the women use the courts to try to obtain a ruling that the Nineteenth Amendment applied to Puerto Rico.[51]

The possibility that the U.S. amendment granting woman suffrage included Puerto Rican women had already been investigated. In September 1920, Governor Yager sent a cablegram to the Bureau of Insular Affairs, asking for a ruling "whether it applies to Porto Rico," adding that the matter was "urgent." General E. H. Crowder, the judge advocate general of the army, gave the Bureau of Insular Affairs his opinion, saying the Nineteenth Amendment did not include Puerto Rico. The "heart of the question," as he saw it, was the fact that the Constitution had never been fully extended to Puerto Rico. He repeated the "insular cases" doctrine: "In the light of two decades of American rule in the tropics, it may be stated as an axiom of government of our dependent peoples that a prerequisite to efficiency is adherence to the doctrine of the nonapplicability of the Constitution as a body of organic law to outlying possessions of the United States."[52] Mrs. Ida Husted Harper, who had been important in the woman suffrage movement in the United States (especially in California), wrote to outgoing Secretary of State Bainbridge Colby in January 1921, asking him to explain the difference between Alaska "and our former territories" and Puerto Rico in relation to woman suffrage. Colby referred Mrs. Harper's letter to General McIntyre of the Bureau of Insular Affairs, who explained to her that Alaska and Hawaii, and the "former territories," were all "organized, incorporated" territories, over which the Constitution ruled in full, whereas Puerto Rico was not.[53]

The woman suffrage bill of 1927, like the earlier ones, began in the insular Senate. This time the bill passed through the Senate, but failed in the House of Representatives.[54] The lower house represented more of the lower economic class in Puerto Rico, among whom the *macho* tradition (masculine superiority) could be expected to be stronger. When this bill was quashed, many of the women decided female suffrage was never going to come from the insular politicians. Turning to the U.S. government, they sent a four-page memorial to President Calvin Coolidge. In it the women reported the discouraging situation they faced in Puerto Rico, and argued that the many educated women and women schoolteachers in the island proved the propriety of female suffrage there. They asked Coolidge's help in getting the U.S. Congress to remedy the wrong.[55]

Two governors over Puerto Rico urged the passage of a woman suffrage law. Governor E. Mont. Reily called for it in his inaugural address in 1921, and Governor Horace Mann Towner did the same in a message to the Puerto Rican legislature in 1927. However, there is no evidence that they, or any other governors, ever suggested that the reform come from the U.S. Congress. Another official who was closer to the administrations in Washington, General Frank McIntyre, was sympathetic toward woman suffrage, but again there is no proof that he moved to promote activity in Washington.[56]

Some members of Congress felt that it was time to take the woman-suffrage question out of the hands of the Puerto Rican legislators. Early in 1928 Senator Hiram Bingham introduced a bill amending the Jones Act to provide for female suffrage. The Senate of Puerto Rico sent a resolution protesting Bingham's bill on the grounds that it dealt with "matters of local interest" which should be handled by the Puerto Rican legislature.[57] The bill died in committee. But even before Bingham's bill in the Senate, Congressman Edgar R. Kiess of Pennsylvania had introduced a similar bill in the House of Representatives. This bill, H.R. 7010, slowly worked its way through to passage in December 1928. In the Senate, H.R. 7010 was reported favorably out of the Committee on Territories and Insular Possessions within a month. But with the bill came a minority report from five senators in the committee, including Carl Hayden and Millard E. Tydings. In the debate over the woman suffrage bill, these two men pointed out to the Senate that they too wanted to see the women of Puerto Rico given the right to vote, but that "the Legislature of Porto Rico is the proper authority to remedy the evil, rather than the Congress of the United States." Senator Tydings appealed to the ideal of states rights, and said the federal government should not use "coercion or guidance" on "every little matter of local self-government in which we may differ with them."[58] After an extended debate over H.R. 7010 and the reading of the minority report and some telegrams opposing the bill from Santiago Iglesias and Rafael Martínez Nadal (head of the Republican Party at that time), the Senate went on to other matters without voting on Puerto Rican woman suffrage. Nothing further was done or attempted by the U.S. Congress to push woman suffrage into the Jones Act, but the point had been made: the Puerto Rican legislature should get the job done, or it would be taken out of the hands of the islanders.

On the same day the Senate debated H.R. 7010, February 11, 1929, Governor Horace Mann Towner gave his annual message to the insular legislature, and in it he warned the members: "Action on the question of Woman Suffrage in Porto Rico should no longer be delayed by the Legislature. The Congress of the United States has the matter under consideration, but if you take prompt action here at this time your judgment will be respected and Congress will not be called upon to act."[59] On April 16, 1929, the insular legislature passed a bill to give Puerto Rican women the right to vote. The law provided, however, that this privilege would not begin until 1932, and that the elective franchise would at that time be open to all Puerto Ricans of either sex who could read and write in Spanish or English.

What were the effects of woman suffrage in Puerto Rico? First, it did not end the existence of the feminist organizations. Some merely changed their names; for example, the Puerto Rican Association of Suffragettes became the Insular Association of Voting Women. They worked now for female literacy and awareness of civic issues and duties.[60] Second, some women began to be included in the work of Puerto Rican political parties. When a commission came to Washington to represent the cause of the Republican Party of the island early in President Hoover's administration, one member of the group was Dr. Marta Robert de Romeu, "Committeewoman."[61] Mrs. Ana Roqué de Duprey worked with Antonio Barceló, the Unionist leader, urging Puerto Rican women to petition the U.S. Congress for a status offering complete autonomy for Puerto Rico.[62] Barceló, who claimed to be the author of the bill which gave the vote to Puerto Rican women, advised Mrs. Roqué de Duprey against starting a separate women's political party.[63] Third, while the women of Puerto Rico may have been largely responsible for the increase in the 1932 election in the total votes cast (383,657 as compared with 264,734 votes in the 1928 election and 253,520 in 1924), there is no evidence to prove women had anything to do with the important political changes that occurred within the insular parties during those years.[64]

Within a dozen years after the passage of the Jones Act, Puerto Ricans had adopted two American reforms—prohibition and woman suffrage—and had been involved in American participation in the First World War. Were these, for Puerto Rico, merely "loyalty oaths"? In the case of prohibition, such a conclusion is most reasonable. Santiago Iglesias, head of the major labor union and the Socialist Party on the island, had an important role in the outcome of the 1917 referendum because his Socialist Party was the only political group which took a definite stand on the question, and it was for prohibition. And Iglesias was pro-American to an almost ridiculous degree. He reveled in the nickname, "Mr. Liberty," given him by American troops in 1898. He named some of his daughters (Iglesias had eleven children) "America," "Justice," "Equality," and "Liberty."[65] Beyond the referendum of 1917, prohibition was never supported in Puerto Rico by groups other than those who least fit in with Puerto Rican culture: the Protestant churches.

Puerto Rican participation in the World War was not such a clear case of copying the imperial power. There is every indication that Puerto Ricans were proud of their American citizenship and looked on their part in the war as a matter of *partnership* with the United States. If it resulted in mere patriotic bombast, perhaps the fault lay with the United States in not using Puerto Rican troops in more direct confrontation with the enemy.

The feminist organizations of Puerto Rico originated on the island, even though they adopted the tactics of "the cause" in the United States. The women who were active in the Puerto Rican suffrage movement were native Puerto Ricans, not women from the United States who were residing on the island. The success of the woman suffrage movement was a direct result of pressure from the U.S. Congress, but there were Puerto Rican politicians such as Barceló who had worked toward woman suffrage for at least a decade before women won the vote. Neither the feminists nor the insular politicians who helped them indicated that they wanted woman suffrage simply to show the United States how American they were. Like American feminists, they wanted the right to vote because they believed it was a step toward bettering the condition of women.

"Americanization" was a major controversy in Puerto Rico during the years between the Jones Act and the New Deal. Whether prohibition, woman suffrage, and Puerto Rican aid in the American war effort represented Americanization or not, there were definite attempts by some Americans who dealt with Puerto Rico to promote the metamorphosis of Puerto Rico from a Spanish to an American culture. The most flagrant and offensive of these attempts came with the governorship of E. Mont. Reily.

3

"100% Americanism"

Comes to Puerto Rico

In December 1920, Governor Arthur Yager gave the Bureau of Insular Affairs his assessment of the Puerto Rican political situation. During the preceding seven years there had been increasing use of oratory for independence, accompanied by a one-star flag to symbolize independence.[1] There were many Americans who took this talk seriously, and thought of it as a threat of rebellion.[2] But Yager understood that independence was merely an electioneering tactic, and warned that the governor who succeeded him should not believe the Puerto Rican Republicans' claim to be the only loyal American party on the island. Yager saw that the Republicans wanted President-elect Harding to give them a governor who would take the Unionists' independence rhetoric seriously and would help the Republicans "win at Washington what they lost in the local elections." If the president would choose a superpatriot who would show resentment at anything expressing preference for Puerto Rico over United States, the governor counseled, he would run the risk of driving the Unionists into being actually an anti-American organization.[3] Unfortunately, the Republicans did "win at Washington," for the man Warren Harding chose as the new governor for Puerto Rico was exactly the loud superpatriot Arthur Yager had feared.

Neither Yager nor the Bureau of Insular Affairs saw any urgency in putting a new man in the governorship. Yager told President Harding that it would be wise to wait to replace him until summer, when the fiscal year would end and the governor's annual report would be prepared.[4] General McIntyre of the BIA told the administration the same thing.[5] The legislature of Puerto Rico sent a resolution to the new president saying they wanted no change at all, but would be happy to see Yager retained as governor.[6] On April 9,

1921, Harding assured Yager that "there will be no hurry in making a change of executives for the island."[7] But President Harding saw the office as a political tidbit to be handed out, and on May 6 the White House announced that E. Mont. Reily of Kansas City was the nominee for governor of Puerto Rico.[8]

Emmett Montgomery Reily apparently never used his full name, but always went by E. Mont. Reily. He was born in Sedalia, Missouri, in 1866, and had lived in Kansas City since about the age of thirty. He had been assistant postmaster for Kansas City for a short period around 1902, and was in business as a mortgage broker for several years prior to his gubernatorial appointment.[9] Reily had increasingly involved himself in politics, first on the local and state levels, then on the national scene. He claimed to have organized the first "Roosevelt for President" club in America in 1901, and later he supported T.R. as a Progressive candidate against Wilson and Taft.[10] As early as the summer of 1919, Reily had begun to work toward the nomination and election of Warren G. Harding. Harding at that time asked Reily to discontinue this effort, because he felt that he himself lacked "that availability which is based on geographical locality" or "the elements of leadership or the wide-spread acquaintance necessary for victory." But of Reily, Harding said: "I have come to understand full well your very marked political influence and the effectiveness of your political activity and I know too, some of the rare political friendships which you have enlisted."[11] Reily continued to promote Harding, using his time and money as Harding's "pre-convention Western campaign manager"—probably a self-appointed position.[12] He later claimed to have personally contributed $11,000 to the Harding campaign fund.[13]

Once Reily's appointment to the governorship of Puerto Rico was known publicly, it was assumed he would promptly go to the island. Paul G. Miller, the commissioner of education, urged General McIntyre to try to get "Mr. Riley" to Puerto Rico by the first of June. He stressed that if the new governor should arrive any later, the new fiscal year would open without an insular budget, and in the matter of education this could be disastrous.[14] General McIntyre's

reply to Miller was labeled "CONFIDENTIAL" and properly so, for its contents would not have pleased the Puerto Ricans. Reily, who had been in Washington (conferring with President Harding about Puerto Rico, presumably), had already left for Kansas City. His plans, as he had divulged them to the Bureau of Insular Affairs, were to take the oath of office as governor of Puerto Rico in Kansas City on May 16 and then attend to business in Texas and other parts of the West. He had told the BIA that it would not be possible for him to go to Puerto Rico before July, and he hoped the legislature and the acting governor, José E. Benedicto, could manage without him until then.[15]

Governor Reily was back in Kansas City by late June, and at that time wrote to George Christian, Harding's personal secretary, asking him to call to the president's attention the three appointments Reily wanted for the insular government. For commissioner of education he wanted Juan B. Huyke to replace Paul Miller, as "the present educational organization there is very much opposed to President Harding and . . . I will not work with any organization that is against the President." For commissioner of immigration Reily asked for the appointment of Roberto H. Todd, the Puerto Rican politician whose career was characterized by his attempts to tie the insular Republican party to that of the states. Reily chose William L. Kessinger, a friend from Kansas City, as his auditor in the insular government.[16] The Harding administration conferred with the War Department about these appointments and was advised not to be in a hurry; the position of auditor should not be changed until Reily was actually in Puerto Rico.[17] Secretary of War John Weeks also gave Governor Reily some direct advice, warning him not to be quick to commit himself to "certain acts and appointments" before going to the island.[18]

All administration counsel to Governor E. Mont. Reily was apparently in vain. By July, Reily had already made some Puerto Ricans very aware of him. The Puerto Rican press had begun to quote (and possibly misquote) the new governor as saying there were "thousands" of abandoned children in Puerto Rico; that he would press for better enforcement of prohibition; that he wanted woman suffrage in Puerto Rico; that he desired ultimate statehood for the island; that the politicians who wanted anything other than statehood were professional agitators and not native Puerto Ricans; that with his strong influence with the president, Reily would make his military aide, presently a captain, a colonel in the army; that he was not going to let the Puerto Ricans run their affairs as they had under Yager, because he was "the boss" now; and that the governorship of Puerto Rico was "the best appointment that President Harding could award," as its salary and "perquisites" would total $54,000 a year.[19] If Reily had said such things, declared *La Correspondencia,* then he had "demonstrated not only the negligent ignorance which he possesses in matters regarding our island, but his greater incompetence in the discretion and tact which a person in his position should have." The newspaper's editor was sure that Reily was simply being repaid by Harding with the governorship for "past electoral services."[20] Even at this early date, the Puerto Ricans had spotted the two characteristics that were to become synonymous with Reily's name—tactlessness and an Americanism that *La Democracia* called "of the double sort," that is, superpatriotism.[21]

Reily was in Washington again for a few days in late July, and while there he called on both President Harding and BIA Chief Frank McIntyre. With his wife and two daughters, he sailed from New York on July 23, and a week later he landed in Puerto Rico. A few hours after his arrival Governor Reily delivered his inaugural address—some two and a half months after taking the oath of office.

E. Mont. Reily's inaugural speech is interesting and important. It is important because it shows the mind of the new governor, because it was the cause of a great deal of bitterness on the part of Puerto Ricans, and because it was apparently edited by President Harding. Among the Reily manuscripts in the New York Public Library is the original draft of his inaugural address, typed on long pages. With it is an envelope which bears the hand-written label "President Harding's Correction of my Inaugural Speech." The speech itself is marked in many places with blue pencil. At the top of the first page is a hand-written note in ink, which says, "The corrections in 'blue' were made by President Harding. EMR"[22] Thus, Governor Reily claimed that a president of the United States took time out from his busy schedule to read and edit a speech to be given by a colonial governor. There is no reference (to the best of my knowledge) in Harding's own papers at the Ohio Historical Society to this editing job, but certain internal evidences and other facts would indicate that he did in fact correct Reily's address.

Governor Reily apparently wrote the speech while in Kansas City between his first visit to Washington and his journey to Puerto Rico, for the heading of the first page of the original draft reads: "KANSAS CITY, MISSOURI. JUNE 30TH, 1921. (INAUGURAL ADDRESS OF E. MONT. REILY, GOVERNOR OF PORTO RICO.)" He might have sent the proposed speech to the president then, or he might have handed it to Harding when he visited Washington the second time that year, just before going to the island.

Reily's oration was to have begun: "My Fellow Americans: It is with the deepest and most profound pride that I can address you to-day as my 'Fellow Americans.' In so doing, I feel that I am bestowing upon you an incomparable compliment." The blue pencil changed this patronizing phrase to read, "I feel that I am uttering the highest respect which I can bestow." Farther along, Reily had intended to say, "I have ideas of my own as to what the conduct of a Governor or ruler, under these circumstances, should be." The word "ruler" was deleted and the less offensive word "executive" substituted for it. A few paragraphs later, when Reily had spoken of the territory "over which I may rule," his speech critic wrote in "administer."[23]

Many of the statements made by Governor Reily in his inaugural address offended the Puerto Ricans, or at least the Unionists. He advocated woman suffrage for the island; this was looked on as purely a local matter and none of America's business. He bluntly remarked that "there is no sympathy or possible hope in the United States for independence" for Puerto Rico, and that anyone who advocated independence was probably a foreigner, not a Puerto Rican.

He firmly stated that there was no room for such individuals in Puerto Rico, nor was there room for flags other than Old Glory, which had "come to stay." He made a lengthy pledge that he would insist upon "Americanism" in Puerto Rico, and that this would include making "the language of Washington, Lincoln, and Harding" the primary one in Puerto Rican schools. None of these harshly worded parts of the speech was changed or dropped by the presidential blue pencil.

There was one other aspect of the address which bears importance, for it is the internal proof that President Warren G. Harding was Reily's speech critic. Four times in his speech the governor referred to Puerto Rico as "these Islands." While it is true that Puerto Rico includes a host of tiny islands (many uninhabited) which surround it, nevertheless Puerto Rico has, since earliest times, been known as "the island of Puerto Rico." Of all the Puerto Rican and non–Puerto Rican figures who dealt with Puerto Rico from 1898 to 1940, only two of them dubbed Puerto Rico "these Islands"— E. Mont. Reily and Warren G. Harding.[24]

As Reily delivered his inaugural address, he paused at each paragraph while a Puerto Rican read the Spanish translation. Sitting on the platform from which the governor spoke were Barceló and some other prominent Unionists. They pointedly refused to applaud when Reily said Puerto Rico must seek statehood and at the end of the speech.[25]

Reactions to the speech were prompt. The very pro-American *El Tiempo* (which always was published with an English version, *The Times*) happily reported that Reily's firm stand against independence had begun the "liquidation" of the Union Party.[26] The Republican Party organ, *El Mundo,* considered part of the inaugural address as "marvelous paragraphs, revealing his high spirit of Justice, his great equanimity and sincerity of soul, proclaiming the best and most sane desires . . . for the promotion of the welfare and the happiness of the island." In other words, the Republicans liked what he said about statehood. But *El Mundo* did admit that the address was the most widely discussed message ever delivered by a governor in Puerto Rico, and that this discussion dealt mostly with Reily as a "strong man." Reily's "hard and threatening tone," said the paper, was not apt for "noble, faithful and loyal" Puerto Rico, symbolized always by a kneeling lamb. Finally, the Republican newspaper counseled against being too quickly exasperated with the new governor; it stressed that he might turn out to be very good after he had a chance to observe the Puerto Rican people and see that they were loyal to American institutions.[27]

The reaction of the Unionists to the inaugural address was predictable—they were already "laying for him." *La Democracia* saw the speech as "the work of a bold man who has been allowed to speak, taking the ridiculous pose of a schoolteacher, of things that he doesn't know about." Reily had made a "lamentable" mistake in thinking that he had come among a primitive people whom he could dazzle with the "splendors of a superior civilization" or that he could conquer their "poor weak spirits with a brutal threat." He was absolutely ignorant of Puerto Rican culture and history. In short, according to the paper, the inaugural address showed that Governor Reily did not have the open mind he claimed, and this was an "insult, provocation and threat."[28]

La Correspondencia agreed that Reily demonstrated that he had no knowledge of "our manner of being." He had showed Puerto Ricans his "aggressiveness, and the tendency of his nature, to intend to change, through his administration, the *ideals* of Puerto Ricans." Reily was a "battlefield politician, not a statesman." Reily was a patriotic American, preferring the United States to Puerto Rico; but he should have realized that Puerto Rican patriots similarly preferred Puerto Rico.[29]

The Unionist Party proceeded to push Governor Reily into the clash that dominated his year and a half in office. Barceló, the president of the party and president of the Senate of Puerto Rico, used the issue of appointments to press Reily. On August 13, 1921, Barceló sent to the governor a recommendation of three men (all good Unionists) for Reily to pick one for a vacancy on the Workman's Relief Commission.[30] Reily saw this—probably correctly—as an attempt to "dictate" appointments to the governor. He replied to Barceló in a letter saturated with venom; the letter, soon known as "the Barceló letter," was published in the insular press. It sarcastically told Barceló that whether he knew it or not, with Reily's coming "the old order has changed and will return no more. . . . The plan of the politicians here has been to control and to break every governor that has been sent to this Island. . . . I hope all concerned here understand now it will not work out on me." He told Barceló: "Sever your connection with the independence party and become a loyal Porto Rican American or we cannot have any friendly political relations."[31]

Barceló sent the text of this letter and his own earlier letter with the three nominations to President Harding, via the War Department. Harding promptly wrote to Governor Reily, mildly telling him the letter to Barceló had been "indiscreet," and cautioning him to deal carefully with "a rather delicate situation." The president assured Reily that this was not a condemnation or lack of confidence in the governor's good intentions and courage, but just a suggestion for more "thoughtful prudence."[32]

A few days later Reily defended his actions to the president. He had, he said, the "greatest provocation" before writing his letter to the Unionist chief, for Barceló's demand was that all appointments made by Reily had to be submitted to him first. (There is no proof of this beyond Reily's word, for Barceló's letter to him had merely contained the three names of possible selections for a post and had not made any demand beyond that.) Next, Reily told Harding that after his inaugural address, he received "a number" of threatening letters. This was the first time Governor Reily claimed to have received such letters; there is no proof, for never did he send one of these letters on to Harding or the War Department, and never did anyone else claim to have seen the letters. Reily told Harding that "the Barceló letter" was considered to be too weak by the prominent Americans who resided in Puerto Rico.[33]

Thus, by the end of his first month in office, Reily was helping to draw up the opposing sides in the island, by identifying himself thoroughly with the little clique of American residents there. These "continentals" (as Americans who were not native Puerto Ricans were termed) soon formed Reily's opinion of Félix Córdova Dávila: "He is a professional double-crosser, so every American on the Island tells me."[34] They and their wealthy Puerto Rican friends backed the governor. The Saddle and Motor Country Club of San Juan sent President Harding a resolution condemning the Yager administration for a loss of prestige for the United States flag and for the increasing sentiment for independence, and lauding Reily for reversing these trends.[35] One of Governor Reily's most prominent sycophants was Roberto H. Todd, a member of the insular Republican Party and also of the National Committee of the Republican Party of the United States. Todd wrote and cabled Harding on several occasions, praising Governor Reily and trying to give the impression that all but a few disloyal and corrupt Unionists among the Puerto Ricans were wildly happy with their new governor.[36] Another of Reily's backers was Willis Sweet, who published and edited the extremely pro-American dual-language newspaper *El Tiempo–The Times*.[37]

For a short period late in September, there was a lull in the Unionist pressure upon Governor Reily, and the governor thought he had won; he reported this to the president.[38] Harding was glad to hear that the turmoil in Puerto Rico was at an end, and that the "foolishness" of independence talk there was put down. He confided to Reily, "When you first plunged into the situation, you did it rather more frankly than I should have been disposed to do, but we can't all do things precisely alike, and I am not sure but yours was the quickest and most effective way of getting the desired results." Now, he was sure, Reily could settle down to do "constructive as well as corrective things."[39]

The lull was only a temporary one in the political hurricane, and in October, Barceló and other Unionists began an unremitting campaign against the governor in their press. Stinging articles in both Spanish and English appeared in *La Correspondencia* and *La Democracia*. The latter newspaper carried a series of "open letters" to Governor Reily in English, some of them titled "Letters to the Emperor" and beginning "Darling Caesar."[40]

President Harding had told Reily that he would have to be very tactful and either thick-skinned in the face of this satire or able to stop it in some way; otherwise he would not get any real work done as governor.[41] Unfortunately, Reily was above all lacking in tact and patience (as even President Harding ruefully admitted), and he was able neither to stop the Unionist barbs nor to ignore them. For several reasons E. Mont. Reily was not a very successful or productive governor.

Reily spent an inordinate amount of his time writing letters and sending cables to President Harding, justifying himself. In the first year after his arrival in Puerto Rico, Governor Reily sent at least thirty-four letters, some of them as much as nine pages in length, and six cables to President Harding. No other governor of Puerto Rico ever had such a massive correspondence with the president he served under, not even Arthur Yager, who was a far closer friend of Woodrow Wilson than Reily was of Harding.[42] This flood of correspondence with the president included large doses of effusive flattery. On October 19, 1921, Reily wrote Harding, "When a man is away off in a place like this and is doing what he thinks is best and is backed up by ninety percent of the people, . . . it is mighty fine to have his President say the beautiful things you said in your letter. I knew absolutely when you got the facts you would sustain me, on account of your real Americanism." In the same letter, he told the president why he was not sending him a copy of a speech he had made: "I do not desire to appear as patronizing. You know I cannot make a speech anywhere without saying something about you."[43] At another time Reily sympathized with Harding's personal troubles, making them his battles too: "By the way, Mr. President, I wanted you to know that that vile attack made on you by the New York World has been reproduced in the Barcelo papers of Porto Rico."[44] He sent the president an oil portrait of Harding and on at least one occasion some Puerto Rican cigars.[45]

An implication of Reily's voluminous correspondence with the president was that he was bypassing the proper channels of communication with the administration in Washington. His direct superior was Brigadier General Frank B. McIntyre, chief of the Bureau of Insular Affairs, and above him John Weeks, secretary of war. Reily realized after some time that McIntyre was aware of this slight, and he wrote the general a rather lame excuse: he had been forced to send "a number of cables" to the president directly because he did not trust the Puerto Rican in the office of the executive secretary who handled cables. Reily assured McIntyre that he had nothing to keep from him and offered to show him all the cables he had sent directly to Harding.[46] This was not a logical excuse, for surely the governor could have by-passed or transferred the suspect Puerto Rican. Neither does the excuse give any reason for the many letters Reily sent directly to the president.

McIntyre and Reily were completely at odds by early in 1922. The BIA chief suggested in a confidential memorandum to Secretary of War Weeks that the federal government "plant" a man in the insular cabinet, to advise the governor and help him avoid any future blunders of magnitude.[47] For his part, Reily wrote to the president's personal secretary accusing McIntyre of trying to get a certain Unionist appointed to the Puerto Rican Supreme Court; Reily claimed that this would put the Court in Barceló's hands, whereas with the appointee the governor wanted, "we will have control of the Court."[48] Whether or not it was true that McIntyre was actively working against Reily, certainly the general was not going out of his way to make things easier for the governor. President Harding became aware of this, and on one occasion asked Secretary of War Weeks to

invite [McIntyre's] cooperation in immediately clearing up this situation. I cannot escape the conviction that the General can be helpful in putting aside all the disagreeable things which have developed during the early period of Governor Reily's administration. I do not mean by this that General McIntyre is in any way responsible or that he has been in any way sympathetic with the opposition. I am only trying to say that I believe he has great influence and the exercise of that influence at the present time will prove very helpful.[49]

Harding was correct; as the one man who had a controlling influence in United States–Puerto Rican relations, administration after administration, the chief of the Bureau of Insular Affairs could make a governorship smooth or extremely difficult. Reily's break with General McIntyre was an important second reason for his lack of success in Puerto Rico.

Another factor in Reily's ineffective governorship was that he divided his attention between Puerto Rico and Kansas City. Many of his letters and cables to the president dealt, wholly or in part, with Missouri politics and patronage. On September 21, 1921, he sent Harding both a letter and a cable, warning that certain men should not receive Kansas City appointments because they were not "Harding men," and telling the president he concurred in a recommendation made by "our friends from Missouri" that Assistant Secretary of State Dearing be appointed minister to Portugal.[50] When Reily came to the United States in November 1921, he was slated to return to the island within a month; he did not leave Kansas City until January 13 or later, excusing himself on the grounds that he was busy "selecting forty deputies" there and getting all Republican factions to agree on the selections.[51]

Not only was Reily's mind on Kansas City politics, but it was too much on United States politics. In November 1922 he wrote a long letter to the president with his interpretation of the historical significance of the recent Republican election victories. He showed how for each president from Grant through Wilson the "off-year" elections had been disastrous for their parties. But this, Harding's off year, was the grand and glorious exception—which proved that Harding was the most popular president at least since Lincoln.[52] A few weeks later the governor again shared with President Harding his expertise in American politics. He told Harding that

I have been thinking a good deal about 1924, and have noticed that a number of loud talking "Progressives" have had a great deal to say, so I have in mind that if we should nominate Hoover for Vice President in 1924, it would be, not only a great stroke politically, but would close the mouth of every alleged progressive who thinks he has been called especially by the Lord to save the country. . . . Vice President Coolidge could be taken care of in some other way, and perhaps would be glad to make a change.[53]

Reily's presidential advising was hardly necessary to proper performance of his own job.

Symptomatic of Reily's unhappy administration was the little time he actually spent in Puerto Rico. Of the 642 days from his oath of office as governor of Puerto Rico, May 16, 1921, until the date of his letter of resignation to President Harding, February 16, 1923, Reily was absent from the island for 204 days. Part of this time was the ten weeks which elapsed before he first went to Puerto Rico; the rest was made up of two trips back to the United States, one of ten weeks and the other seven.

Governor Reily could not or would not let the Unionists make their charges and have their satire, and ignore them. Instead, he was generally on the offensive against his enemies. Besides his "Barceló letter" there are several examples of this. When in February 1922 the Puerto Rican Senate turned down his non-Unionist cabinet nominations, he waited until it adjourned and then reappointed them.[54] Another example of Reily's aggressiveness was his frequent removal from office of Unionists or any other people he suspected of opposing him, without any legal basis or public backing for such action. When in August 1922 the governor made a big issue over his attempt to oust his attorney general, Salvador Mestre, Secretary of War Weeks admitted to President Harding, "I am somewhat disturbed to see that the Governor seems to be making a clean sweep of officers in Porto Rico."[55] Reily was on the offensive, too, whenever he told Puerto Rican audiences, as he did in his inaugural speech and again in speeches made on a tour of the eastern portion of the island, that if individuals could not get justice from an insular court or judge, they should come directly to him, and he would give them justice and also "immediately destroy" such a judge.[56] Since most—if not all—of the judges in Puerto Rico were Unionists, this amounted to saying that the governor did not trust them to carry out their duties properly.

The governor's consciousness about flags was an additional symptom of his ineffectiveness. Throughout his gubernatorial term flags were a major issue. He mentioned flags in his inaugural address and in many later speeches. He boasted in November 1921 that from 1918 to 1921, under Governor Yager, only 1,300 American flags were sold in Puerto Rico, but that in his first four months, natives had bought 16,000 American flags.[57] Félix Córdova Dávila, resident commissioner from Puerto Rico (and second in the Unionist Party, behind Barceló), questioned Reily's neat statistics on flags.[58]

Knowing that Reily would react to the one-star Unionist flag like a bull to the toreador's *muleta,* the governor's opponents used this issue to goad and distract him. When Reily began his speaking tour of Puerto Rico in October 1921, his cavalcade passed by the University of Puerto Rico in Rio Piedras. Many of the students greeted him there with "an infinity" of the one-star flags, holding them aloft as they chanted " *Viva la independencia!*"[59] A frequent Unionist charge was that in at least one speech he had called the one-star flag of their party a "rag."[60] The insular press also frequently hinted that Reily had given orders to suppress this flag, and that his personal bodyguard, George S. McClure, the chief of the Secret Service in Puerto Rico, tore one of the lone-star flags from an automobile during his first day on the island.[61] By making this flag so much the center of his attention, the governor was instrumental in converting it from a Unionist flag into the Puerto Rican flag, so that even a Republican newspaper, *El Mundo,* was offended at the report that Reily had asked the insular political leaders to design a new flag to be used as a "regional ensign."[62] Secretary of War John Weeks accurately predicted the outcome of Reily's anti-Unionist flag campaign: "Continual depreciation of the Porto Rican flag may easily give that flag a position in the eyes and minds of the people of Porto Rico which it has never had and would not otherwise acquire."[63]

A major feature of Governor Reily's poor administration was his thinly disguised contempt for Puerto Ricans. At first Reily showed his lack of respect only for his political opponents: Barceló was "absolutely unreliable and treacherous and a crook" and so was Córdova Dávila.[64] Later, Reily told President Harding, "I find here that Porto Ricans are much the same, whether they are Republicans or Unionists."[65] Reily increasingly identified with the "continentals" against the "natives," and in his letters to the president he more and more used the same generalizations the "continentals" did to characterize the Puerto Ricans. Warning Harding against a meeting with Resident Commissioner Córdova Dávila, he stated that "*every* Porto Rican professional politician carries a pistol, and I do not think you should ever see Córdova unless your Secretary or someone else is present."[66] At different times Governor Reily told the president:

> Porto Ricans, as all Continentals say, are "children" and change their attitudes almost daily.

> I want you to understand, Mr. President, these people are so unlike North Americans it is impossible to make any comparison. They make agreements one day, and break them the next; they stand for certain principles one day and reverse them the next.[67]

There were four Puerto Rican political figures who sided with Governor Reily at the beginning of his term: Santiago Iglesias Pantín, Juan B. Huyke, Martín Travieso, and Roberto H. Todd. When Reily went to the United States in November 1921, he took Iglesias and Todd with him. It was Todd who made lengthy statements to the American press at that time, accusing Reily's enemies of trying to "get" him by starting a fire on the ship carrying the governor's party.[68] Huyke and Travieso were scorned by their fellow Puerto Ricans as bootlicking traitors.[69] Of this group, apparently only Iglesias and Huyke escaped having Reily later turn against them. As early as May 1922, the governor told President Harding that Travieso was "a good fellow in many ways, but like most Porto Ricans is unsteady."[70] A few months later Reily and Travieso were staunch political enemies, and Travieso sent to the president a twenty-two page summary of charges against the governor.[71] Todd, appointed by Reily to the post of immigration commissioner, never had a complete break with the governor. Todd apparently considered his relationship with Reily excellent, and probably never knew that the governor said of him to President Harding: "Mr. Todd is a half-blooded negro, and sometime ago deserted his wife and is living with a woman of the streets. Personally, I am quite friendly with him, but you can see that he is the kind of man I cannot associate with or consult with much."[72]

This accusation may have been quite true, but it is very similar to the reasons Reily gave Harding for removing José Benedicto from his post as treasurer of Puerto Rico. Benedicto, he said, "lived all the time with a negro woman" instead of his wife, and so the "better women of the Island, Continentals," had "hounded daily" the governor to remove Benedicto.[73]

Governor Reily's ineffectiveness was compounded by the fact that he undermined the War Department's confidence in him by lying to the administration. There were at least two clear instances of this. Senator William H. King introduced a resolution on December 6, 1921, that the secretary of war be directed to submit a list of non–Puerto Ricans who had been given official or clerical posts in the insular government by Reily, because "the great number" of such "carpetbaggers" was the "cause of complaint" in Puerto Rico. The next day this resolution passed the Senate.[74] This looked serious to Harding, and he immediately asked Reily to forward this information before things went further. On December 17 the governor sent Harding his list of non–Puerto Rican appointments. According to it, the accusations were false, for, said Reily, the number of "continentals" in the insular government had decreased by four since his coming. He told the president that in all his appointments to various offices in the Puerto Rican government, only two were not Puerto Ricans, and these were men who had resided on the island for over a quarter of a century.[75] Harding quickly relayed this information to Senator King, before the War Department could do as the Senate had requested. When King read these figures to his Senate colleagues, he cheerily announced that this settled the question of whether Reily had taken a host of carpetbaggers with him from Kansas City; Harding and Reily plainly had the best interests of Puerto Rico in mind.[76]

But this did not end the question. A few days later, Resident Commissioner Córdova Dávila wrote to President Harding to argue that Reily had not given him all the facts, and named five carpetbaggers: John R. Hull, the governor's nephew and private secretary; George S. McClure of Kansas City, the chief of the Puerto Rican "Secret Service"; William Kessinger of Kansas City, auditor; Kessinger's son, "an inexperienced youth," the assistant auditor; and a Mrs. Liggett of Kansas City, assistant commissioner of education. None of these people, said Córdova Dávila, had a knowledge of Spanish.[77] General McIntyre also concluded that Reily's count of non–Puerto Ricans in his government was incorrect, and he informed Secretary of War Weeks of this. Weeks mildly suggested to the president that "there was evidently some error" in the statement given Harding by Reily and reported by him to Senator King.[78] Rather than reprimand Reily for having been untruthful, the president turned on the man who had exposed him:

> I know full well concerning the high motives of Governor Reily, and if he can have cooperation instead of mere partisan opposition I believe he will institute and conduct a very wholesome administration in the islands. . . . It is possible that there were some trivial inaccuracies in my letter to Senator King concerning the distribution of patronage in the Islands. I do not suppose Governor Reily thought it important to report to me the very minor clerical and police appointments to which General McIntyre has made reference. Permit me to express the hope that the Head of the Bureau of Insular Affairs here in Washington is not disposed to too deeply sympathize with the opposition forces in the Islands. It is highly important to have cooperation and harmony of effort at this end of the line. I will be very glad if you will say as much to General McIntyre.[79]

What probably irritated Harding even more was the fact that Secretary of War Weeks had already complied with the Senate resolution and sent complete information on non–Puerto Rican appointments.[80] Harding and Reily had not, even with their fast actions, headed off this embarrassing situation.

On at least one other occasion Governor Reily definitely lied to the administration in Washington. A Unionist attorney who resided in Washington, Pedro Capo-Rodriquez, wrote to the War Department, prodding it with questions regarding the Harding administration's plans for Puerto Rico's eventual status. Secretary of War Weeks sent a rather huffy reply which intimated that he felt Capo-Rodriquez did not sincerely wish answers to his questions as much as a chance to put the Harding administration on the spot. General McIntyre sent Governor Reily a copy of the letter from Weeks to Capo-Rodriquez. On February 8 Reily wrote to ask McIntyre if he could use the letter publicly to embarrass the Unionists. He assured the general, "However, I would not think of using it unless permitted to do so by you or the Secretary of War." General McIntyre responded to Reily's query in a letter of February 16, in which he forbade the governor to use the Weeks–Capo-Rodriquez correspondence publicly.[81] Nevertheless, Willis Sweet's English-language newspaper in San Juan, *The Times*, on February 11 included an editorial excoriating the Unionists for persisting in asking about Puerto Rico's eventual status. The letter from Secretary of War Weeks to Pedro Capo-Rodriquez was printed in full.[82] There is no proof that the War Department ever learned of Reily's deception in this case, but if it did, it certainly must have lost additional confidence in the governor.

Several of Reily's other statements to President Harding or the War Department have a phony ring about them, but there is no evidence to prove that they were lies. For example, the governor claimed on at least two occasions—immediately after his inauguration and when he came to the United States in November 1921—that he had received many letters threatening his life. Further, he justified his desire to replace a Puerto Rican with a "continental" as postmaster of San Juan on the grounds that his letters from the United States were "constantly opened." Another such suspicion Governor Reily entertained was—as we have already seen—that some of his cables to and from the United States were made known to the Unionists; yet in February 1922 he boasted to Harding that "I have seen all of the cables that have passed between Barceló and Córdova."[83] Governor Reily hardly had room to complain of violation of private correspondence!

Had E. Mont. Reily been an able, dedicated administrator, he could have carried on the functions of governor of Puerto Rico in a constructive way in spite of the opposition of the Unionists. But his shortcomings exacerbated the opposition. Reily's emphasis upon "Americanization" and "Americanism" was turned against him in vicious satire. A nickname for the governor that spread throughout the island was "Moncho Reyes," which meant "Monty the superking."[84] Reily's statement that he wanted Puerto Ricans to learn the language of "Washington, Lincoln and Harding" (in both his inaugural speech and his annual report for 1920–21) was made a joke by Luis Muñoz Marín, son of the founder of the Unionist Party. Muñoz Marín stated that the governor was ignorant of the fact that "there's many a Porto Rican schoolboy who speaks the language of Washington and Lincoln better than Harding does."[85]

When letters and cables protesting against Governor Reily began to come to the president, George Christian, Harding's secretary, sent back form replies that read, "Your protest to be of value must be accompanied by specifications."[86] Subsequently, at one time or another five specific accusations were made against Reily: that he had brought with him a horde of "carpetbaggers" from Kansas City; that he arbitrarily removed members of the insular government from their offices to enforce his own wishes; that he had identified his administration with men who were one with the Russian Bolsheviks; that he and other members of his government misused public funds for their own private purposes; and that he showed no tact or discretion in his words or actions as governor of Puerto Rico. The first two of these, carpetbagging and tyrannical removals, have already been discussed.

Santiago Iglesias, who headed the Socialist Party of Puerto Rico, apparently made a statement at some time that he was a follower of Lenin. If he did not, such a remark was at least attributed to him. Two things would argue that he was not a dangerous radical: (1) Iglesias was also the founder and head of the Free Federation of Laborers, the greatest labor union in the island, and in that capacity was considered by Samuel Gompers (with whom he carried on an extensive correspondence) the Puerto Rican representative of the American Federation of Labor. Gompers would not have worked with a "Bolshevik revolutionary." (2) On many occasions Iglesias argued that the right course for Puerto Rico was closer ties with the United States. It was this latter position, plus Iglesias' desire for electoral success, that brought his Socialist Party in 1920 to begin increasing cooperation with the insular Republican Party, traditionally the party of the upper class.[87] But the charge that Iglesias was a wild-eyed revolutionary Communist was still powerful, and the Unionists used it. When Iglesias did his best to defend Reily's government, and when he was given certain privileges by the Harding administration, the Unionists tried to embarrass Reily and Harding by trumpeting loudly the words "Communist" and "Moscow" in regard to Iglesias.[88]

On April 7, 1922, a grand jury in San Juan climaxed several months of investigation by bringing formal charges of misuse of public funds for private purposes against Governor Reily, Auditor William Kessinger, and Reily's secretary John Hull. The grand jury accused these men of using the fiction that Puerto Rico owed the Governor $5,000 to gain that amount in a series of withdrawals, ranging from $400 to $1,000, from the insular treasury over the months from August through November 1921. When Reily realized the investigation was serious, the report charged, he returned part of the money—$1,449.03—in a personal check to the auditor's office.[89]

Reily wrote to President Harding the next day, justifying the withdrawals as legal, and labeling the grand jury's action as inspired by Barceló. He told Harding that the district attorney of San Juan, Ramón Díaz Collazo, had told him he had found some irregularities in the auditor's office, but would drop the matter if Reily would make him chief of police or district judge. Reily claimed that he virtuously refused Díaz Collazo's proposal, as well as a later one in which Díaz offered to resign so the governor could appoint a new (pro-Reily) district attorney in return for a specified amount of money.[90] Fortunately for Governor Reily, District Judge Charles E. Foote was on his side; the judge twice refused to accept the report of the grand jury, saying it was up to the district attorney to make a formal indictment if he wished. Reily forestalled this action by removing District Attorney Díaz Collazo from office. When the D.A. argued that he was being removed illegally and without cause, and refused to leave his office, Reily had the police forcibly eject him.[91]

Congressman Horace Mann Towner, chairman of the House Committee on Insular Affairs, wrote to Harding that the grand jury's report and Reily's subsequent actions were "most embarrassing."[92] However, the president was not embarrassed; he announced to the press on April 15 that he had the utmost confidence in Governor Reily's integrity.[93] He did admit in letters to the governor that he found events in Puerto Rico "confusing."[94]

Governor Reily promptly asked the president for a new attorney general for Puerto Rico. He needed a man, preferably a "continental," who would be "in sympathy with my views and my policies."[95] It was true that Reily badly needed a change of attorney generals, for the one he had, Salvador Mestre, held the papers of the evidence and report of the abortive grand jury, and shortly presented them to Judge Foote, saying he would turn them over to a new grand jury to meet on June 6, 1922. Reily's new district attorney, Arrillaga, loyally refused to include this case among the responsibilities of that new grand jury. Attorney General Mestre then had Arrillaga transferred to Mayagüez, a city on the western end of the island. Arrillaga ignored the transfer order, and so did Judge Foote, who ordered the papers containing the evidence against Reily given to Arrillaga.[96] But Mestre, who had given the papers to José Benedicto, did not turn over the papers to Reily's district attorney.

The only thing which kept this deadlock from bursting into a worse scandal was that the Harding administration, apparently without Reily's knowledge, used Martín Travieso as a liaison with Attorney General Mestre. Each side had a sword over the head of the other: Mestre had the incriminating papers, and the Harding administration had the power to replace Mestre as attorney general. Travieso managed to get Mestre to agree to "let the Grand Jury proceedings remain in abeyance during the vacation of the [San Juan District] Court, thus giving the President an opportunity of finding a satisfactory solution to the unfortunate political chaos of Porto Rico." For these "good offices" President Harding thanked Martín Travieso.[97]

Reily, meanwhile, was pressing for the removal of Attorney General Mestre, whom he called "a little sneak." Harding declined, explaining to the governor that

> the federal government would not like to be in the attitude of removing a man who pretends to be safeguarding the public interests, even though most of us thoroughly believe that his motive is in every way unworthy. As soon as we get in the clear and there is time for a deliberate and thorough discussion of this problem I mean to take it up with the Attorney General and the Secretary of War.[98]

True to his promise, the president in late September told his attorney general, Harry Daugherty, that he thought it was time to name a new attorney general for "the Islands of Porto Rico."[99] But the stalemate went no further; no grand jury again took up the case of Reily's use of funds, and Salvador Mestre remained in office as attorney general. In late November, Governor Reily mentioned that he no longer used Mestre's services: "When I need a lawyer, I call in my own counsel."[100]

The earliest, most potent charge brought against Reily by the Puerto Ricans was that he was tactless, and it was this that began to erode Harding's confidence in him. The insular press attacked the governor for indiscreet words even before he reached Puerto Rico. And in July 1921, Senator Medill McCormick warned Secretary of War Weeks that "want of tact and good taste may work havoc there."[101] When Reily came to the United States in November 1921, the mainland press noted that the governor was saying about the same things to the Puerto Ricans that Governor Yager had told them, but simply with less diplomacy. The *New York Times* claimed that, while the Harding administration was behind Reily in his policies, it was unhappy about his tactlessness.[102] This was correct, for at about this time Secretary of War Weeks gave the president his opinion that Reily lacked discretion.[103] Weeks tried to remedy the situation with a letter of final instructions as Reily returned to the island in December. In as nice a way as possible, he told the governor that the "lack of restraint" in his actions and speeches could prove embarrassing for the Harding administration, and forbade him to speak publicly on political issues. He reminded Reily at length that the situation in Puerto Rico required "tact, courtesy and patience."[104] Reily could, and possibly did, ignore this counsel and credit it to the hostility of General McIntyre. But from the man who repeatedly expressed, publicly and privately, his confidence in Governor Reily's honesty and ability came again and again the word "tact." In March 1922, President Harding told Reily: "I never for a moment lost faith in your honesty or good intentions. I did apprehend that you had been lacking in tact on some occasions."[105] In May the president admitted to Puerto Rican Auditor Kessinger that Reily had acted with "very poor discretion" and in August to Congressman Towner that Reily had failed to handle matters with "all the tact and poise that conditions require."[106]

In the winter of 1921–22 there were several attempts to pass resolutions through the United States Congress which would call for a congressional investigation of Governor Reily's government. These were introduced by Resident Commissioner Félix Córdova Dávila and Congressman Benjamin G. Humphries of Mississippi, and were accompanied by resolutions of the Puerto Rican legislature requesting an investigation. President Harding was apprehensive of an investigation when the subject was first broached, but later concluded that it could be "a helpful thing" in clearing the air. Reily insisted that he welcomed an investigation, if it would also cover the charges he was making against Barceló and Córdova Dávila, but he also told the president:

I believe it would be better for the Rules Committee [in the House of Representatives, where Humphries's resolution had gone] now not to order this investigation on account of the fact that they would claim it a victory. . . . I think it would be better to let this die in the Committee, and later I will ask for an investigation of my administration, and also an investigation of all of my official acts, including why I removed certain men from office.[107]

The resolution calling for an investigation did die in the House Rules Committee; whether President Harding had anything to do with its death is unknown. But Governor Reily never called for an investigation of his administration.

Barceló, Córdova Dávila, and the other opponents of Governor E. Mont. Reily wanted more than an investigation of his administration; they wanted his removal.[108] At first newspapers in the United States showed either a pro-Reily or a neutral attitude, but by November 1921 a Puerto Rican newspaper could boast, "The American press is helping our cause."[109] This was true, for from that time on papers like the *New York Times* were printing such information as rumors that the administration was unhappy with Reily's lack of tact and that he might soon resign to take some administrative post in Washington.[110]

Many of Governor Reily's letters to President Harding contained assurances that "everything is running along most serenely here now."[111] President Harding repeatedly expressed his hope that this tranquility was a fact; but his doubt was expressed by the frequency of these wishes and in such statements as, "I hear concerning the troubles in Porto Rico from one source or another every day."[112]

To people other than Reily, the president talked of the rumors of Reily's removal. In April he admitted to Congressman Towner that if Reily was a failure, he would recall him, but he did not want the governor driven out by "a lot of political conspirators."[113] Five months later Harding made a cryptic but perhaps significant comment to Secretary of War Weeks: "I do not see but one cure for the situation in Porto Rico, and that one cure I shall have to apply very shortly."[114] From June through the rest of 1922 letters came to the War Department and the president with suggestions for a governor to replace Reily.[115] In January 1923, Senator Albert B. Cummins promoted the appointment of his fellow Iowan, Congressman Horace Mann Towner. President Harding admitted to Cummins that he had been considering Towner because of his "tact, patience and quiet way."[116] On many occasions it had been Towner with whom Harding had conferred about the problems of Reily's governorship. Further, Towner was chairman of the House Committee on Insular Affairs and had been in Puerto Rico on at least one occasion.

There is nothing in Governor Reily's official correspondence to indicate that he was aware of the gradual decision of President Harding to replace him. However, by the middle of 1922 the Harding administration was no longer sharing everything with the governor. This is seen in the fact that Harding was using and thanking Martín Travieso for working out some *modus vivendi* with Attorney General Mestre at about the same time Reily was describing Travieso as another of his enemies.[117]

On December 12, 1922, Governor Reily left Puerto Rico for the United States, ostensibly to talk to the administration about the application of federal farm laws to Puerto Rico. Since neither Reily nor Harding had heretofore shown any interest in Puerto Rican farmers, it is possible that the president wanted to chat with Reily about something other than the coffee crop. After a short time in Washington, Reily went to Kansas City for the Christmas holidays. While in his old hometown, the governor was riding in a taxi which was involved in an accident.[118] Some weeks later Reily returned to Puerto Rico, where he was met by a large welcoming crowd (he claimed 20,000 people). Almost immediately he wrote to the president, saying his injuries—he claimed to have had six broken ribs and a nervous breakdown caused by shock—were such that he should never have traveled back to the island, and therefore he wished to resign from his position. He modestly told Harding that his resignation would be "a great set-back" to Americanism in Puerto Rico, unless the president was careful to choose "an upstanding American" to follow him.[119]

Reily was not pleased with Harding's selection for his successor. On March 4, 1923, the president named Representative Horace Mann Towner of Iowa to the post. In June, Towner cabled Secretary of War Weeks that he understood that Reily was "making trouble in Washington," and asked him not to let the ex-governor influence the president against making a visit to Puerto Rico during his return from a trip to Alaska.[120]

Four years later Reily was still trying to bother Governor Towner. He wrote to Everett Sanders, the private secretary of President Calvin Coolidge, offering to send photographic copies of "a number of letters" from "good President Harding," which would show Harding's "deep regret and humiliation" over having appointed Towner.[121] There is no indication that the Coolidge administration asked for Reily's papers. When Theodore Roosevelt, Jr., was named to succeed Towner in 1929, Reily (from Kansas City, of course) wrote two letters to him. In the first he merely patted Roosevelt and himself on the back and strongly criticized Towner. The second letter was a vicious commentary on each of the local political figures with whom Roosevelt would have to deal in "the Islands"; Todd was "utterly unreliable," and so on, with only Harry Besosa "honest." It was his hope, Reily said, that when Roosevelt finished his governorship and left "the Islands," he would say, "Well, Reily had them all down absolutely correct."[122]

Several questions arise in an evaluation of Reily's governorship. Were the accusations against him correct? The charge that Governor Reily had taken to the island a number of "carpetbaggers" seems well founded; no other governor had a personal bodyguard (under any title), and hiring his nephew and the son of Auditor William Kessinger was also unnecessary. The fact that none of these people knew Spanish or much about Puerto Rico was compounded by their lack of experience in positions similar to those they filled in Reily's government. The charge of misuse of public funds is not so easily judged, for it was a handy accusation to throw at a governor— Theodore Roosevelt, Jr., who was personally very wealthy, was accused of the same thing. But Reily, unlike Roosevelt, went to great lengths to obtain the evidence compiled against him by a grand jury, and with the help of a very "continental" American judge, was able to stop the legal proceedings. His anxiety to get the papers would suggest some fear about their contents.

What was E. Mont. Reily's policy for Puerto Rico? As nearly as it is possible to ascertain, he looked on his job as primarily involving the "Americanization" of Puerto Rico: Puerto Ricans should speak English, not Spanish; they should stop considering any alternative status for Puerto Rico but eventual statehood; American standards of political and social conduct should be accepted as the norm for Puerto Rico. However, Reily's tactlessness and ineptitude caused such an uproar against him from the start of his governorship that there is no way one can say he had a "policy." His administration never "got in the clear" (to use Harding's phrase) to be able to engage in constructive legislative or executive activity. Reily's time in Puerto Rico was spent in defending himself and attacking his enemies.

Finally, what was President Harding's role in the Reily debacle? Why did Harding hang on to Reily so long, refusing to hear un-flattering truths about him from General McIntyre and others? The answer to this question probably lies in the type of politician Warren G. Harding was; the pattern of his defense of Reily fits in naturally with the man who refused to stop his friends—the "Ohio gang"—from involving his administration in activities like the "Teapot Dome" and other affairs which were to become front-page scandals after Harding's death. Harding's personal loyalty to Reily could have easily overlooked such incidentals as malfeasance of office and worsened relations between Puerto Rico and the United States, and Reily's loyalty to Harding could have made the president more lenient of the governor's shortcomings. Another interesting aspect of Harding's part in this situation is that his efforts to counsel Reily and to take the dangerous portions out of Reily's inaugural speech do not fit the image of the Warren Harding we know as the man with the "bungalow mind." Some scholars have recently questioned Henry Mencken's view of Harding as a "boob"; perhaps his role in Reily's troubles adds to their reevaluation.[123] Harding may have had no moral backbone, but perhaps he was not the oaf he has been assumed to have been.

Harding's choice for the Puerto Rican governorship and his defense of Reily, however, were not judicious actions. And the Reily administration immediately set a strained tone to the Puerto Rican–United States relationship in the 1920s. The shifting course of Puerto Rican politics in that decade did nothing to ease this strain.

4 | The Kaleidoscope of Puerto Rican Politics, 1923–1929

One of the observations made by Theodore Roosevelt, Jr., during his governorship (1929–32) was that "parties down here in no way correspond to parties in the continental United States. They chop and change, combine and split, with great regularity."[1] He described these frequent changes as "kaleidoscopic."[2] This was an apt generalization, not only about the Puerto Rican political scene during Roosevelt's years, but equally in the 1920s. (See figure 1.) Politics were kaleidoscopic in terms of the disappearance of some parties, the birth of new ones, and the merger of others. They were kaleidoscopic in terms of personality clashes, factions within parties, and changing political credos. But always—and here lies the difference between Puerto Rican politics and the political activities of most Latin American countries—the kaleidoscopic changes operated within the framework of United States control. At least throughout the 1920s not even the Nationalist Party advocated open resistance to that control. Nevertheless, to a man like Roosevelt or any of his predecessors in the insular administrations, accustomed to the political stability of the United States, the frequent changes in Puerto Rican politics seemed as curious as Alice's Wonderland. The political shifts began during the last year of Governor Yager's administration and gained momentum in the Reily era, but their influence upon United States relations with the island was felt first in the time of Horace Mann Towner's governorship.

When Governor Reily resigned in February 1923, the Unionists believed that he had, in effect, been fired, that it was "apparent that he had orders [to resign] before he left Washington."[3] When Reily sent his final message to the Puerto Rican legislature, the strongly Unionist legislature refused to have it read by Acting Governor Juan

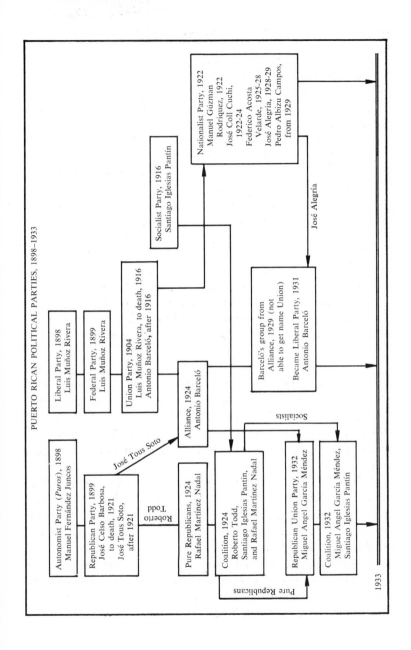

PUERTO RICAN POLITICAL PARTIES, 1898–1933

B. Huyke, and it was simply printed.[4] Huyke, though a Unionist, by that time had so identified himself with the despised Reily that he was considered a virtual Judas by his party.

The Republicans who were very pro-American, José Tous Soto and Roberto Todd, were not happy to see Reily leave. They stated in a cable to President Harding that they regretted that "illness" had forced Reily to resign, but that they trusted the president would continue the policies of the past two years in regard to Puerto Rico.[5]

Having been outvoted in every insular election since 1904, the Republicans worked sedulously in the 1920s to identify themselves with the Republican administrations in Washington, trying "to win at Washington what they lost in the local elections."[6] Their hope was for a governor who would side with them—especially in patronage—against the Unionists. Reily had fought the Unionists from his earliest moments as governor, and he had kept Tous and Todd close to him during much of his administration. But his offensiveness and general anti–Puerto Rican attitude had made him less than useful to the Puerto Rican Republicans. Perhaps his successor would be their answer.

The Republicans were disgruntled to find Horace M. Towner named the new governor, because in his position as chairman of the House Committee on Insular Affairs he had worked fairly smoothly with Unionist Félix Córdova Dávila, the resident commissioner. When he picked Unionists for his counselors and for many other positions, the Republicans shrieked in complaint to President Harding.[7]

Although Harding had been plagued by troubles in Puerto Rico since he had appointed Reily as governor, he could logically assume that the protests against Governor Towner would not prove too serious. Towner's knowledge of Puerto Rico and his tactful nature would gradually win over some opposition and hush the rest, and in any case only the minority insular party was voicing unhappiness, not the Unionist majority. Harding's prediction about Towner's administration turned out to be accurate. Towner worked with the Unionists (as had Governor Yager), and he had a relatively trouble-free governorship. In June of Towner's first year in office, Puerto Rico's political situation appeared calm enough for President Harding to look forward to a visit to the island in August.[8] This proposed stopover did not occur, for on the first leg of his trip to Alaska and the Pacific Northwest, President Harding suddenly died.

Todd and the Republicans confronted Governor Towner with a problem at the beginning of his administration, that of patronage to post-office positions on the island. Todd claimed to have made all such appointments during the Reily administration, and demanded that the governor give him a free hand. Towner offered to let Todd choose people for post-office jobs in towns that were predominantly Republican, if Unionists were selected for the positions in towns where their party was most powerful. Todd refused and threatened to take the matter to the national Republican Party of the United States. Governor Towner was not alarmed at this, for, as he explained to the private secretary of President Coolidge:

> The strength of Mr. Todd's claim is that he is a Republican and represents the Republican party here, which is recognized as a branch of the party in the States. That is true only as a matter of courtesy, because there is no identity between the Republican party here and in the States. Here they are a small group, who have no chance to succeed except as they unite with the Socialists. Both combined are in the minority in the Island and in most of the towns. The Unionist party is the dominant party, and is much more identified and in sympathy with the United States than the Republican-Socialist Combination. Nothing could be more unfortunate than for the administration to give its support to that malcontent group.[9]

President Coolidge wisely refused to let the matter of patronage be blown into a row of the type Governor Reily had known; he had his secretary write almost identical letters to Towner and Todd, asking them to "work out an amicable solution of appointment matters."[10] Unlike Harding, Coolidge did not demand a complete victory for the governor, but merely a satisfactory compromise. Also unlike in Reily's time, the War Department firmly supported the governor's stand as "a perfectly fair proposition."[11] At the end of his first year in office, Governor Towner was finally able to make the happy announcement to the Coolidge administration that he had worked out an arrangement with the leaders of all the insular parties in regard to post-office appointments in Puerto Rico. It was a fine agreement: the man with the highest grade on the civil service examinations would henceforth get the job, regardless of party affiliation.[12]

An even more dramatic change from the Reily era is evident from Towner's description in 1925 of the Unionist Party as "the conservative party, to which belong most of the educated and property-owning men of the Island."[13] At any time in the two decades before Towner took over this would have been an apt description of the Republicans, not the Unionists. Was Governor Towner being naive? Or had Reily erred in considering the Republicans more loyal to the United States than the Unionists, and Yager in believing the Republicans were the conservative and wealthy class of the island? The answer is that Towner's description merely pointed out one aspect of the major political changes in Puerto Rico between 1920 and 1925.

In the 1920 insular elections the Republicans and Socialists had worked together in an attempt to defeat the Unionists.[14] They were unsuccessful; the Unionists won sixteen of the nineteen races for seats in the Senate, twenty-seven of the thirty-nine positions in the lower house, and the office of resident commissioner. During the next election year, 1924, two new parties were formed from the three political organizations: some of the Republicans joined with the Unionists to become the Alliance Party (*Alianza*) and other Republicans went with the Socialists to become the Coalition Party (*Coalición*). (See figure 1.) How had these strange shifts come about? What concord could be found between the Republicans, traditionally the party of the wealthy landowners, and the Socialists, led by a man who had made his whole career one of fighting against those landowners in the bitter labor struggles of Puerto Rico? And the Unionists and Republicans, who had treated one another harshly since 1904, how could they now be in alliance?

The answers are found primarily in the rising political consciousness and electoral strength of the Socialists. For many years Santiago Iglesias had kept his Socialist Party out of active insular politics, concentrating on the labor movement that was synonymous with the party. But in the first elections under the Jones Act, in 1917, he entered the political arena. Samuel Gompers, who kept close contact with the Puerto Rican labor movement, tried to talk Iglesias out of this, saying: "I do wish that you would not accept any political office. If you desire to be of best service to Porto Rico, her working people and her people generally, you can do so most effectively outside of any political position."[15] This was a natural position for Gompers; he personally stayed out of politics, and under his leadership the AF of L took no partisan political stance, except for one disappointing flirtation with the Democrats in 1908. Each local union, including those in Puerto Rico, was left free to back any local politicians who seemed to offer advantage to the labor movement.[16] As a result of this AF of L policy, Iglesias was not required to follow Gompers's advice in political matters, and he did not, but won a post of senator-at-large, thanks to a recount of the ballots by the insular Senate. In that election the Socialists won only two other places in the insular government, positions in the House of Representatives. But in 1920 they doubled their votes and put an additional man in the lower house. The future seemed to indicate a gradually rising Socialist vote in Puerto Rican elections.

Since the Republicans had polled only about four thousand votes more than the Socialists in 1920, perhaps they were nervous that the Socialists would replace them as the major opposition party, and they began to see some common grounds for cooperation between the two groups. First was their common desire to defeat the Unionists. Second was the fact that both the Republicans and the Socialists had long expressed hope for eventual statehood in the United States.

A third factor that drew the Republicans and Socialists together was the way Governor Arthur Yager favored the Unionists over either of their parties.

Not all Republicans could bring themselves to work with the men they thought of as wild-eyed Bolsheviks, the Socialists. But neither could these conservative Republicans find comfort in the Unionist Party as long as it espoused independence. In 1922, however, Barceló pushed his party to drop the "eventual independence" plank from its platform and replace it with a goal of obtaining the status of *Estado Libre Asociado* ("Free Associated State" or "Commonwealth").[17] (A militant minority of the Unionists refused to follow Barceló and formed the Nationalist Party.) There was now not enough difference between the Unionist idea of an autonomous commonwealth connection with the United States and the Republican statehood dream to keep the two groups apart. In March 1924, Barceló's Unionists and the wealthy, conservative majority of the Republicans, led by José Tous Soto, merged to become the *Alianza*. Two months later Roberto Todd and Rafael Martínez Nadal, with about thirty Republicans who preferred to try to soften the radicalism of the Socialists rather than be junior partners with the Unionists, formed the Pure Republicans (*Republicanos Puros*) or Constitutional Historical Party, which with the Socialists was known as the *Coalición*.

The desire for success was the reason why each of these Puerto Rican political organizations took the moves it did in the period between 1920 and 1924. The Republicans were split between those who accepted instant success by joining forces with the party that had dominated insular elections since 1904, and those who saw in the Socialists an opportunity finally to defeat the Unionists. The Unionists knew that the Socialists and Republicans together had polled only about four thousand votes less than the Unionist total in 1920, and saw success in burying the hatchet with their ancient foes to stop the rise of the Socialists. Santiago Iglesias admitted to General Frank McIntyre in 1920 that electoral success was the only reason for his cooperation with the Republicans.[18]

Besides the Socialists, there was a second new political force which made itself felt in Puerto Rico during the 1920s—the Nationalists. There had long been an independence wing of the Unionist Party, tenuously held in check by Luis Muñoz Rivera and after his death by Barceló. This group of *independentistas* forced the Unionist Party to use independence in its political repertory, even though men like Barceló knew it was a useless dream. The independence portion of the Unionist Party attracted the most attention from Americans such as Mary Weld Coates, who wrote an article in 1922 which made it seem that the island was on the verge of revolution.[19] Early in that same year the independence wing of the Unionist Party split with Barceló's majority.

The catalyst for division among the Unionists was the Campbell bill. A group of Unionist legislators went to the United States and enlisted the aid of Congressman Philip P. Campbell of Kansas in furthering the political autonomy of Puerto Rico. On January 19, 1922, Campbell introduced his bill, H.R. 9995, "to declare the purpose of the people of the United States as to the political status of the people of Porto Rico, and to provide an autonomous government for the said island, creating the associated free state of Porto Rico."[20] The bill went to the Committee on Insular Affairs, from which it never emerged. Even though President Harding and Governor Reily each indicated to the Puerto Rican leaders that they favored the bill, the Harding administration did not push for its passage. As in the cases of some pre-1917 bills to give Puerto Rico more autonomy, a Puerto Rican bill was not likely to get far without forceful backing from the administration. And Governor Reily privately showed himself to be against the Campbell bill, when he told General McIntyre that rumors by Barceló's party of prompt passage of the bill were regarded as "mythical" by the "Americans and the American–Porto Ricans" on the island.[21] In such a case passage of the bill would seem a victory to Reily's enemies, Barceló and the Unionists. The lack of support for the Campbell bill by both the president and the governor certainly must have dampened enthusiasm for it in the Committee for Insular Affairs.

For a few months, however, there was the possibility that the Campbell bill would move on toward passage. It was the subject of much controversy in both the United States and Puerto Rico. The enthusiasm it created among the conservative portion of the Unionist Party was largely responsible for the writing of the "Declaration of Political Principles," which proclaimed that "the creation of the *Free Associated State of Puerto Rico* is from today the Program of the 'Union of Puerto Rico.' "[22] This declaration came out of a Unionist assembly held February 11, 1922. The *independentistas* of the party refused to affirm the "Free Associated State" principle, and left the Unionist Party, but they did not begin to form separate parties until April, when it was becoming obvious that the Campbell bill was dead. There were two separatist groups, the *Asociación Independentista* and the *Asociación Nacionalista,* but apparently only the latter formed a distinct political party. At the organizational meeting of the Nationalist Party (*Partido Nacionalista de Puerto Rico*), September 17, 1922, José Coll Cuchi was elected president and José S. Alegría (who had been prominent in the *Asociación Independentista*) vice-president. (See figure 1.) The Nationalist Party made no particular impression on either Puerto Rican politics or United States relations while under the leadership of these men. But a young Unionist, Pedro Albizu Campos, came into the Nationalist Party after the merger of the Unionists and the Republicans in 1924; and it was he who caused attention to be focused on the Nationalists within the next three years.

The story of Pedro Albizu Campos is one of a Puerto Rican who from 1917 to 1933 progressed from strong pro–United States views to rabid and violent anti-Americanism. Albizu Campos came from Ponce. Thanks in part to some scholarships of $500 per year from the insular government, he graduated from Harvard University in 1916.[23] Until the United States entered World War I, Albizu Campos attended Harvard Law School, but in May 1917 he dropped his law studies to take a three-month course (apparently at Harvard) for officer training, after which he waited for a commission. When it failed to come, he took a second year at Harvard Law School, and wrote to General McIntyre of the Bureau of Insular Affairs, asking him to look into the matter of his military service. McIntyre replied that he was sure Albizu Campos would soon be made an officer in the army. In the spring of 1918, the young Puerto Rican was drafted in Cambridge and transferred to Puerto Rico for mobilization. He was still not an officer, though he was at last in the army, so once more he talked and wrote to several high-ranking officers, including McIntyre. By autumn Albizu Campos was in an Officers' Training Camp at Camp Las Casas, near his hometown of Ponce. He received his commission, remained in Puerto Rico the last month of the war, and emerged a first lieutenant.[24] After the war, Albizu Campos continued his legal studies at Harvard and finally got his law degree in 1923. He returned to the island and gradually became involved in politics, first as a Unionist, then from 1924 as a member of the small Nationalist Party.

Earl Parker Hanson has repeated the popular idea that it was racial discrimination and segregation which Pedro Albizu Campos, who was part Negro, first encountered in the United States Army that turned him against America.[25] Roberto F. Rexach Benítez disputes this thesis. As Rexach points out, Albizu Campos came out of the army *proud* of his military service.[26] It is inconceivable that this was the first time he had encountered racial discrimination. Puerto Rico was not immune to racial prejudice (although, like many other Latin Americans, Puerto Ricans claim to have no racial prejudice in their society); Mary Weld Coates, who lived for a year with an upper-class Unionist family in Rio Piedras, reported that "the better class Porto Ricans bemoan the general intermingling that has been going on for generations."[27] In 1921, an article in the *New York Times* which laid stress on the Negro blood in many Puerto Ricans was protested by one Ralph George Gatell of Puerto Rico, who claimed that "the native Porto Rican is 100 per cent. white and is a descendant either from Spanish or French people," and asked that continentals not judge San Juan by the "colored" section of that city.[28] Certainly there was a degree of racial prejudice in Puerto Rico. A second reason why Albizu Campos's experience in the army could not have been responsible for his conversion to nationalism is that as late as January 1923 he was a faithful member of the Unionist Party, making public speeches in favor of the *Estado Libre Asociado* status and deploring the formation of the Nationalist Party.[29] Within the next year and a half, however, Albizu Campos became a Nationalist.

Rexach points to several things which he believes account for the bitterness that Albizu Campos developed toward the United States. First, there was an element of racial prejudice, but not primarily in the U.S. Army; rather, there is strong indication from some of his statements that both in Massachusetts and in Puerto Rico, Albizu Campos had felt a snobbish social rejection. Significant is the statement by Franklin B. Frost of the United States Embassy in Santo Domingo: "I have a slight recollection of him when he was a member of the class with which I was graduated from Harvard Law School where he appeared to be a quiet, studious and cultivated Porto Rican."[30] In other words, perhaps the shy and nearly poverty-stricken foreign student, Albizu Campos, found that he did not fit in with his classmates, had few friends, and took it as a personal affront.

A second factor, says Rexach, was Albizu Campos's frustrating road to becoming a lawyer. His law studies were broken up by the war and strung over a six-year period. When he did receive his law degree from Harvard, he was not admitted to the bar in Puerto Rico until he took the situation into the insular courts.[31] His struggles to be allowed to practice law took place during 1923 and 1924, the period of his change from Unionism to Nationalism. Occurring in that same time span were two more events which Rexach says helped to turn Albizu against the United States and the orthodox Puerto Rican political parties: his failure in 1924 to be nominated by the *Alianza* as a senatorial candidate and his marriage to a radically anti-American Peruvian woman.[32]

Once in the Nationalist fold, Albizu quickly became its most prominent member. The United States War Department took cognizance of his trip to Santo Domingo and Haiti in 1927, and of the publicity his travels and speeches received in Cuba and South

America.[33] He was by that time vice-president of the party. Under his leadership, the Nationalist message became more radical and violent each year. Early in 1927 Nationalist tactics were still geared to sending to American leaders protests which were typical of the Unionists and other insular parties.[34] But by 1932, when Albizu Campos was unsuccessfully running for office in the insular government, public advertisements of his speeches read: "Nationalism solicits the unity of Puerto Ricans against the common enemy: THE YANKEE. All the problems of Puerto Rico, such as the economic situation, absentee landlordism, latifundia and the *nationalization of capital,* will all be resolved the day that Puerto Rico becomes a NATION with SOVEREIGNTY to legislate for itself."[35] The one-star flag, once a Unionist banner, was by the 1930s proclaimed the flag of nationalism.

When the outcome of the election of 1932 was overwhelmingly against the Nationalists, Albizu became even more radical. He proclaimed United States sovereignty over Puerto Rico completely illegal, saying he had "revived" the Republic of Puerto Rico which had been proclaimed in the abortive revolt at Lares in 1868.[36] In 1935 he formed the "Liberation Army," and in 1936 and 1937 some of his Nationalist followers heeded his calls for violent resistance, and assassinations and assassination-attempts alternated with murders of Nationalists by the insular police.[37] Pedro Albizu Campos was responsible for bringing bloodshed to the island that had prided itself on being peaceful.

The Nationalists were loud and distracting, but as far as insular politics were concerned (and even U.S. relations until 1936), they were largely ignored. In 1928 the Nationalists received a total of 343 votes of the 264,734 cast in Puerto Rico, and by 1932 this was raised only to 5,257 of over 380,000 votes.[38] The traditional parties and traditional political methods were dominant, and so were the traditional issues, such as the demand for an elective governor.

In April 1919, a group of twenty-five members of the U.S. House of Representatives had visited Puerto Rico and held public hearings. Four months later they signed a petition which called for President

Wilson to name as the next governor of the island a native recommended by his fellow Puerto Ricans.[39] One of the members of that delegation was Horace Mann Towner of Iowa, then chairman of the Committee on Insular Affairs. Towner did not forget his conviction that there were many Puerto Ricans qualified to hold the gubernatorial post. The insular legislature passed a joint resolution in July 1923 to send a commission, which would include Towner, to Washington. Its purpose was to ask the American government for a statement of intention in regard to the final status of Puerto Rico and for an elective governor, and to request that appointments to the insular government then made by the president be made by the governor with the advice and consent of the Puerto Rican Senate, "that the Legislature of Porto Rico be granted power to legislate without restriction on all local matters," and that all United States laws promoting education, agriculture, and other matters of public welfare be applied to Puerto Rico.[40] Similar commissions had gone to Washington hat in hand in years past, but this was the first one that included the governor of the island. A total of fourteen men comprised the delegation, including the three leading Unionists (Barceló, Córdova Dávila, and Miguel Guerra Mondragón), the two top Socialists (Iglesias and Frank Martínez), José Tous Soto of the Republicans, and Governor Towner.

The commission did not go to the United States until January 1924. In Washington the Puerto Rican members of the group presented their requests to President Coolidge and Congress.[41] Coolidge's reply was typically "cool" in his refusal to be cornered on the status question:

> You have spoken of desiring to know what may be your condition in the future. In that you have a curiosity common to all of us, and the answer is naturally a common one. Your lot in the future will depend entirely upon your actions in the present. . . . My suggestion is that you cooperate one with the other, and attempt to harmonize your difficulties, if any arise, and all work together for the common welfare. Your island is prosperous,

it is making great progress, it is learning the art of self-government, your people are becoming more and more educated, your living conditions are growing better, and your whole atmosphere is one of prosperity, and ought to be one of contentment. The only way to prepare for something better tomorrow is to do well the duties that come to us today.[42]

Perhaps the best commentary on President Coolidge's reply to the commission was the letter he received from a "continental" in Puerto Rico, Harold I. Sewall. Sewall congratulated the president for the reply and said:

It was adequate, just, and so safe! You may be sure you have made many followers and friends down here.

We have been following the trouble over in the Philippines with sympathetic eyes doubly glad that such a debauch in autonomy did not occur here and hopeful that the wise but inexperienced legislators in Washington have finally got a vivid object lesson in the capacities of these people for self-government.[43]

President Coolidge's statement to the commission was indicative of the attitude of the administration toward possible changes in Puerto Rico's status. But the commission had come to the United States as much to deal with Congress as with the president. On January 26 and 29, Resident Commissioner Félix Córdova Dávila and Senator William H. King of Utah spoke in the House and Senate in favor of complete self-government and an elective governor for Puerto Rico. On February 2, Córdova Dávila introduced H.R. 6583, a bill which included both these goals. The bill was reported out of the Committee on Insular Affairs on March 13 with a favorable report which published the testimonies heard from the members of the Puerto Rican commission (including Governor Towner), Edward F. McGrady of the American Federation of Labor, and some delegations of Puerto Ricans living in New York City.[44] This was as far as the bill went—it was never brought up for debate. But by this time Senator King had introduced a similar bill, S. 2448, in the Senate. King managed to get it out of committee and up for debate in the Senate on May 15. In its original form, S. 2448 would have set the date of Puerto Rico's first gubernatorial election at 1928, but at the insistence of General McIntyre and Secretary of War Weeks, Senator Frank Willis of Ohio had an amendment tacked on which changed the date to the 1932 elections (or when the illiteracy rate on the island would drop below 30 percent, if that came before 1932).[45] The bill passed and went to the House of Representatives.

Supporters of Puerto Rican autonomy were full of hope. Secretary of War Weeks backed the bill in its amended form and informed the president of his approval.[46] On June 3, C. Bascom Slemp, the secretary of the president, asked Weeks for a form which would be proper for Coolidge to sign, endorsing passage of the elective-governor bill.[47] The first hope of the supporters of the bill was that it would pass when it came up on a unanimous-consent calendar. But when it did, Guinn Williams of Texas, a member of the House Committee on Insular Affairs, objected to it, and the bill was forced into the normal committee-before-consideration route.[48] The elective-governor bill was given to the Committee on Insular Affairs, from which it failed to emerge; at least one member, Guinn Williams, was opposed to it, and it is possible that he could have kept it in committee until the end of the session.[49] Governor Towner's attempt to help the Puerto Ricans put him and other continentals out of the Governor's palace, "La Fortaleza," had failed.

There were other petitions from the Puerto Ricans asking for an elective governor during the Coolidge years; and there were other bills for that reform, initiated by Félix Córdova Dávila of Puerto Rico and Fiorello H. La Guardia of New York.[50] But President Coolidge and his administration never publicly endorsed the later bills, and for this and other reasons Puerto Rico did not come near to getting an elective governor during that time. Just as the long struggle to replace the Foraker Act had shown, presidential leadership and perhaps additional factors were necessary for any major changes in the United States' relationship with Puerto Rico. Neither presidential interest nor special immediate forces were present during the Coolidge administration to help Puerto Rico's case.[51] And Governor Towner had increasingly enough problems of his own, without adding more.

Whenever people think of "smooth-sailing" governorships in Puerto Rico, the names of Arthur Yager, Horace Mann Towner, and Theodore Roosevelt, Jr., come up. Certainly in comparison with the administrations of Regis H. Post, E. Mont. Reily, and Robert Hayes Gore, the Towner years were trouble free. But in comparison with the governorships of most continental American territories, Towner's official career was most unhappy. This says something about the position of the American governors of Puerto Rico: the nature of it, the very fact that it was held by an outsider appointed from the outside, precluded native satisfaction.

Governor Towner's problems arose from two of his policies. His willingness to work with the *Alianza* (Unionists and some of the Republicans) infuriated the *Coalición* (Todd's Constitutional Historical Republicans and the Socialists); and his tax policies did not bow to the desires of the continental-owned agricultural corporations, which dominated the insular economy. (In this context, it is interesting that Santiago Iglesias did not see Towner as a friend of Puerto Rican labor.)

One of the common ploys of the political enemies of continental governors in Puerto Rico was to circulate rumors that the governor was either about to resign or in imminent danger of being recalled by the president. In Towner's case his opponents found a handy way to do this so that it sounded accurate and not malicious; they said his health was broken. Roberto Todd, who represented the *Coalición,* and Federal Judge Arthur F. Odlin, who represented the continentals, another group upset with the governor, were the first to inform Washington of Towner's "precarious" health. In November 1924, Todd wrote to Ira K. Wells, United States assistant attorney general, that Dr. Bailey K. Ashford, the governor's physician, had told Towner's wife her husband's life was in danger if he stayed in

Puerto Rico. Odlin spread the rumor first to John Barrett, the federal prohibition director for the island, and then to a lawyer friend, L. R. Wilfley of New York City. Both men relayed the "confidential information" to the administration, either directly or indirectly.[52] Todd and Odlin (and others who spread the rumor of a governor near death) always tied the idea of physical weakness to that of weakness in the face of duty, and usually went on to say that the president should appoint as Towner's successor a "strong good man." By this one can only assume that they meant a man ready to carry on a government in Puerto Rico which would ignore the *Alianza* electoral majority and cooperate instead with the strongly pro–United States Republicans of the *Coalición* and the even smaller number of continentals residing on the island.

By the spring of 1925 friends of the governor were alarmed at the story of Towner's failing health. A Chicago lawyer, James W. Good, wrote to Everett Sanders, secretary to President Coolidge, that Towner was doing a fine job in Puerto Rico and it would be a mistake to replace him. He was especially concerned that, as rumor had it, the new governor might be Senator Thomas Sterling of South Dakota, who had upheld Reily's regime. He assured the administration that even though Towner had been ill with dysentery in the summer of 1924, he was presently much improved, and would not need to leave the island unless the illness should recur.[53] A few weeks later Governor Towner and Dr. Ashford wrote separately but on the same day in an attempt to dispel the rumor. Towner told the president that he wanted to "set at rest erroneous impressions regarding my health," that he had "never been seriously ill, either before or since I came to Porto Rico," and that the "attack of indigestion such as is very common to people who come from the north into this tropical climate" had subsided and he had felt no physical problem for several months.[54] Ashford, a famous expert on tropical diseases and a man who had been in Puerto Rico almost since the United States occupation, corroborated the governor's statement.[55]

Although Coolidge and his administration apparently took no stock in it, the rumor of Governor Towner's broken health persisted.

A year after Ashford and Towner had denied it, Charles R. Neidlinger, a New York insurance executive, wrote to E. T. Clark, a secretary to Coolidge, to suggest a member of the Columbia University faculty for Towner's replacement. Neidlinger maintained that he and a group he claimed to speak for had nothing against Towner, that "we respect him and we like him and know that he has done much good while Governor of Porto Rico and can continue to do much good were it not for his failing health. We understand he is on his way from Porto Rico to Washington to resign."[56] Clark replied: "While I have no reason to doubt the accuracy of your prediction, we have heard nothing here which shows that a vacancy is impending, and I doubt if anything is to be gained by anticipating it."[57]

At the same time that Todd's Constitutional Historical Republicans and the continental business interests both were working to spread the story that Governor Towner was near death, they were equally diligent to attack him on his pro-*Alianza* and tax-reform policies. Each of these differences between the governor and his enemies was slanted in an ugly way. Immediately after the 1924 election Todd's Pure Republicans screamed that the governor had allowed a corrupt election to put Félix Córdova Dávila into the office of resident commissioner again, and that the Unionist (*Alianza*) victories for seats in the insular legislature were merely results of "smiling Towner's" weak submission to the crooked ways of Barceló, Córdova Dávila, and other Unionists.[58]

Henry Wells states categorically that the 1924 election was very corrupt, with vote-buying and *Alianza* control of the voting places at an all-time peak.[59] Wells, however, is quoting Bolívar Pagán, and that Socialist historian is hardly an objective scholar in this case. First the *Coalición* leaders failed to get an appointment with President Coolidge for José Coll Cuchi, who had intended to ask Coolidge for a contest in the U.S. House of Representatives over the seating of Córdova Dávila as resident commissioner.[60] Then Pagán cabled President Coolidge that Puerto Rican Attorney General Herbert P. Coats had refused a court order to let the Insular Canvassing Board (of which Pagán was a member) recount the ballots.[61] One scholar has commended Pagán for keeping himself out of his history of Puerto Rican political parties (written in 1959), but in this case he kept himself out to the extent that he made Wells believe he had no personal involvement when in fact he was a chief actor in the election controversy. This knowledge casts some doubt on the corruption charges in Pagán's book; they are at least partisan.

Governor Towner and Attorney General Coats denied the charges of Bolívar Pagán. They maintained that the case of Pagán and the *Coalición* versus the Insular Board of Elections was still not decided; for even though a district court on the island had issued a writ of mandamus ordering a ballot recount, the board had appealed to the Supreme Court of Puerto Rico, which was to shortly decide the case.[62] The higher court ruled against Pagán's group, and—in effect—so did the Coolidge administration, for the president and the War Department ignored Pagán's complaint.

From this time on the *Coalición* attacked Attorney General Coats with even more venom than they displayed toward Governor Towner. Guy M. Winslow, a continental businessman residing in Puerto Rico, charged that Coats was "shifty" and a "tool of Barceló" in a letter sent to Frank Stearns of Boston (but which ended up in Coolidge's hands).[63] Winslow said he spoke for the "residents" of Puerto Rico—the continental clique. And one Harold I. Seusall of this same group wrote a slashing letter to Coolidge against Coats and Towner.[64] Former Governor E. Mont. Reily wrote from Kansas City to inform the president that "Coates [*sic*]" was "a degenerate. . . . I should not say this unless I really knew."[65] All this was enough to worry President Coolidge at least to the extent of having his secretary ask Governor Towner whether he had appointed Coats as acting governor at the time of Towner's recent trip to the United States.[66] Towner and his friends apparently were feeling uncomfortable about Herbert Coats by this time, for in his reply the governor noted that the naming of Coats as acting governor had been normal procedure, but admitted that at the present time he held Coats in a different light: "It should be remembered that there was never any stain on Mr. Coats' character until now. He was criticized, of course, but never until now was cause afforded sufficient to ask for his removal."[67] Coats was removed quietly, and President Coolidge did not have to look far for a successor. E. Mont. Reily had pumped for his old friend George C. Butte, dean of the University of Texas, and the president appointed Butte the new attorney general for Puerto Rico. Coolidge may have been merely taking the easiest course immediately available, but it is also possible that Reily had some political pressure in Washington even at this date.

We have seen how the reaction of the *Coalición* against Governor Towner's policy of accepting the *Alianza* and its victory in the 1924 election was an attack first on the election results and second on the member of Towner's government who was both most closely involved with the election and most vulnerable—Attorney General Herbert Coats. In the same way Towner's other opponents, the continentals and the corporations they represented, sought avenues of attack on the governor. In addition to chiming in with the chorus of accusations that Towner was both physically and politically weak, they used two more charges: that because of his inept handling of the insular government, mass starvation was occurring in Puerto Rico; and that his government was not only engaged in a spending spree financed by harshly taxing the businesses that were trying to build up the island's economy, but also guided by corrupt native political bosses.

On December 24, 1924, Secretary of War John Weeks cabled the governor: "Reports have reached the President that in sections of Porto Rico many of the people are suffering from want of food. He requests that you promptly make investigation and report by cable."[68] In denying this report, Towner was backed not only by members of his administration such as Dr. Pedro N. Ortíz, commissioner of health and sanitation, and Dr. Carlos E. Chardón, commissioner of agriculture, but also by Edward P. Mitchell, who was sent to Puerto Rico personally by President Coolidge to report on economic and political conditions. Mitchell concluded that Towner's claim of "general prosperity" in Puerto Rico was true; to be sure, there was "poverty and sometimes hunger and suffering," but not worse than in previous years. The causes of these were not faults of Towner's government, but "anemia and inertia" which were prevalent on the island, and for which "no legislative remedy is conceivable."[69] Calvin Coolidge had a different manner from that of Warren G. Harding in dealing with complaints against a colonial administrator: instead of stubbornly refusing to hear anything against Towner, he quietly sent a trusted subordinate to investigate the situation, and then sent confidential word to the governor that he had no intention of replacing him.[70]

The second complaint of the continentals against Governor Towner, and the one which came closer to their real reasons for opposing him, was that of irresponsible taxation and extravagant expenditure on the part of his government. From 1924 through 1927 Towner worked to get stiffer tax laws applied to corporations in Puerto Rico, as well as new income tax laws. The predominantly Unionist (*Alianza*) legislature agreed with Towner in this effort; but Todd's Pure Republicans, long identified with the United States corporate interests and the continental "high society" clique on the island, was outraged. Some of its members were shamelessly open in their pleas for tax exemption; P. J. Rosaly, manager of the Bank of Ponce, complained to General McIntyre that "no importance" was given his suggestion that the Central Mercedita, "the most important sugar mill near Ponce," be given tax exemption when he wrote to "several conspicuous members" of the insular legislature about it. Now he asked the head of the Bureau of Insular Affairs to put pressure upon Governor Towner to accomplish his desire.[71] Many of these corporations and individuals were feeling for the first time the weight of taxation (Governor Towner and his successor, Governor Roosevelt, spent a lot of time pushing for the collection of delinquent taxes), and they enlisted as much aid as possible in attacking Towner for his policies.

Judge Odlin, who had opposed Governor Towner, had been forced to resign (he had some idiosyncrasies that suggested senility[72]), and in his place as judge of the United States District Court in Puerto Rico came Ira K. Wells of Kansas. Wells had been the

United States attorney for Puerto Rico during E. Mont. Reily's administration; and if he had not kept up communication with the ex-governor, he at least was still in Reily's corner—and that of the rest of the continentals. Several months after his appointment, Wells wrote to Attorney General John G. Sargent, stating that the Puerto Rican economy was in trouble because of Governor Towner. The letter came to the attention of General McIntyre, who suggested to the new secretary of war, Dwight F. Davis, that Wells be "diplomatically advised to avoid criticism of the Government of Porto Rico and the people of Porto Rico, even in private letters."[73] Early in 1926 Judge Wells continued his attempts to undermine Towner's administration by writing a letter to United States Supreme Court Justice Harlan F. Stone. Stone forwarded the letter to presidential secretary Everett Sanders, saying, "For obvious reasons, I do not encourage this kind of letter to me."[74] Wells had complained to Justice Stone that Towner's government had "taxed everything to the limit" and assured him that "the business interests of the Island are waking up and taking notice and protesting against the high taxation and if the Coolidge policy of economy was put in force here the administration would have the business interests of the Island square back of it. There must be a change. . . . all it takes is a Governor who will stand square on the Coolidge platform of economy in Government."[75] There is every indication in the letter that Judge Wells wanted it to reach the president—but not in the way it did.

Another member of the Puerto Rican government who disloyally helped the continentals and business interests try to oust Governor Towner was Norval P. Nichols, who had been appointed immigration commissioner late in 1924. Nichols was given the post on the warm recommendation of Judge Arthur Odlin. Nichols, whose chief qualification was said to have been his twenty-four years of business experience in Puerto Rico,[76] reflected his "continental clique" background in a letter to President Coolidge, when he said that he was "more and more impressed that we need in Porto Rico a man who has not only business judgment but also would feel seriously his stewardship to the people of the United States and Porto Rico."[77]

Considering President Calvin Coolidge's near reverence for business, it is a wonder that Nichols's cunningly worded sentence did not persuade Coolidge to replace Towner immediately!

Finally, E. Mont. Reily continued to write from Kansas City in efforts to dislodge Towner from his post. As noted in chapter 3, he offered in 1927 to send Everett Sanders some letters in which Harding had expressed regret at naming Towner as governor.[78] By this time, the Teapot Dome and various other scandals of the Harding era had changed a lot of people's attitudes toward the president from Marion, Ohio; Coolidge was not in a mood to replace Governor Towner at the posthumous behest of "good President Harding." Reily's letter was apparently ignored.

Perhaps one reason why President Coolidge trusted Governor Towner was that Towner was not forever writing to him to protest his innocence in matters or to bring the president into the problems of Puerto Rico. Unlike Reily, Towner realized that the president had enough problems with his own job, without having to worry about those of the colonial governor too. As a result, Towner's contacts with the Coolidge administration were spaced well apart and were usually communications from the governor to the Bureau of Insular Affairs, the Secretary of War, or one of the president's secretaries. Only rarely did Towner write directly to Coolidge. The governor, of course, defended his position in matters such as the 1924 election, the rumors of starvation in Puerto Rico, and the attacks on his taxation policy.[79] But he also let his official reports tell the story for him in an appropriate way.[80]

Others wrote to President Coolidge in Towner's behalf, whether the governor knew of it or not. Former Governor Beekman Winthrop (1904–07) told the president that on a recent trip to the island he had talked to many friends of all classes who had convinced him that Towner was well liked and had a "thorough grasp of the situation."[81] Henry Kittredge Norton, writing a series of articles on the American empire for *The World's Work,* praised the governor: "That the present is a time of comparative quiet is due largely to the vision and tact of Governor Horace M. Towner. . . .

If business is not enthusiastic in his support, Governor Towner has won the regard of the Porto Ricans, and if they were to elect a governor to-morrow and he were to run, he would probably be elected."[82] *The American Review of Reviews* lauded Towner in articles and editorials.[83] And of course the *Alianza* did what it could to uphold the governor.[84] Except for the members of the Pure Republicans, who saw eye to eye with the continental businessmen in Puerto Rico, it would seem that most Puerto Ricans realized that Towner's tact, his respect for Puerto Ricans, and his unwillingness to be a tool for the American business interests made him an exceptionally good colonial administrator. Perhaps Santiago Iglesias regretted the strange bedfellow that politics had made for his Socialist Party in its coalition with the Pure Republicans, for he admitted early in 1929 that a change of governors would not better Puerto Rico's situation. In spite of Towner's preference for the *Alianza* over the *Coalición,* admitted Iglesias, he was at least aware of the economic problems of the island.[85]

Had Iglesias, his labor union, and his Socialist Party not been merged with the anti-Towner Pure Republicans, perhaps the governor and the labor chief would have realized that they had basically the same ideas about the needs of Puerto Rico. But as it was, when Iglesias sought action, he turned to the administration in Washington. There, his pleas for an investigation of the economic conditions of Puerto Rico were received with less than enthusiasm.[86] Secretary of War Dwight Davis told the president's secretary: "Similar petitions from the same source since 1916 have urged this. . . . The conditions in Porto Rico which call for remedy are receiving the attention of the Department."[87] The BIA chief, Frank McIntyre, agreed with Davis and stated: "Perhaps no place under the American flag is so fully reported on as is Porto Rico. The economic conditions of Porto Rico are decidedly simple. The remedies have been recited from time to time."[88] Governor Towner concurred in believing that Iglesias' appeals for an investigation were not wholly sincere in motive; he called Iglesias "our chief trouble-maker," and said Iglesias' announced intention of getting an appointment with President Coolidge was just "so he can boast of his having seen the President and so strengthen his position here with his deluded followers."[89] Santiago Iglesias probably did not know of Towner's low esteem for him, for he did not join the Pure Republicans in trying to unseat the governor. On the contrary, when the Puerto Rican legislature passed a memorial asking President Coolidge not to replace Governor Towner, along with the names of the members of the *Alianza*—Barceló, Guerra Mondragón, Tous Soto, and others—was the signature of one member of the *Coalición*—Santiago Iglesias Pantín.[90]

As continental governors went, then, Horace Mann Towner was a popular one, and as governorships went, his was a quiet one. Unfortunately, President Calvin Coolidge did not have that same popularity with the Puerto Ricans. Coolidge had anything but an innovative, daring, and liberal personality. His outlook toward the American overseas possessions was much like that of President William Howard Taft: leave things as they are for now, for native peoples cannot be expected to have the Anglo-Saxon capability of self-government.[91] On three occasions Coolidge gave Puerto Rican political leaders the impression that he was opposed to any further autonomy for Puerto Rico. The first was when he responded coolly to the commission that came to Washington in 1924 seeking an elective governor and a definitive statement of Puerto Rico's future direction.

The second was when he vetoed a Puerto Rican legislative action, the only time this was done in the 1917–33 period. The Jones Act gave the governor of Puerto Rico a "backstop"; if the insular legislature should pass a bill over his veto, a governor could send the bill to the president of the United States. The approval or disapproval of the chief executive would determine the fate of the bill. In 1925 the Puerto Rican legislature passed a bill to establish an industrial school in San Juan. It was Governor Towner's opinion that the insular government had insufficient funds at that time to undertake further programs in industrial education. (Among other institutions, there was already an agricultural and mechanical college at Mayagüez, and rural grade schools and high schools concentrated on practical vocational education.) So Towner vetoed the bill. When the legislature overrode the governor's veto and passed the bill with the necessary two-thirds majority in both houses, Towner took the recourse left him according to the organic act, and sent the bill to Coolidge, along with a full explanation of his reasons for vetoing it and a request that the president do the same.[92] Coolidge saw the situation in the same light as the governor, and the bill was killed.[93] It was probably an unwise bill, but the squelch was certainly not designed to smooth the Puerto Ricans' ruffled feathers. Towner's action in sending the bill to Coolidge and the president's veto were denials of self-government for Puerto Rico.

The third occasion of Coolidge's wet-blanket policy toward Puerto Rican agitation for political reforms was the most widely publicized of the three. This was in part because it began with the visit in 1928 of the most famous hero of the time, Charles Lindbergh. The Puerto Rican legislature met in ceremonial joint session in Lindbergh's honor, with speeches and a special medal struck for the occasion. The legislature gave the aviator a message to deliver to President Coolidge. Among its flowery phrases were some very blunt words about Puerto Rico's colonial position, including the request to "grant us the freedom that you enjoy, for which you struggled, which you worship, which we deserve, and you have promised us."[94] To make sure its point got across, the legislature on that occasion also passed a special concurrent resolution (not requiring the approval of the governor) written by the leaders of the *Alianza,* Barceló and Tous Soto. This resolution was cabled by those two men to President Coolidge. It congratulated the president for the proclamation by the United States of "justice and self-determination" at the recent Sixth Inter-American Conference held at Havana. In language bordering on sarcasm it asked that the United States now "make effective . . . the wonderful language of that brave speech" (Coolidge's speech at the Havana Conference on January 16) by constituting Puerto Rico as a "free state concerting thus with your great republic such good and fraternal relations as may be necessary for the mutual welfare of the United States and Porto Rico, and to the dignity of our citizens." The resolution closed with the words, "Justice and nothing but justice is what we ask."[95]

The message sent to Coolidge via Lindbergh and the resolution which followed did not help matters for the president at a meeting with some Latin American delegates who came with hostile anti-American attitudes and intentions. And Coolidge was not the type to let his humiliation go unrevenged. He made his rebuke of the Puerto Ricans as public as had been the Barceló–Tous Soto criticism of the United States. On February 28, 1928, Coolidge sent an eleven-page letter to Governor Towner, in which he responded to the actions taken during the Lindbergh visit. He said:

> The cablegram and resolution seem to be based largely on a complete misunderstanding of concrete facts. It would not be difficult to show that the present status of Porto Rico is far more liberal than any status of its entire history; that its people have greater control of their own affairs with less interference from without; that its people enjoy liberty and the protection of law; and that its people and its government are receiving material assistance through its association with the continental United States. The Treaty of Paris, of course, contains no promise to the people of Porto Rico. . . . *The Porto Rican government at present exercises a greater degree of sovereignty over its own internal affairs than does the government of any State or Territory of the United States. . . . The people of Porto Rico are citizens of the United States with all the rights and privileges of other citizens of the United States.*[96]

The president had this letter printed in both English and Spanish, and many copies were distributed in Puerto Rico.

The reactions to Coolidge's smashing refutation of the Puerto Rican cry for autonomy were predictable. During the first few weeks after he wrote it, the president received many letters and cables warmly congratulating him. He received commendations from such people as former governor Charles H. Allen; Harry Besosa, past commander of the Puerto Rican American Legion; James Bliss Coombs, with a Wall Street address ("The economic wisdom of this message will make it a real contribution to our state papers. It possesses a dignity and splendor that cannot fail to have a profound effect. I am grateful in having my interests so impartially and well protected."); Solon A. Davison, manager and treasurer of the Porto Rican Fruit Union; James R. Sheffield of New York City ("The Latin mind may attempt to distort the picture, but it cannot escape the facts as you have presented them."); and Dr. Ramón C. Goyco, the president of the Ponce Committee of the Pure Republicans.[97]

Except for the Pure Republicans of Roberto Todd, the insular political figures were indignant at President Coolidge's open letter. Alfonso Lastra Charriez of the Puerto Rican House of Representatives wrote Coolidge that the president had had an opportunity to win for himself "the love of a whole people" by an encouraging reply to the Lindbergh message, but instead he had shown the other Latin Americans "the *paternal* manner in which the United States treats our country."[98]

Félix Córdova Dávila criticized the president's letter in careful detail in a speech in the United States House of Representatives on April 12. Coolidge, he said, had left a mistaken impression as to Puerto Rico's condition when the United States took it over in 1898, by using the worst parts of a description written in 1892. The president placed great emphasis upon all the things the United States did for Puerto Rico, said Córdova Dávila, especially upon such trivial blessings as the Lighthouse Service operations on the Puerto Rican coasts. And the statement made by Coolidge that Puerto Rico enjoyed more autonomy than any American state or incorporated territory was patently false: (1) Puerto Ricans had no choice over whom they would have for governor, and could be sure he would be a man who did not speak their language and who had no understanding of their customs and culture; (2) only in Puerto Rico could a governor's veto be reinforced with a presidential nullification; (3) the Puerto Rican governor held enormous power over the insular budget, so much that "the legislature in this case is nothing more than a debating society"; (4) the insular legislature had no power to create, consolidate, or abolish an executive department of its government; (5) Puerto Rico had no real representation in Congress, and there, even though it was difficult to get up interest enough to push through a bill helpful to the island, "there are always powerful interests in behalf of the bills restricting our liberties," such as bills legislating for Puerto Rico on local matters. Finally, Córdova Dávila quoted some of the phrases President Coolidge had spoken at Havana: "We have put our confidence in the ultimate wisdom of the people. . . . We are thoroughly committed to the principle that they are better fitted to govern themselves than anyone else is to govern them. . . . It is better for the people to make their own mistakes than to have someone else make their mistakes for them."[99] In the light of Coolidge's veto of Puerto Rican legislation, and in the light of the other hard facts named by Córdova Dávila, the president's words sounded hollow.

One interesting feature of this third clash between President Coolidge and the Puerto Rican politicians is that it, like the first, gave to the Puerto Ricans the impression that Governor Towner was the good friend of native aspirations and Coolidge the enemy. This is evident when one notes that it was the group that was against the governor—the Pure Republicans—that applauded the president's letter, and it was the *Alianza* political leaders, who liked Towner, who completely broke faith with Coolidge as a result of this incident. Towner seems to have had the best of both sides of the fence: he was trusted by the Puerto Ricans because he wanted an elective governor, yet he used the administration in Washington to undercut insular autonomy when he wanted a bill stopped. In one other respect, too, Horace Mann Towner was lucky. He did not bear the onus for having been the governor of Puerto Rico at the start of the Great Depression of the United States; he left office in September 1929. This is perhaps another reason why Towner's name evokes no hostile emotions among Puerto Rican memories. And yet, surprisingly, neither does the name of the man who followed him in the governorship, Theodore Roosevelt, Jr. The basic reason for the absence of antipathy against Towner was his lack of public personality; conversely, it was Roosevelt's fully public personality that achieved the same success and made him a colonial administrator who left Puerto Ricans with no bitter memories.

5 | The Insular Economy, 1917–1933

President Warren Harding's hope that Governor Reily would some-day be able to concentrate upon "constructive work" was never ful-filled. There was a lot of constructive work to be done in Puerto Rico, and the political issues that dominated Reily's governorship did not have a great deal to do with the central problems of the island. Both governor Roosevelt and his successor, James Rumsey Beverley, saw that the basic problems of Puerto Rico were economic, and focused their energies upon these, but other American adminis-trators who dealt with the island seemed to assume either that the economic troubles were being solved (the colonial success story of more schools and less hookworm) or that they were endemic to Puerto Rico. A Bureau of Insular Affairs memorandum in 1921 con-tained the rather nonchalant remark: "Porto Rico is progressing normally. The problems existing there are of such duration that they might properly be called chronic."[1] The persistent nature of Puerto Rican economic ills was commonly attributed by Americans to "the people themselves, who are not markedly discontented with their present condition."[2]

Many problems plagued the Puerto Rican economy in the period between 1917 and 1933: overdependence upon a few agricultural products, high prices for consumer goods, domination of the econ-omy by a relatively small number of American and other absentee corporations, highly destructive hurricanes every few years, popula-tion growth that strained the capacity of Puerto Rico to feed all its people, the drain of an important segment of the money of Puerto Rico to foreign lotteries, increasing unemployment aggravated by an underemployment factor built into the insular economy, an un-favorable impact of the world war upon the economy, and nine-teenth-century conditions for the great mass of the island's workers.

106

Prior to 1898 the major export crops of Puerto Rico were sugar, coffee, and tobacco; there was a European market for each of these products, and Puerto Rico was favored by its position in the Spanish tariff system. Most of the island's crops were sold to European markets, and less than 30 percent was exported to the United States.[3] After the American take-over of Puerto Rico the insular economy increasingly revolved around one crop—sugar. Sugar exports to Europe rapidly declined as Puerto Rico ceased to be a part of the Spanish mercantile family, and sugar exports to the United States climbed with the free-trade clauses of the Foraker and Jones organic acts. In 1901 Puerto Rico exported a total of 68,909 tons of sugar; in 1928, 605,620 tons. But the price of sugar dropped seriously after 1920. In that year 419,388 tons of sugar were exported for $98,923,750, but in 1922 Puerto Rico exported 469,889 tons of sugar for only $40,820,333, and in 1929 the same figures were 471,244 tons for $35,222,162.[4] In a report on Puerto Rican agriculture in 1925, Carlos E. Chardón pointed out that the price for sugar had dropped from 6.58 cents per pound the year before to 4.43 cents per pound, even though the cost of sugar production in Puerto Rico was 4.04 cents a pound.[5] It is not hard to see that only a high United States tariff against sugar from Cuba and elsewhere could enable the Puerto Rican sugar industry to survive. Fortunately for the sugar producers of the island, both the Fordney-McCumber Tariff in 1922 and the Hawley-Smoot Tariff of 1930 were highly protectionist in nature. Sugar production continued to be profitable, in spite of low prices, because the United States tariff protection enabled Puerto Rican sugar to be produced in "excessive" quantity.[6]

Puerto Rico's coffee market was seriously upset by the events of 1898. Americans were accustomed to other coffees, and the United States therefore failed to replace the European market enjoyed by Puerto Rico before its coffee was taken from the Spanish trade system. The number of acres planted in coffee in Puerto Rico fell from 197,031 in 1899 to 186,875 in 1909.[7] In an effort to prevent a virtual one-crop economy, the insular government gave tax advantages and passed other laws favorable to coffee production. As a result, in the years immediately before American entrance into the First

World War, coffee exports rose to as much as fifty-one million pounds in 1915.[8] The markets for Puerto Rican coffee were principally in Cuba, Spain, Germany, and Italy; almost no coffee was imported into the United States.[9] Probably in part as a result of the European war, the amount of coffee exported from Puerto Rico fell during the early 1920s to within the range of twenty to forty million pounds.

There were four things that coffee planters in Puerto Rico needed. The first three had to come from the United States. They wanted the United States to seek free importation of Puerto Rican coffee into Spain and other European nations, in the course of making commercial treaties with any of those countries.[10] On the other hand, the Puerto Ricans wished that the United States would erect a thorough tariff barrier against coffee from any foreign country.[11] And in 1928 and 1929, the resident commissioner from Puerto Rico, Córdova Dávila, helped by Congressman Fiorello La Guardia of New York and Senator Hiram Bingham of Connecticut, pushed for a law to stop unscrupulous entrepreneurs from importing coffee into Puerto Rico and shipping it to Europe as "Porto Rican coffee." Together they tried for a ten-cent-per-pound duty on all coffee imported into Puerto Rico, but finally obtained an amendment to the Hawley-Smoot Tariff of 1930 that empowered the insular legislature to impose tariff duties on coffee imported into Puerto Rico.[12] The fourth desire of the Puerto Rican coffee planters was for calm weather, for a major problem for the island's coffee industry was the damage done by hurricanes. The coffee crop was more susceptible than other crops to ruin by these hurricanes, and in some years as much as 40 percent of the crop was wiped out. This was all the more important because coffee plantations were not only farms, but also "about the only forest we have," and so served a conservation purpose by holding the soil against erosion.[13]

In spite of the efforts of the insular government to stimulate coffee production, many growers during the 1920s turned large portions of their coffee lands over to tobacco production. Tobacco was the only one of the three traditional Puerto Rican crops that seemed to offer promise for a strong future. While the *value* of coffee exported from the island during the 1920s never exceeded nine million dollars, and was often half or one-third of that, tobacco and finished cigar exports combined ranged from a low of $15,282,000 in 1922 to $24,815,000 in 1927. Put another way, in 1901 leaf tobacco and manufactured cigars comprised only 8 percent of the Puerto Rican exports, and coffee made up 19.5 percent; but in 1929 only 0.6 percent of the exports were coffee, and the tobacco products represented 20.4 percent.[14] The United States depression which began in 1929 brought to an end the high hopes of many Puerto Ricans that tobacco would be a consistently profitable product for the island. So bad did conditions become by 1931 that tobacco buyers were no longer purchasing tobacco from insular farmers, school superintendents reported to Commissioner of Education José Padín that "there is actual hunger," and groups of laborers up to five hundred strong were marching into towns in the tobacco regions with black flags and demands for either work or food.[15]

After the American occupation of Puerto Rico, there was an effort to build up two other agricultural industries—fruit and cotton. Neither had been important in Spanish times. In spite of the promotion of these crops by both the insular government and the U.S. government, by 1929 they had climbed to only a total of 4.2 percent of the total exports from Puerto Rico.[16] The failure to make cotton an important crop in the island was particularly disheartening to those who wanted agriculture to be less a matter of large landholders and corporations, for cotton was seen as "a small farm crop."[17]

Luis Muñoz Marín, son of the most famous individual in Puerto Rico's political history, wrote in 1925 that "the story of Porto Rico is . . . economically, the triumph of after-dinner delicacies—coffee, sugar, tobacco—over the dinner itself."[18] Not only was the insular economy dominated by those three crops, but the primary food products used by the people were not grown in Puerto Rico. During the 1920s foodstuffs made up from 32.1 to 39.5 percent of Puerto Rico's imports. What made this an even greater problem for the Puerto Rican consumer was the fact that nearly all of this food was imported from the United States, whose products were relatively expensive. In the 1920s, Puerto Rico received from 86.3 to 94.1

percent of its imports from the United States.[19] Agricultural workers on the island often complained of the prices they paid for food products such as rice and lard.[20]

The economic problems of Puerto Rico were most often attributed to the presence of a number of agricultural corporations or partnerships that held lands in excess of the "500-acre" law that was added to the Foraker Act. The "500-acre" law was retained in the Jones Act, but only after a great deal of discussion in Congress and probably because its opponents realized it was a dead letter. The law, which forbade ownership by a corporation of more than five hundred acres of land in Puerto Rico, contained no provision for enforcement, and well into the 1930s was ignored, largely because most people familiar with Puerto Rican agriculture understood that a limit of five hundred acres was unrealistic for profitable sugar production.

The "500-acre" law was tacked on to the Foraker Act by Congressmen William A. Jones and other members of Congress with Populist or Progressive sentiments. Jones voiced the fear that motivated the "500-acre" amendment when he told the House of Representatives in April 1900, "I have reason to believe that syndicates are now being organized to buy up practically all the rich sugar, coffee, and tobacco lands."[21] A few years later one C. H. Forbes-Lindsay complained that "the bugbear of 'exploitation,' the fear of which has retarded the progress of the Philippines," brought about the 500-acre clause which "entirely nullified" the "original design" of the Foraker Act, which had been, he said, "to facilitate the introduction of American capital into Puerto Rico" and "the development of the Island upon the most promising lines."[22] Forbes-Lindsay's worries were in vain; American and other outside capital was invested in the "most promising" manner in Puerto Rican land, and by 1920 only 1.2 percent of the farms in the island held 36 percent of the cultivated land—a total of 716,490 acres, far beyond an average of five hundred acres per plantation. [23]

The great sugar operations were called *centrales* and lived up to their name: they did not need to own all the land from which they derived crops; they merely bought the crops of small farmers whose lands were near their refining mills. Without the refining, grading, transportation, and marketing abilities of the large corporate *centrales,* sugar production would have been a very inefficient and probably unprofitable business for the small landholder. At any rate, this is what General McIntyre believed. He did admit, however, that even though large landholdings were necessary, the great sugar companies should prepare for the day when "a breaking up of their properties will be necessary and practicable," and advised that preparations by them for that day would "still criticism" of their holdings.[24] Theodore Roosevelt, Jr., put forth as a worthwhile ultimate goal the creation of an important small-farmer class in Puerto Rico. But he believed that this development was only a future possibility, and that it should not even be considered on good sugar cane lands: "I am convinced of the value of the homesteading on the marginal lands. I am fearful of the sugar, for my general experience tends to prove that sugar is profitable in direct relationship to the size of the holdings." Roosevelt feared that a sudden land-redistribution project in Puerto Rico, or an attempt to achieve land redistribution by a system of taxation designed to drive out the agricultural corporations holding over five hundred acres of land, would bring about a collapse of the insular banking system and an inability of the insular government to continue its activities.[25]

Governor Towner believed that "the big profits made and the small wages paid by the Sugar Centrals" seemed to prove to many people that "the island is held by the United States merely for exploitation."[26] Certainly a few giant agricultural corporations were very noticeable. Four corporations, all non–Puerto Rican in organization and capitalization, dominated the sugar industry: the South Porto Rico Sugar Company (often called Central Guánica), the Aguirre Central, the Fajardo Sugar Company, and the United Porto Rican Sugar Company. This last company was typical in its holdings; by owning from 83 to 100 percent of the stock in four sugar *centrales,* it controlled over sixteen thousand acres of cane producing land; it owned four modern sugar-refining mills; and it also owned over a hundred miles of railroad, sufficient railroad cars to carry its goods to a port, and warehouses and terminals at the port to provide "adequate harbor facilities" for shipping its sugar.[27]

Sugar companies were not the only type of foreign corporation involved in Puerto Rican operations. In 1918 about 349 corporations existed in Puerto Rico. Of these, 195 were domestic—organized in Puerto Rico (but not necessarily by Puerto Ricans). These were all small operations or at the most such businesses as ice companies, newspapers, or laundries. The 154 corporations existing in Puerto Rico that were organized elsewhere, however, were mainly import and export companies or insurance, banking, or machinery companies. Well over a hundred of these were incorporated in the United States, but there were several from other nations: thirteen British corporations, seven Canadian corporations, and others from France, Switzerland, Scotland, Spain, Cuba, and Belgium.[28]

A major reason why many of the "continentals" in Puerto Rico were important people was their connection with agricultural corporations. A good example of this was the way Charles Hartzell, a corporation lawyer, remained on the fringes of the insular government throughout the 1917–33 period, being considered for posts in the insular government and acting as a trusted informant about conditions there.[29] Victor M. Cutter of Boston, the president of the United Fruit Company (which had many investments in Puerto Rico) showed corporation power from the mainland in 1926 when he wrote to President Coolidge, recommending three names for possible choices as the new auditor of Puerto Rico. Coolidge thanked Cutter for "the trouble you have taken to secure for me such full information," and noted in pencil at the bottom of the letter, which he forwarded to Secretary of War Dwight Davis, "Sec. War give this immediate attention." Davis did, and within ten days Frederick G. Holcomb, one of Cutter's recommendations—and for many years the auditor of Cutter's United Fruit Company—was appointed auditor of Puerto Rico.[30]

The men who were involved in these corporate enterprises were irritated with the attempts of the insular government during this period (except during Reily's administration) to apply existing tax laws fully and even institute new ones that sliced off some of their profits. During the 1917–18 fiscal year alone forty-two companies brought suit to recover a total of $135,000 they had paid in tax money under protest.[31] This tactic was not successful, and neither was a petition for an injunction against the insular government brought by the Porto Rican American Tobacco Company in that year, asking nonenforcement of a law which required the purchase of official stamps to guarantee that cigars labeled "Puerto Rican" were actually manufactured on the island.[32] More frequently the corporations simply delayed payment of taxes—often for years. Governors Towner, Roosevelt, and Beverley all spent a great deal of effort in getting these back taxes collected. Indeed, the Puerto Rican government did understand the need for capital investment in the island, and from time to time granted tax exemptions to specific companies; but sometimes a corporation did not get the tax exemption it believed was its due.[33]

Through a variety of means, the offended corporations sought to attack and discredit the governors who pressed for back taxes. They used contacts in the United States and in Puerto Rico to spread the ideas that the insular government was being maladministered, that it was on a spending binge that would only be encouraged by collecting back taxes, and that the governors themselves were incompetent.[34] It would appear that many of the American-based agricultural corporations would have preferred as governor a "tame" Puerto Rican (one who would be very pro-American and who would perhaps be a lawyer retained by one of the sugar companies) to a "continental." Governor Towner knew the corporate interests were working for his fall, and on at least two occasions he felt it necessary to write confidential letters to President Coolidge to defend himself. He pointed out that, contrary to the reports, corporate taxes were still lower in Puerto Rico than in the United States, and governmental expenditures were only proper—there was no extravagant use of public funds.[35] The great corporations were never able to mount a sufficiently strong attack to have any governor dismissed or even—as far as can be ascertained—considered for dismissal on the basis of their charges and gossip attacks.

The effect of the absentee corporations upon the Puerto Rican economy was a matter of dispute, but no one failed to see the effect of tropical hurricanes upon it. Full-scale hurricanes hit Puerto Rico in 1910, 1916, 1926, 1928, 1931, and 1932. Thanks to storm warnings by the government, there was generally a relatively low loss of life, but property damage was another matter. Perhaps the coffee crop suffered the greatest losses, especially from the storm of 1928. This was because the blow to coffee production was felt for more than one year. In 1926 Puerto Rico had exported over twenty-six million pounds of coffee with a total value of seven million dollars, but in 1928 it shipped only seven million pounds and in 1929 even less, one and a quarter million pounds. The total value in 1929 was only $456,831, even though the price of coffee was ten cents per pound higher than in 1926.[36] The same hurricane destroyed about 32 percent of the island's sugar crop.[37]

The long-range cost of hurricanes to Puerto Rico can never be determined accurately, for it would have to include the disruption of the insular school system, the enormous loss of homes and other buildings, the time lost from agricultural labor, and the possibility that some of the financial relief given Puerto Rico by the United States might have been given the island for more constructive ends had a hurricane not hit. The immediate relief work was usually accomplished by a combination of the insular police, the National Guard, the Sixty-fifth Infantry Division (formerly the "Porto Rico Regiment"), and the Red Cross. There were sensational reports in the United States of food riots, of martial law, and of a refusal by Washington to send aid to the island, but all of these were denied by the insular authorities.[38] In every case after the American take-over in 1898 when a hurricane struck Puerto Rico, the people of the United States responded generously to appeals for relief. The vice chairman of the American Red Cross stated that the American people gave $5.4 million for Puerto Rican relief after the hurricane of 1928.[39] Whether he was including in this figure the four million dollars of relief aid put into Puerto Rico by the federal government at that time or whether he was speaking only of donated money spent through the Red Cross is not certain. In any case, the amount of relief, even though it was generous, was far from enough—the hurricane left between $85 and $100 million dollars in damage to property.[40]

Hurricanes alone could not paint a totally gloomy picture of Puerto Rico's economic possibilities; after all, they did not hit the island *every* year. And to many people the powerful absentee corporations and the increasing dependence of Puerto Rico upon sugar did not seem to be problems. One could argue that the corporations meant vitally necessary capital for the island, and that the one-crop economy meant Puerto Rico was concentrating on what it could do best. But the population growth of Puerto Rico presented nothing but a bleak picture to many people who saw statistical or personal evidence of it. In many of the governors' reports mention was made of a lowered infant mortality rate and of American success in checking diseases among the Puerto Ricans; with this came a dramatic rise in population (as so often happens in underdeveloped nations). The 1899 population of Puerto Rico had been 953,243; in 1910 it was 1,118,012, ten years later 1,299,809, and in 1930 up to 1,543,013.

This increase does not seem alarming or really meaningful until put in other terms. First, it meant that in 1930 the population density of Puerto Rico was 451 persons per square mile. (The population density for the United States in the same year was only 41.2.) This was especially high in view of the fact that Puerto Rico has a considerable amount of rough, mountainous terrain which is not inhabited. Second, it meant that from 1899 to 1910 the annual rate of population growth in Puerto Rico had been 1.54 percent, in the next decade 1.56 percent, and in the 1920–30 period 1.69 percent.[41] During the periods when nations such as France, Sweden, Germany, Japan, and Great Britain were entering into sustained economic growth, they all had annual rates of population increase under 1.5 percent; only Russia and the United States exceeded that rate during their transition from underdeveloped nations to countries with independent economies.[42] The population growth of Puerto Rico was not far in excess of the 1.5 percent rate, but even a slightly higher figure meant a burden that the economies of many nations had not been forced to bear during economic transition. Third, Puerto Rico's population growth caused an urgent housing problem. In a study of Puerto Rico made in 1928–29 by The Brookings Institution, a survey of rural housing showed that 62.4 percent of the 32,710 people included in the study were living in circumstances of from three to six people per room, and 13.9 percent were living in dwellings with six to fifteen people per room.[43] In this general time of urbanization in Puerto Rico, it must be assumed that urban housing was in no better condition. A fourth factor in evaluating Puerto Rico's population boom can be seen by looking at another side of the public health and infant mortality statistics, paraded by each governor in his annual reports—perhaps the people were being saved from diseases to suffer from hunger. In the very grim days of 1932, the population growth of Puerto Rico seemed to Governor Beverley to be of paramount importance.[44]

With its burgeoning population, Puerto Rico needed all its capital for economic development. The sale of illegal lottery tickets in Puerto Rico took between one and three million dollars a year from the island.[45] The tickets were mostly for the national lottery of the Dominican Republic, but perhaps one-tenth of the money went to the Spanish lottery. One could argue that this money was taken almost exclusively from the poor people of Puerto Rico, and was not disruptive of capital formation because these people would not have invested it in some business in Puerto Rico. But this thinking is inaccurate, for had the money been spent for products manufactured in Puerto Rico, it would, in effect, have gone for capital formation. And the lottery was, in any case, a very pronounced dollar drain from the island. People who bought lottery tickets were generally not affluent; on the contrary, they were hoping for some luck to fall their way because they had too little money. (One proof of this is that the Spanish tickets, which cost twenty dollars each, were not very popular in Puerto Rico, and even the four dollar tickets from the Dominican Republic were usually sold in tenths.[46])

One reason why many Puerto Ricans wanted some luck was the unemployment and underemployment on the island. With bad international market conditions for sugar, tobacco, and coffee, the sugar mills, the tobacco plantations, and the docks began to lay men off or give them less than full days of work. In 1927 Dr. F. H.

Newell, one of The Brookings Institution researchers, indicated in a preliminary report that he believed the unemployment level of Puerto Rico to be 70 percent, with underemployment included in the figure. The Bureau of Insular Affairs took issue with this high figure and asked Governor Towner to collect information to prove its accuracy. Towner wrote that the 70 percent figure was obtained by Newell from a pamphlet written in 1927 by one Andrés Justicia, a socialist. He reported that a survey by his administration of sixty-nine of the seventy-seven *municipios* of Puerto Rico showed only 7.1 percent unemployed at the peak of sugar harvesting, and his Commissioner of Agriculture, Carlos Chardón, estimated no more than 37 percent as a maximum possible unemployment figure for the year.[47] General F. LeJ. Parker, chief of the BIA, wrote some highly caustic letters to Professor Newell, and the final form of the Brookings report did not contain any full estimate of unemployment in Puerto Rico. Nevertheless, Towner's administration did admit that unemployment had doubled since 1910 and risen considerably since 1920.[48] A study made in 1929–30 by seven members of the Puerto Rican legislature stated that in 1926 30.2 percent of the 485,337 males over ten years of age in Puerto Rico were unemployed.[49]

How much of the unemployment problem was due to the advent of prohibition in Puerto Rico is not possible to ascertain. The rum industry of the island may not have employed many workers, even though it did provide considerable governmental revenues in the form of excise taxes. Some of the workers who lost their jobs as a result of prohibition continued to find employment as a small commercial alcohol industry arose. In 1914 only $21,000 worth of alcohol was exported from Puerto Rico, and in 1928 this figure had climbed to $405,000.[50] Whatever other effect prohibition had upon employment on the island, it did affect the insular economy adversely. First, it was believed that prohibition hurt tourism, which was a source of income that was increasingly looked upon as important, if not a panacea for all the island's economic problems.[51] Second, as it became more and more likely that prohibition would be repealed, both in the United States and in Puerto Rico, some philanthropists were reported as feeling that their gifts to Governor Theodore Roosevelt's child-feeding program were not necessary, "if it is true that prosperity will return to the Island with the removal of restrictions on sale of liquor."[52] Third, as noted in chapter 2, prohibition seriously reduced the revenues of the insular government, and forced the government to find new sources of income.

The effects of the First World War upon the Puerto Rican economy included a labor shortage, a moderate amount of food scarcity, price control by the insular government, and an effort on the part of the insular government to promote the cultivation of agricultural goods for local consumption rather than cash crops for export. The Puerto Rican government hoped to make the island more self-sufficient in foodstuffs, in part because fewer vessels came to the island, either from the United States or from other countries. As in the United States, prices rose during the war; this is seen in the fact that for most food items, there was a much lower volume imported during the war, but with a higher value.[53] There was hope that after the war the acreage which had been converted to subsistence crops would remain in that category, but the high post-war prices of sugar, coffee, and tobacco resulted not only in the replanting of the old sugar cane lands, but even in the conversion of grazing and fruit land to sugar cane.[54]

Perhaps one reason for the higher prices of imported articles during the war was that Puerto Rican importation from the United States rose from 89.5 percent in 1914 to 94.7 percent in 1920, with the European nations losing the difference; and U.S. products were generally far more expensive than comparable European goods. This was not a permanent trend, however, for by 1928 the domination of Puerto Rico's imports by the United States had gradually declined to 86.3 percent—still a formidable figure, but not so huge as before.[55]

The Puerto Rican workers who had to pay higher prices for imported foods during the war did not experience a comparable increase in their wages. For at least two reasons it is difficult to determine the wages actually paid to workers in Puerto Rico for the first third of this century. First, wages apparently differed among the various sections of the island, among the several types of agriculture, and even from one plantation or sugar mill to the next. Second, the figures listed for wages at any period vary depending upon their source: Santiago Iglesias consistently claimed much lower prevailing wages for Puerto Rican workers than did the governors. For example, Governor Towner stated that during the 1923–24 fiscal year, field hands in sugar-cane production made between one and four dollars per day, those in tobacco farming one dollar a day, and those working on coffee plantations fifty cents per day during the dull season and one dollar a day during harvest, plus a house, land, and bananas.[56] During the same time, Iglesias wrote that wages on the sugar, coffee, and tobacco plantations ranged from twenty-five to seventy-five cents per day.[57] But Iglesias may have been correct; in Towner's report the previous year he had mentioned the fact that "even at these wages unemployment is a constant condition," telling how sugar workers normally had less than six months of work each year and other workers not even that much.[58] Perhaps the lower wages recorded by Iglesias were obtained by figuring in the months of little or no work, and the higher wages reported by Governor Towner were taken from the peak earning season only.

An editorial in *The Survey* in 1920 asserted that "wages, hours of work, and industrial relations [in Puerto Rico] recall the eighteenth century United States."[59] One respect in which this was the case was the use of women and children in labor, at wages considerably below those paid to men. In 1919 some women working in a tobacco factory reported pay of sixty to eighty cents a day for nine to ten hours of work.[60] Four years later wages for the same kind of work ranged from fifty cents to four dollars a day for men, but only fifty cents to two dollars a day for women.[61] Well into the 1920s reports of working conditions in Puerto Rico consistently mentioned working days of ten and twelve hours, both in plantation field work and in factories and sugar mills. Many of the laborers on the island were paid by the piece or by the pound, depending on their type of work.[62]

There were some small independent farmers in Puerto Rico, but their independence was extremely limited. They usually were called *colonos* ("colonist"), a status not quite like that of a sharecropper or tenant farmer or yet of a completely independent farmer. The *colonos* were almost part of a *central,* as they brought all their crops to it for sale (hardly a competitive market). An age-old complaint of the *colonos* was that the *centrales* cheated them on the weight and quality of their sugar cane. Governor Yager admitted that in this "accuracy is exceedingly difficult and fraud very easy to practice, hard to discover, and still harder to punish." Yager's government worked toward acceptance by sugar *centrales* of regulations for scales and other measuring instruments.[63]

Governor Yager also tried to get the insular legislature to pass a law for enforcement of safety regulations for Puerto Rican industrial workers (including workers in cigar factories and sugar mills).[64] Nevertheless, the laborers of the island felt that Yager and his government were hostile to labor, primarily because of the police role in labor strikes on the island.[65] Neither did the Puerto Rican workers have faith in the Unionists or Republicans (or their successors by any name); one labor leader expressed their attitude succinctly— "The political parties do nothing for us."[66] This was in great measure true; not only did neither of the two major parties actively promote necessary legislation for bettering the lot of the island's laborers, neither party even *claimed* to have a good record in respect to labor in their campaign propaganda.

Two other reasons for labor's lack of interest in the traditional political parties of the island were related to Santiago Iglesias. The first was that the Puerto Rican workingmen accepted to a great extent the credo repeated many times by Iglesias that the political formulas (independence, statehood, or autonomy) proposed by the Unionists and Republicans were not the answers to Puerto Rico's problems.[67] Second was the existence of the Socialist Party in Puerto Rico as a Siamese twin of the Free Federation of Laborers (*Federación Libre de los Trabajadores*). As was noted in the first chapter, Iglesias founded both the labor union and the political party, and the memberships of the two were virtually identical. This gave the masses of Puerto Rican workingmen a political identification apart from the "bourgeois" parties—especially after 1917, when the Socialist Party formally reentered active politics.

Iglesias was a controversial figure in Puerto Rico. As he was beginning the merger of the Free Federation of Laborers with the American Federation of Labor in 1901, he was jailed on charges of conspiracy to raise the price of labor. (In the United States, from the 1842 case of *Commonwealth* v. *Hunt* on, mere labor union organization had not been sufficient grounds for conspiracy; in Puerto Rico the Spanish law had held unionization to be conspiracy, and it was on this pre-1898 basis that Iglesias was jailed.) The court, reflecting the conservative bent of the insular political leaders, found Iglesias guilty and sentenced him to over three years in prison. The American Federation of Labor helped Iglesias appeal his case to the Puerto Rican Supreme Court, where the decision of the lower court was reversed.[68] This victory allowed Santiago Iglesias in the subsequent years to carry out the thorough job of creating and publicizing a labor movement in Puerto Rico, but it did not end attempts to discredit him by members of both traditional parties on the island. The charges against Iglesias were that he was a dangerous rabble-rouser, a Moscow-directed Marxist, a proponent of anti-Americanism, and a self-seeking hypocrite, really more interested in his own political success than in the lot of the Puerto Rican laborers.

A Puerto Rican socialist, writing in Iglesias' party organ, *Justicia,* in 1924, answered the charge of agitator that was thrown at the labor-Socialist leaders. He said they appeared so only because their constituency, the masses of laborers, were in great number illiterate, and therefore the leaders used speeches instead of written arguments.[69] There is no accurate record of any wildly irresponsible ideas uttered by Iglesias in any of his speeches, but it is possible that he made some such inflammatory statements.

Santiago Iglesias' Marxism was a favorite target for the barbs of his enemies. (This was especially true in the early postwar period, when the United States was in the midst of a "Red scare" of epidemic proportions.) Félix Córdova Dávila, for example, denied that he was anti labor, but declared that his personal correspondence with William Green, who had succeeded Samuel Gompers as head of the American Federation of Labor, was an attempt to show Green that the AF of L must disconnect itself from Iglesias, "which means the repudiation of Bolshevism and the red flag."[70] A more objective and probably more correct assessment of Iglesias' Marxism was made by Robert W. Anderson in 1965, when he said it was "largely pragmatic and untouched by the subtleties of European Marxist Socialism . . . [and] stimulated by a sincere, almost primitive, sense of social justice."[71] Iglesias had faith in the ideals of the United States and in the possibility of improving conditions within the structure of a close relationship between Puerto Rico and the United States. His appeal to the secretary of war in 1926 reflects his attitudes: "The injustices now inflicted upon the great bulk of Porto Ricans would shock the social conscience of the American people, if they were acquainted with the facts."[72]

Very closely tied to the accusation that Santiago Iglesias was a full-fledged Bolshevik was the accusation that he was anti-American. Actually, nothing could have been further from the truth. One of his biographers has proudly claimed that Iglesias was possibly the first Puerto Rican to become an American citizen.[73] In a long letter to Samuel Gompers in 1920, quoted by Gompers in his correspondence with President Wilson, Iglesias complained that the Unionist Party showed leanings against "American institutions and the American flag."[74] One of the points of harmony which helped to bring about the coalition between Iglesias' Socialists and one wing of the Republicans was their confidence that a close relationship with the United States, leading even to statehood, was the best path for Puerto Rico.

Arthur Yager, the governor most bitterly opposed to Iglesias, did not use the first three of these charges. Instead, Yager accused the labor leader of insincerity in his mission to help the workingmen of the island. On the occasion of one strike in Puerto Rico, Yager said of Iglesias, "I do not believe he cares for anything except his personal ideas and interest, and it seemed necessary for him at this moment, in view of the approaching elections, to try to demonstrate afresh his ability to control the laborers of San Juan."[75] In addition, General McIntyre did not feel that Iglesias cooperated with the BIA, but claimed that "he invariably goes ahead with his own plans without reference to the advice received."[76] Certainly Santiago Iglesias took full advantage of his position as combination political leader and labor leader. He asked the U.S. government for several privileges, among them the help of the War Department in getting free tuition for his oldest son at Pennsylvania State College and free transportation for his daughters on an army transport ship from New York to San Juan.[77] His enemies did not believe that he had need of such financial aid, for they accused him of making $10,000 a year as the general organizer for the American Federation of Labor in Puerto Rico, plus over $3,000 as a senator in the insular legislature and from a retaining fee his son-in-law Bolívar Pagán received as the lawyer for some municipal governments with Socialist members.[78]

When Iglesias was elected to the prestigious post of resident commissioner to the U.S. House of Representatives in 1932, his political opponents even went as far as to drag up an 1898 court case in which Iglesias had been convicted of using a false name to rent a room. The United States officials to whom they sent this information, however, were not impressed by a thirty-five-year-old lie, especially when it appeared possible that the 1898 case was either a matter of harrassment of Iglesias by the Spanish government (labor organization was illegal) or the result of necessary lying about his name to be able to rent a room.[79]

Governor Arthur Yager despised Santiago Iglesias and did not keep his feelings a secret. The animosity was mutual. In 1918 Iglesias went to Washington and mounted an attack on Yager of sufficient force to worry the governor.[80] Iglesias believed that Governor Yager was set on destroying labor unionism in the island, and some of Yager's actions in attempting to keep order appeared that way.[81] The remaining four governors in the period between 1917 and 1933 all had better relations with Iglesias, and Theodore Roosevelt, Jr., actually worked with him toward common ends for Puerto Rico.[82]

Iglesias' labor organization, the Free Federation of Laborers of Puerto Rico, exercised power beyond its numbers and by its growing membership, for in 1924 it was estimated that only about twenty-six thousand of the quarter million workers in Puerto Rico were organized; in 1929 the estimate was at thirty-five thousand.[83] It is possible that the very low wages of Puerto Rican workers discouraged some from joining a local union, because each union required payment of dues. (The sum must have been very small, for some of the amounts reported by a union in 1915 were fifteen to twenty-five cents per man, for a month.)[84] The local unions were organized by craft, as seen by their names (Typesetters' Union No. 478 of San Juan, Bakers' Union No. 150 of Cabo Rojo, Tobacco Box Decorators' Union No. 15367 of San Juan, Agricultural Workers' Union No. 16054 of Ponce, Pier Clerks' Union No. 17001 of San Juan, etc.). Women were very much in evidence in the Free Federation, having their own locals in most cases (possibly because the particular job was done by women exclusively).[85]

The Free Federation had ties with both the Puerto Rican Socialist Party and the American Federation of Labor. Through the socialist connection of the labor union, the Free Federation identified itself with both socialist and labor movements throughout the world, a fact evidenced by many of the headlines and articles in *Justicia* (for example, "World Labor News" and "Albert Thomas in Madrid").

The demands of the Free Federation were obviously dictated by Iglesias; they were pragmatic goals for Puerto Rican labor, oriented toward closer union with the United States. The exact platform changed from time to time, but in 1924 *Justicia* listed the following as "immediate demands": The Puerto Rican legislature should pass a resolution to ask Congress for a loan of fifty million dollars over a ten-year period, beginning June 30, 1926, to the Puerto Rican government for rural schools, public health, cancellation of municipal and insular public debts, and electrical production. The use of this money would be overseen by the U.S. Treasury. Congress should extend the federal income tax to Puerto Rico. And the insular government should place a tax on absentee property holdings in Puerto Rico, and strictly enforce the "500-acre" law.[86]

With such a small percentage of the island's labor force organized, it was surprising to many people how often the Free Federation was able to involve great numbers of the workers in strikes, sometimes of several months' duration. Among the more serious strikes were a stevedore strike in 1917, a railroad workers' strike in late 1919, a general agricultural strike from January to late April of 1920, and two strikes of farm workers in 1922 and 1923. The strikes involving laborers from sugar plantations were usually the most bitter, with violent clashes between police and workers and with fires set in the cane fields.[87] The normal response of the insular government was to increase the police force of the island by a hundred men or more.[88] Officials of the Bureau of Insular Affairs generally were annoyed by these strikes, which they believed were responsible for driving some industries from Puerto Rico and discouraging new capital investment into the economy of the island.[89]

During the strikes the Free Federation supplied some money for legal services for those of its number who were jailed,[90] but it could not provide subsistence money for workers on strike. These funds had to come from elsewhere. Fortunately, the Free Federation had been affiliated with the American Federation of Labor since 1900. So important was this connection that when Iglesias spoke of the Puerto Rican labor movement—at least during the 1920s—he simply referred to the American Federation of Labor.[91] The link between the AF of L and the Free Federation was not appreciated by anyone who was either against Iglesias or against labor organizations. One example of this was the sarcastic conclusion to a report on a forthcoming trip Iglesias would make in behalf of the AF of L in the very conservative San Juan English-language newspaper *The Times:* "Of course, the Legislature meets on the 11th instant, and will probably be in session for three months, but that will probably not interfere with the Senator's more important plans."[92] General McIntyre, who felt that the Puerto Rican labor movement was not especially good for the island because it often meant strikes, correctly told Governor Yager, "So long, of course, as strikers in Porto Rico feel that they will receive from the American Federation of Labor a strike allowance about equal to their earning capacity when working the temptation to strike will be very great."[93] McIntyre was right about the primary role of the AF of L as "parent body" of the Free Federation—it offered strike funds.

Samuel Gompers did not want the Puerto Ricans to see the American Federation of Labor simply as a source for strike subsistence money. He certainly had a larger view of the role of the AF of L, of the Free Federation, and even of Puerto Rico. Like the best of the American governors, Gompers understood Puerto Rico's importance in the relationship between the United States and the independent nations of Latin America.[94] He worked to make the AF of L the agent by which the labor movement in Puerto Rico could not only survive and act, but could also improve itself. Gompers wanted the relationships of the Free Federation with the business organizations of Puerto Rico and with the U.S. government to be something more than harsh confrontations and demands. Thus he used his own fame and strength to ask presidents of sugar corporations, the secretary of labor, several presidents of the United States, and other public officials to hold interviews with Puerto Rican labor representatives or to help in specific or general problems facing the workers of the island.[95] Although he generally backed Iglesias on matters regarding the Puerto Rican labor movement, Gompers did not give him a free rein. As seen in chapter 4, he bluntly expressed his disapproval of Iglesias' personal entrance into Puerto Rican politics when Iglesias ran for the insular Senate in 1917.[96] He also required Iglesias to give him an exact accounting of $2,700 he sent the Puerto Rican for furthering the pan-American labor movement.[97] And Gompers saw to it that strike activity in Puerto Rico followed the policies and procedures of the American Federation of Labor.

The AF of L was willing to help out during strikes in Puerto Rico only as a final resort. One thing Gompers hoped to teach the Puerto Rican unionists was first to look to negotiations and then to consider strikes. A great percentage of the correspondence between Gompers and Iglesias consisted of requests by Gompers for Iglesias to investigate a particular labor situation on the island and to report to him on it, so that the Executive Council of the AF of L could decide whether or not to approve the demands of the workers in the case, and whether or not the local union should go on strike.[98] Unless this approval by the central governing body of the AF of L was granted, no local union received strike benefits from the organization. More than once, Gompers wrote mild rebukes to local leaders in Puerto Rico, reminding them that their precipitate decisions to strike had cost them possible financial aid from the American Federation of Labor.[99] Even after such decisions to strike, however, Gompers asked Iglesias to help the strikers in other ways, especially in getting the strikes ended constructively. The AF of L also refused to send strike funds to local unions that had been affiliated with the American Federation of Labor for less than a year (Gompers was strict about the AF of L constitution) or that had not kept up in payment of dues.[100] An attempted strike of sugar workers in 1918 was flatly opposed by the American Federation of Labor and, therefore, did not become serious; Gompers explained to Iglesias that the AF of L took this action in part because "sugar is essential to the nourishment of our fighting men," and in part because he agreed with the principles of the War Labor Board which stated that there should be no strikes or lockouts during the United States effort in the European war.[101]

The enemies of Santiago Iglesias consistently contradicted his dire descriptions of labor conditions in Puerto Rico or of the Puerto Rican economy in general. Governor Yager predicted at the start of a strike, "Of course we shall have the usual distorted and exaggerated cablegrams from Iglesias to Mr. Gompers."[102] It was true that situations were generally very differently described by Yager and Iglesias, but there is no evidence that Gompers ever doubted a description sent him by Iglesias, or that Iglesias was distorting or exaggerating. Puerto Rico's economic situation was far from promising in the 1917–33 period, and when Córdova Dávila wrote an article "proving" that the island was prosperous, he was reflecting either his ignorance of the conditions of the working classes of Puerto Rico or his callous desire to convince the United States that it need not pay any attention to Iglesias.[103]

Many members of the U.S. Congress wanted to find out firsthand about conditions in Puerto Rico. There were numerous occasions when men introduced resolutions for congressional investigations of the Puerto Rican economy, but none passed.[104] The Puerto Rican resident commissioner, Félix Córdova Dávila, was noted for resolutions of investigations—but always investigations of *political* conditions in Puerto Rico, such as the Reily regime, never of *economic* problems. The economic conditions the "establishment" politicians of Puerto Rico—the Unionists and Republicans—were content to ignore, for to admit their existence would be to admit responsibility for them. It had not been the Socialists who had directed the politics of Puerto Rico since the turn of the century! Iglesias often pleaded for United States investigation of Puerto Rican economic conditions;[105] but the Bureau of Insular Affairs continually advised against acquiescence to Iglesias' appeals on the grounds that "perhaps no place under the American flag is so fully reported on as is Porto Rico. The economic conditions of Porto Rico are decidedly simple. The remedies have been recited from time to time."[106]

There had been investigations, it was true. In 1917 the United States Department of Labor sent F. C. Roberts to Puerto Rico as a mediator and liaison with Food Administrator Herbert Hoover. Roberts was joined in his mission by a Mr. O'Connor who was president of the International Longshoremen's Association, and their work in the island was considered by Governor Yager a further source of labor agitation rather than mediation.[107] In all likelihood, any agreement with the Free Federation by Roberts and O'Connor made the two investigators seem wholly in league with Santiago Iglesias. These men were probably more objective, however, than the next investigating team that came to Puerto Rico. In 1918 the American Federation of Labor sent men named Brady and McAndrew to investigate labor conditions. This pair toured the island with Iglesias, and were dependent upon him for their information because they spoke no Spanish. So active did they become in the strike situation that Acting Governor José Benedicto asked the Bureau of Insular Affairs to try to persuade Samuel Gompers to give them stricter orders about their roles as investigators.[108] There were other, less inflammatory, investigations of the Puerto Rican economic situation during the following dozen years. In 1919 the United States Employment Service sent down Joseph Marcus, whose report was a heart-rending substantiation—with photos equally grim—of the conditions on the island that Santiago Iglesias frequently talked about.[109]

Another investigation on the state of Puerto Rico's economy was conducted from October 31, 1929, until the middle of the following February by a group of seven insular legislators. They labeled their report an investigation into "the Industrial and Agricultural Uneasiness and Restlessness Causing Unemployment in Porto Rico."[110] The investigation and report had been called for by joint action of the two houses of the Puerto Rican legislature. In their report the investigators charged that Leslie MacLeod, the auditor, had tried to block their study by keeping them from receiving the money voted by the legislature to finance the inquiry. The report had as some of its major findings charges against the governors of the island. Several laws which had been passed by the insular legislature between 1921 and 1929, according to the report, had been nullified by the governors' refusals to put them into execution. These laws were mostly deficit-spending items such as issuance of public bonds for six million dollars of municipal public works, three million dollars of rail-road construction, and one million dollars of public-housing projects for low-income families.[111]

The most scholarly and comprehensive investigation of economic conditions in Puerto Rico was that carried out by a team of experts sent by The Brookings Institution of Washington, D.C., in 1928–29. Included in this group of investigators was Victor S. Clark, who had been commissioner of education in the island during the period of American military governorship. The Brookings survey, published in a 700-page book in 1930, contained chapters on subjects ranging from tax appeals to public personnel administration, and its final list of recommendations was equally sweeping. It included recommendations for action by the U.S. Congress (such as providing a one-house legislature for Puerto Rico and repealing the "futile" 500-acre law), for action by the insular legislature (including passing a better civil-service law and an improved municipal law), and for actions by the executive officials of Puerto Rico (such as providing more training in the primary schools in such matters as homemaking, health habits, and community life).

Of all the panaceas advocated by various individuals and groups for Puerto Rico's economic problems, the most touchy and yet one of the most frequently mentioned was the solution of mass emigration of workers from the island. During the period of the Foraker Act there had been suggestions as well as attempts to begin such an operation, but none had been of importance. A law passed in 1919 by the insular legislature provided for approval of emigrant labor contracts by the Puerto Rican Department of Agriculture and Labor. Under the protection thus provided, over 700 workers went to work on sugar plantations in Cuba and 130 women went to Brooklyn for factory work, and in 1921 some Hawaiian sugar agents hired over 300 laborers for plantation work there.[112] Several other negotiations for Puerto Rican laborers to go to California and the Dominican Republic fell through in 1923 and 1924. The dissatisfaction of a thousand Puerto Rican workers who went to Arizona in 1926 as cotton pickers halted further labor emigration into the Southwest.[113]

As late as 1931 the Hawaiian Sugar Planters' Association investigated the possibility of replacing Filipino labor in Hawaii with Puerto Ricans.[114]

Sponsored mass emigration was attacked violently by two groups of Puerto Ricans, the Nationalists and the labor leaders. Pedro Albizu Campos saw emigration as part of a "neo-Malthusian" plot to wipe out the Puerto Rican race so that the island could be taken over completely by "continentals."[115] When Governor Towner and officials of the Bureau of Insular Affairs gave mild approval to emigration, Santiago Iglesias accused Towner of wishing to put Puerto Ricans into the lowly places in the southern states occupied formerly by Negro migrants to northern cities, and William Green and the AF of L stated that the BIA's advocacy of emigration proved conclusively the need for placing Puerto Rico under some other government agency.[116] Most thoughtful Americans, however, probably concluded as did Samuel McCune Lindsay and the Brookings survey staff, that emigration was a very doubtful solution to the problems of Puerto Rico.[117]

The one partial solution for Puerto Rico's troubles which was agreed upon by all was that American panacea of education. But within that general idea, there were several stormy specific issues. The first of these was the question of the magnitude of Puerto Rico's educational problem. For the Unionist or Republican politician, deeply concerned about additional autonomy from the United States, a high rate of illiteracy quoted for Puerto Rico was threatening. One of the points these political leaders repeatedly made was that Puerto Rico was ready and able to direct its own governmental affairs. The Socialists, on the other hand, were not afraid to "tell it like it was," and on at least one occasion Santiago Iglesias publicly contradicted Antonio R. Barceló on the matter of the illiteracy rate.[118] A second controversy concerned Americanization and emphasis on the English language. From the early days of the century, when the attitudes of American colonial administrators in Puerto Rico seemed to be almost missionary-minded in respect to the teaching of English, there were gradual shifts of policy and degrees of deemphasis, but not until José Padín became commissioner of education in 1930 were the goals of Americanization and mass instruction in English really questioned by anyone but Puerto Rican patriots.[119] A third point of disagreement on Puerto Rican education was closely related to the second: What type of education should be stressed? No one complained about the fact that upwards of 37 percent of the insular governmental budget was allotted to public education (and sizeable amounts of money from municipal governments too); the question was on the use of this money.[120] For too long the lion's share of that money went to traditional school systems, training children toward high-school graduation, even though most of the children dropped out of school well before high school.[121] Governor Roosevelt, who recommended the appointment of Padín as commissioner of education, emphasized more than any of his predecessors the need for schools that would simply offer trade education and agricultural training.[122] These, he stressed, were the realistic future possibilities of most Puerto Rican children, not academic or professional careers.

Governor Theodore Roosevelt, Jr., because he cared about Puerto Rico, was never optimistic about the insular economy. He understood that there was always too little federal money available, that there were too few federal laws applicable to Puerto Rican needs, that there were too many mouths to be fed, that there was too much apathy toward economic problems on the part of the Puerto Rican leaders, and that there was too much ignorance of Puerto Rico by American leaders. Other American governors had not been so gloomy in their views. This was in part because they were more involved with other, more political aspects of the Puerto Rican situation. Governor Yager was anxious to replace the Foraker Act with an organic law that would give more self-government and American citizenship to the Puerto Ricans. Governor Reily was determined to "Americanize" the island. Governor Towner was caught in a time of vast changes in the political alignments of Puerto Rico, when there were strong movements for an elective governor and woman suffrage. Governor Beverley saw things in the same way as Roosevelt, but had almost no time to pursue a policy toward any economic goals. The next chapter is a study of Roosevelt's distinctive governorship.

6 | "The Hillbilly in the Governor's Mansion"

There was nothing in the Jones Act which specified a four-year term for the governors of Puerto Rico, or a change in the governorship of the island whenever a new man or party took over the presidency. It would seem natural to expect that at a time when a Democratic president gave way to a Republican (as in 1921) or the reverse (as in 1933), the governorship of Puerto Rico would change hands. But when Calvin Coolidge chose not to run in 1928 and thereby turned over the White House to Herbert Hoover, it was not obvious that Horace Mann Towner would be replaced. The possibility that this would happen was present, however, and leaders of the *Alianza* pushed through a concurrent resolution of the insular legislature asking President Hoover not to make a change in the governorship.[1] Unionist political boss Antonio Barceló, knowing that Nicholas Murray Butler, president of Columbia University, had considerable influence among Republicans, wrote to Butler to say that to remove Towner would be "considered a calamity by our people."[2] Butler forwarded the letter to the president-elect.

There were three considerations, however, which might have prompted Hoover to put a new man into the governor's mansion of Puerto Rico. The first was the persistent question of Governor Towner's health, as well as that of his age. It is highly likely that as a member of the Coolidge administration, Hoover had heard of these doubts about Towner's physical ability to continue in his post. Second was the claim of Governor Towner's opponents, such as Judge Ira Wells of the United States District Court in Puerto Rico, that the island was on the verge of economic disaster.[3] Even if these prophets of gloom were not taken at face value, a careful man like Herbert Hoover would not wish to gamble that they were wrong. The third possible hidden influence toward replacement of Governor

133

Towner was the position of Theodore Roosevelt, Jr., within the Republican National Party. As son of the near-legendary president and as former member of the New York State legislature, former assistant secretary of the navy, lieutenant colonel in the World War, and organizer of the American Legion, Ted Roosevelt had made a host of political friends over the years. Rumor in word and press was that young Roosevelt (he was then just under thirty-two) was in line for some appointment by the Hoover administration, probably the governorship of either Puerto Rico or the Philippine Islands.[4]

Hiram Bingham, chairman of the Senate Committee on Territories and Insular Possessions, was anxious to have himself and Félix Córdova Dávila, the resident commissioner from Puerto Rico in the House, apprised of the names of men Hoover was considering for the Puerto Rican governorship.[5] After President Hoover called Córdova Dávila in to discuss the situation with him, the resident commissioner gave the first word to Puerto Rican newspapers that Roosevelt might be the new governor. This was apparently Hoover's way of sending up a trial balloon to ascertain the popular reaction on the island to such an appointment.[6]

The response of Puerto Ricans was satisfactory. Although their preference would have been for the appointment of a native Puerto Rican or at least someone familiar with their language and culture, Roosevelt at least had a magic name, associated in the popular mind with fair play, friendliness, and energetic activities.[7] His father had visited the island as president, and his famous name seemed to assure the Puerto Ricans that their island was not forgotten, the last resort of political "nobodys." President Hoover had his secretary, Walter H. Newton, send a cable to Roosevelt, asking him if he would accept the position.[8]

Theodore Roosevelt, Jr., was then in the jungles of French Indo-China (Viet-Nam today), hunting animals for the Field Museum of Chicago. It took three days for the American consulate in Saigon to get the president's message to the Roosevelt encampment. In his diary Roosevelt recorded his personal reaction to the offer:

> We arrived at the other camp site at 12. A few moments later
> a messenger arrived with . . . a cable from Hoover offering me

Porto Rico. At first I thought I'd refuse. Then I found a cable from E. [Eleanor, his wife] saying she & mother thought I must accept or be out of politics. I decided they were right but could not reconcile myself to giving up this trip. I decided to go at once to Saigon & send a long cable. The oxcarts came very late. I got my coat & was rushing off when D. found another cable from E. saying I need not return till September. That relieved my mind but I pushed for Saigon just the same.[9]

Once he had decided to accept the appointment, Roosevelt threw himself into it with the gusto that was characteristic of his family. He asked the War Department to send him every publication it could that pertained to Puerto Rico.[10] His wife sailed to the Far East to meet him, and before leaving she had talked to as many people as she could who had been in Puerto Rico. On his return trip, Roosevelt assiduously studied Spanish from some textbooks and from a fellow passenger who knew the language.[11] When he arrived in New York early in September, he asked the War Department for the name of a Puerto Rican who had been a hero during the World War, so he could refer to that hero when talking about the cooperation of Puerto Rico and the United States in the conflict.[12] And he worked for several weeks with the Bureau of Insular Affairs to prepare a good inaugural address, in both English and Spanish. Cognizant of the fact that no governor before him had tried to learn Spanish, and aware of the resentment felt by Latin Americans toward Americans, who expected other people to learn English, Roosevelt delivered his inaugural address on October 7 without an interpreter, reading a paragraph first in English, then in the Spanish translation. As simple as this was (it required no knowledge of the language beyond pronunciation, which in Spanish is very phonetic and regularized), no previous governor had done it, and the Puerto Ricans were immediately given a favorable impression of their new governor.[13]

With a new president in the United States and the prospect of a new governor for Puerto Rico, the Pure Republicans (*Republicanos Puros*) renewed their hope of being the island's political party recognized and aided by the administration in Washington. In August the Pure Republicans sent a commission to Washington seeking recognition and appointment of their men to several positions in Puerto Rico. Senator Hiram Bingham thwarted their plan, however, by advising President Hoover not to make any appointments until Roosevelt had been installed in office, and to consult Resident Commissioner Córdova Dávila about appointments.[14] And Unionist Córdova Dávila was not likely to endorse Pure Republicans or Socialists.

Hoover followed Bingham's advice and waited until Roosevelt was in office to make the three appointments left to the president under the Jones Act (Puerto Rico's attorney general, auditor, and commissioner of education). Then he had the new governor give him an opinion of the three incumbents in respect to reappointment to their offices. Roosevelt recommended that James Beverley, the attorney general and acting governor for a short period between the time Towner left the island and Roosevelt arrived, and Leslie A. MacLeod, the auditor, be left in their positions. But Juan B. Huyke, the commissioner of education, he described as "a well-meaning but thoroughly incompetent fellow," who should be replaced after the expiration of his four-year term on January 15, 1930.[15] To succeed Huyke, who had been one of Governor Reily's ultra-American backers, Roosevelt strongly recommended José Padín, a graduate of Haverford College who had worked for the Department of State as an interpreter and who was presently employed as the head of the Spanish department of D. C. Heath Publishing Company. The Pure Republicans fought for their own candidate, but President Hoover approved Roosevelt's choice.[16]

Dr. Padín went on virtually to revolutionize Puerto Rican education, by dropping the extreme emphases on Americanization as a goal of education in the island and on the teaching of English. He irritated a lot of people, and in the 1930s he was attacked by the continentals as being un-American and the Puerto Rican Nationalists as being un–Puerto Rican.[17]

With independent actions such as his insistence upon José Padín for commissioner of education, Roosevelt slowly showed not only the Pure Republicans but other insular politicians as well that he knew what he wanted to do. As individuals and groups gradually formed their opinions of Governor Roosevelt, he did the same regarding them. In his first letter to the president, Roosevelt described the Puerto Rican political situation as "most complicated," and then tried to outline it for Hoover. He had good words for the leaders of all the main political bodies except the Nationalists, about whom he said nothing: the Socialists, the Pure Republicans, the *Alianza,* and the Unionists—who had recently been led back out of the *Alianza* by Antonio Barceló. Of Santiago Iglesias, leader of the Socialists, Roosevelt said, "I think highly of him." Rafael Martínez Nadal, "the real leader" of the Pure Republicans, was "an excellent fellow." Félix Córdova Dávila, who was leading the *Alianza* at that time, Roosevelt praised as "a good fellow, reasonable, and really interested in conditions in the Island. I have always found him trust-worthy." He did not wholly trust Barceló for the varying views of status which the Unionist boss had held over the years, but said, "We get along excellent [*sic*] together."[18]

This honeymoon stage diminished during the subsequent years, and in October 1930 Governor Roosevelt told a New York Republican leader that Martínez Nadal and some other Pure Republicans all were "worthless" troublemakers.[19] It was in this letter and another written four days later to Walter Newton that Roosevelt described the insular politics as "kaleidoscopic." Speaking of Martínez Nadal and Harry Besosa, both Pure Republicans, but possibly including all Puerto Rican politicians, he told Newton: "Their conception of a party is that no member of it may accept office of any sort except by the permission of the leaders of his party, and that when he has accepted office, all of the appointments under him are to be made not by him, but by them. It's 'bossism' gone mad."[20]

In time Roosevelt became disgusted with Barceló and various other political figures too. In 1931 Barceló went on an anti–United States oratorical binge, as a result of losing a suit before the Puerto Rican Supreme Court. When Barceló announced his intention of seeking an interview with President Hoover, Roosevelt advised the administration not to permit it, as Barceló was "a most dangerous man" to whom lies "mean nothing." After he had left Puerto Rico to become governor-general of the Philippine Islands, Roosevelt wrote back to Governor Beverley that he wanted someday to tell Congress the "full truth" of his opinions about Barceló, Luis Muñoz Marín, Luis Llorens Torres (a famous poet and Unionist politician), and others, and looked forward to seeing the surprise of these men "when they are called upon to face the grim responsibility for their acts."[21] He later told Beverley that "the famous double-cross should be the heraldic emblem of the Island."[22] By the end of his tour of duty, Roosevelt's disenchantment was complete: he felt that any and all Puerto Rican politicians were self-seeking, double-dealing, and irresponsible in the way they casually flung around emotional slogans and accusations.

In spite of Governor Roosevelt's increasing disgust with the Puerto Rican political leaders, he had a relatively smooth governorship, for he was in several ways unique among the continental American governors of his time. More than the others, he saw the problems of Puerto Rico primarily in *economic,* not political terms, and concentrated his efforts on helping the insular economy. In this connection, Roosevelt had a better relationship with Santiago Iglesias than had Towner or Yager, both of whom had opposed the labor leader, or even Governor Reily, whose friendship with Iglesias was based upon political expediency, not a similarity of views about Puerto Rico's economic needs.[23]

During his two and a half years as governor of Puerto Rico, Roosevelt worked toward a number of economic changes and additions for the island: (1) He asked for federal funds to help construct secondary schools for agricultural and trade education, and health units in each *municipio* (a local unit, roughly like a county in the United States), and to help establish small farmers on land of their own. (2) He pushed for application to Puerto Rico of the Agricultural Marketing Act and other United States laws which seemed to offer benefits for the insular economy. (3) During his governorship Roosevelt maintained a New York business expert who kept him informed about market needs and changes in the United

States which might be of use to Puerto Rico. (4) Roosevelt urged the United States to maintain a high sugar tariff, so that Puerto Rican sugar, which was not subject to tariff duties, could advantageously compete against Cuban and other sugar. (5) He successfully fought for a law creating a Department of Labor in the Puerto Rican government, and then gave its first executive post to a Socialist, Prudencio Rivera Martínez. (6) Like Governor Towner, Roosevelt worked hard to enforce the tax laws upon wealthy citizens of Puerto Rico and upon the absentee corporations. (7) He recognized the need in Puerto Rico for a more diversified economy, and tried to interest American capital in the island as a location for manufacturing. (His wife even began an embroidery industry in San Juan, using an abandoned insane asylum for the workroom, personally taking samples of the work to New York stores to get orders, and finally turning it over to some of the native women.) (8) Roosevelt and his wife spent a great deal of time and effort raising money for school lunchrooms and lunches for Puerto Rican children, in cooperation with the American Child Health Association and the Golden Rule Foundation. In the 1930–31 fiscal year, they were able to raise over two hundred thousand dollars for this purpose. (9) For this child-feeding and other projects, Roosevelt and his wife frequently went to the United States to speak at universities and to talk to philanthropic foundations and private individuals about how they might help Puerto Rico. (10) Finally, Governor Roosevelt carried on a campaign to educate the United States to the plight of its Caribbean colony; he wrote articles for American newspapers and magazines, issued press statements, and made speeches telling it "like it was." For doing this, Roosevelt was roundly criticized by many Puerto Ricans and continentals alike, but he defended himself by saying that one major reason why the United States had never done its best for Puerto Rico was "due to the very fallacious attitude adopted in the past, of giving people to understand that everything was fine in the Island and that there were no problems."[24]

Theodore Roosevelt, Jr., was an unusually imaginative governor in dealing with the problems of Puerto Rico. For example, he tried some unique ways to boost tourism to Puerto Rico. At the suggestion of Don Marquis, he arranged to have a movie made showing the natural beauty of the island.[25] With Grantland Rice, he publicized the golf course which surrounded the fortifications of historic Morro castle.[26] And with his wife, he entertained the people aboard cruise ships which stopped at San Juan, seeing to it that those tourists would leave full of good words about Puerto Rico as a fine place to visit and explore.[27]

A minor example of Roosevelt's creativity in office was his asking permission to travel to Washington on the government mail plane, rather than using five or six extra days each way traveling by boat.[28] A more important outlet for his imagination was directed to increasing both self-confidence in the Puerto Ricans and knowledge about the island in mainland Americans. He arranged for Antonio Reyes Delgado of the Puerto Rican House of Representatives to speak before the National Conference of Civil Service Commissioners in New York City, and asked Dean Ezra Pound of the Harvard Law School to invite Cayetano Coll Cuchi to lecture there on the Puerto Rican mixture of Spanish and American legal systems.[29]

Some of the things Roosevelt did would have been impossible for a governor with fewer friendships and connections. The Roosevelt name and his own political background gained him an invitation to go trout-fishing with President Hoover and brought a donation of a thousand dollars from J. P. Morgan, Jr., to be used for economic improvements in a Puerto Rican community.[30] Roosevelt himself admitted that none of these many activities and ideas by itself solved Puerto Rico's problems, but all of them collectively were a step in the proper direction.

Another unusual feature of Theodore Roosevelt, Jr., as governor of Puerto Rico was the attitude he took toward Puerto Rican culture. He knew that Americans were often offensively guilty of scorning other people's ways of living and thinking. There were several ways in which Roosevelt tried to show the Puerto Ricans that he respected their culture. He was the first governor to study Spanish. The continentals told him when he arrived in Puerto Rico that it was better to force "the natives" to speak English or use an interpreter, as this position kept up an imperial relationship of American superiority.[31] Roosevelt, however, did not mind making errors in his attempts to use Spanish—rather, he proudly joked of his grammatical blunders, making the point that he did not consider himself above the Puerto Ricans. He used Spanish in public speeches, and Mrs. Roosevelt proudly wrote of how Ted made a speech "without notes" to introduce President Hoover when he visited the island.[32] One might reasonably wonder about the actual extent of Roosevelt's fluency in Spanish by the end of his governorship, but there is no doubting his real effort to learn it (his wife said he memorized twenty words each night, and tried to use them in conversation the next day) nor his conviction that learning the language was necessary for the best United States–Puerto Rican relationship.[33] It is also certain that Governor Roosevelt's attempt to use only Spanish in his dealings with the people of Puerto Rico went a long way toward making them feel he was more than an imported dignitary from Washington.[34]

Besides the language there were other aspects of Puerto Rican culture which Roosevelt consciously strove to emphasize. The Latin American tradition of poetry was an important one, and since Ted himself liked poetry, it required no artificial effort on his part to show his appreciation for it. Roosevelt, urged on by Ernest Gruening, collected some of the poems of Luis Pales Matos and Luis Llorens Torres and tried to have them published.[35] He started a "Roosevelt Poetry Contest" to find the best poems in each of the two languages written by someone in Puerto Rico each year.[36]

In all his contacts with the United States public, Roosevelt hammered away at the idea that Puerto Ricans were highly civilized, culturally sensitive people with many contributions for American society. At the same time he assured the Puerto Ricans he did not want to "Americanize" them; in many ways he cut back on the programs and policies designed to accomplish this. On the contrary, he consciously "Puerto-Ricanized" himself, often saying "we" for Puerto Ricans, learning Spanish, and proudly calling himself (his wife said the common folk gave him this sobriquet) *"el jíbaro de La Fortaleza"* ("the hillbilly of the Governor's Mansion").[37]

Theodore Roosevelt, Jr., believed that the United States relationship with Puerto Rico was not just an internal matter, but a part of the overall diplomatic situation for the United States in Latin America. Roosevelt told President Hoover he knew the president shared his feeling for "the larger aspect of the situation in Porto Rico," which was that "on Porto Rico depends a great deal our diplomatic relationships with much of South and Central America."[38] He used his position as a listening post for reactions in Latin America concerning the United States, and on one visit to Washington stated that he wanted to talk with Hoover about "the general diplomatic situation." He commented that "a great deal of one sort or another seems to be coming in to me informally from the heads of the various surrounding Latin countries."[39] He believed that Puerto Rico could be "our show window looking south," a meeting place between the cultures of North America and Latin America.[40] From American dealings with Puerto Rico could come a greater appreciation for Latin American "culture, traditions and habit of thought."[41]

Roosevelt's awareness of the Latin American republics was reciprocated. *La Prensa,* a very important newspaper in Buenos Aires, Argentina, said of him:

> The recognition on the part of Mr. Roosevelt of the political errors of the government of the United States in its relations with neighboring countries and his fine desire that the people of the United States abandon this psychological attitude of superiority over other people and understand the necessity of harmony . . . are, by being put forward by a politician of his importance, very admirable declarations and should contribute to an entrance upon the road to a real panamericanism.[42]

Roosevelt was correct in assuming that President Hoover saw Puerto Rico as part of "the large picture." This is seen perhaps in the appointment of Roosevelt as governor. Of his eight predecessors (not counting the military governors), only Horace Mann Towner had some national reputation before receiving the governorship; all the others had been relatively unknown. The importance President

Hoover saw in Puerto Rico as part of U.S. diplomacy with Latin America is seen, too, in his three-day visit to the island in 1931— he was only the second president to go to Puerto Rico (President Theodore Roosevelt visited Puerto Rico in 1906; however, only Harding's death stopped him from going there in 1923). During his visit Hoover allowed Roosevelt to advise him regarding the context of his speeches (the opposite of the Harding-Reily relationship). The governor happily reported to Ernest Gruening that Hoover "grasped the cultural aspect . . . and went out of his way to stress the fact that Porto Rico should not abandon its distinctive characteristics."[43]

Ted Roosevelt accepted the Puerto Rican position with the idea that it meant remaining in politics. His numerous articles and speeches in the United States in regard to Puerto Rico increased his public exposure, and by 1931 there were rumors that he would be Hoover's running mate in 1932.[44] Believing these rumors to be good copy, the press picked them up. Governor Roosevelt found himself getting advice both for and against seeking the vice-presidency; he was counseled not to take the nomination because the Republicans were sure to lose in 1932, and he was urged to seek it for that very reason ("it would undoubtedly mean that you would head the ticket in 1936").[45] Disclaiming any knowledge of plans afoot to put him up for vice-president, Roosevelt righteously stated, "I have very little patience with the individual in government who spends his term in one office scheming to get another office."[46] Nothing further came of the prospect, for by the summer of 1932 Roosevelt was not in San Juan, a few hours' hop by mail plane from the continental United States, but rather half the globe away in the Philippines.

While Governor Roosevelt had been too busy with his job to pursue further political ambitions (which, of course, he had), the Puerto Rican political leaders were too busy with their political ambitions to have much time for their legislative duties. The political kaleidoscope had been complex since 1929. In the 1928 elections the *Coalición* victories approached those of the *Alianza,* both in popular vote totals and in seats in the insular legislature (there were eight men from the *Coalición* in the Senate and eighteen in the House of Representatives, against eleven members of the *Alianza* in the upper house and twenty-one in the lower house).[47] Then in 1929 Antonio Barceló led most of the ex-Unionists out of the *Alianza,* with the intention of reforming the Unionist Party. Barceló's group first asked for statehood; then under the goading of Luis Muñoz Marín and some other young firebrands, it turned toward independence or at least a demand for a Puerto Rican plebiscite over the choice of statehood or independence. Barceló expressed himself thus:

> You know that I am the author of the "Free Associated State" solution and I understand that it implies for us independence within a formula that would permit us to resolve our problems ourselves under the protection of the United States, but neither this nor any other formula has been accepted nor even urged by the Federal Administration, which has demonstrated, and demonstrates today more than ever, its intention of maintaining us bound to a regime that is repressive and immoral, which kills our initiative, drowns our sentiments and carries us down the degrading road of becoming a submissive colony, politically and economically, before the great interests that absorb our life, monopolize completely all the business of the colony and reduce us day by day, to the mere condition of pariahs under the feudal power of the new lords of the fief.[48]

Unfortunately for Barceló, in his new break with the *Alianza* he was not even able to make use of the name "Unionist Party" or the symbols the Unionists had created when they had merged with the ex-Republicans to form the *Alianza.* He lost a court battle (which he carried all the way to a federal court of appeals in Boston) over these issues. Barceló's group then named itself the Liberal Party. (See figure 1, page 77.)

Meanwhile, the remainder of the *Alianza,* most of whom were ex-Republicans, joined with the Pure Republicans to form a party named the Republican Union, and this coalition sought an electoral agreement of cooperation with the Socialists. In 1932 it got that co-operation. The only gains for Barceló's Liberals were some moderate Nationalists (José Coll Cuchi and José Alegría, among others) who could not stomach the vicious turn their party was taking under Pedro Albizu Campos, and returned to whence they had begun politically, to the Unionists—now Liberals.[49]

All these shifts and turns in Puerto Rican politics had two contrary effects upon Ted Roosevelt's governorship. A bad effect was the preoccupation of the insular legislators with their political fortunes, so that constructive legislation against the troubles of the depression was not easily obtained. On the other hand, this same preoccupation apparently left Roosevelt free to apply what executive remedies he could to the island's economy; the politicians simply ignored him to go at each other's throats.

The one Puerto Rican political figure who had a bitter public clash with Roosevelt was Roberto Todd of the Pure Republicans. After less than three months in office, Roosevelt had concluded that Todd was "a man of very limited attainments and very loud mouth, who fortunately, carries but little influence on the Island."[50] The relationship between the governor and the self-styled "National Republican Committeeman" never improved, and when Todd was ousted from his post as mayor of San Juan, he blamed Roosevelt. Todd immediately accused the governor, publicly and in a caustic letter, of using government funds for his private purposes, and itemized a list of expenses totaling $2,182.48 of such misused money.[51] Lieutenant Colonel Cary I. Crockett, Roosevelt's military aide, sent the governor a testimonial statement refuting Todd's charges. Among other things Crockett told of having been present on one occasion when the governor used $200,000 of his own money to pay the salaries of government employees when there were temporarily insufficient funds in the government treasury.[52] In any case, Todd's accusations were ignored, and he did not make a formal legal complaint against the governor, in spite of the fact that he claimed to have papers which proved his charges. Months later, Todd and Barceló (strange bedfellows indeed!) were sending attacks against Ted to the newspapers in the Philippine Islands; however, Roosevelt did not feel that the letters, even though published, had done him much harm.[53] Eventually both Puerto Rican politicians lost interest in revenge against Roosevelt, and he heard no more of them.

The Puerto Rican newspapers, just as they had before he was appointed governor, began in late 1931 to report that Theodore Roosevelt, Jr., was soon to be made governor-general of the Philippine Islands. Ernest Gruening felt Ted out about the veracity of these reports, saying that he would consider such a move a "tragedy" because Roosevelt was just beginning in Puerto Rico, and because Puerto Rico, unlike the Philippines, was "unequivocably and permanently United States territory."[54] Roosevelt evaded the Philippine question in his next letter to Gruening; but when he went to the United States in December, leaving Attorney General James R. Beverley as acting governor, President Hoover appointed him to the Philippine position. Roosevelt immediately suggested that Beverley, who spoke fluent Spanish (he was a native Texan) and who had been in Puerto Rico since September 1925, be his successor, and the administration followed the suggestion. Roosevelt did not return to Puerto Rico, but set out at once for the Philippines.[55]

Why did Ted Roosevelt take the Philippine Islands governorship and interrupt his work in Puerto Rico, when everyone agreed he was just beginning to make headway? In doing so, he removed himself from any possible part in Republican election plans for 1932. And he surely realized he would be in the Philippines only about a year, unless Hoover should win again—and even Ted admitted that this did not look likely. The only answer seems to be that the position was, as far as Roosevelt was concerned, a step up. He indicated this in a letter to Beverley in 1932, when he tried to persuade the governor of Puerto Rico to resign that post and become vice-governor in the Philippines, saying, "I believe that the Vice Governorship of the Philippine Islands would be treated as a distinct promotion by the country at large."[56] Beverley declined the offer.

This idea—that the vice-governorship of the Philippine Islands was more important than the governorship of Puerto Rico—may indicate something of the light in which Roosevelt held Puerto Rico: the most difficult of the colonial positions under the American flag, both in economic problems and in local political figures.[57] Ted Roosevelt kept up a brave front while he was governor of Puerto Rico, but he really had some gloomy ideas about Puerto Rico's economic possibilities:

> There seems really to be a very hopeless prospect ahead for Porto Rico, even under the regime that you and I were trying to follow. Everything had to go right in order to put the Island anywhere,—i.e., there had to be a long administration of people like yourself; there had to be an even tenor of prosperity, rising if anything, in the United States; there had to be a change of heart on the part of ninety percent of the political element, a change of heart which would imply the abandonment of the habits of thought and action of a lifetime; there had to be an increased desire to work in the rank and file of the people. If all these things had come to pass, then Porto Rico might have come through.[58]

This pessimistic evaluation of Puerto Rico's economic situation was hidden by Roosevelt during his governorship, and even more hidden was a less-than-flattering evaluation of Puerto Rican characteristics. In discussing James Beverley's future after he too had finished as governor of the island, Roosevelt told Beverley that he hoped he would not stay in Puerto Rico permanently, not only because it was not a proper place for him to use his abilities, but "besides that, I don't think you will want those children of yours to grow up in the community."[59] When Beverley mentioned to Ted the celebration in Puerto Rico of the "*Día de la raza*" ("Day of the race"— that is the Latin American "race"), during which it was common for Puerto Ricans to say, *"Somos nobles por nacimiento"* ("We are noble by birth"), Roosevelt snorted, " 'Nobles por nacimiento'!— Sin verguenzas por nacimiento!—that is what it should be. Isn't it gorgeous? I don't know anything more comic or irritating than Puerto Rico!"[60] In this exchange Roosevelt declared that Puerto Ricans should truthfully say, "We are *shameless* from birth"; even more importantly, he thought of them as "comic." The worst thing one can do to a Latin American is make him the object of humor, for the Latin American value of personal self-esteem does not allow laughter at oneself.[61] The correspondence between Roosevelt and Beverley contained warnings to destroy the letters (which fortunately for the historian were at least sometimes ignored), and both men took care to keep such explosive statements as these from leaking out among Puerto Ricans.[62] Nevertheless, it is depressing to find a man like Theodore Roosevelt, Jr., who had spent so much of his governorship trying to advertise the outstanding features of Puerto Rican culture, harboring some very typically "ugly American" sentiments.

Ted Roosevelt was proud to be the only man who had been governor over both Puerto Rico and the Philippine Islands. His short experience in the Philippines confirmed what he believed about Puerto Rico on the status question: that both possessions should be made self-governing dominions. He did not think either could survive economically as an independent nation, but neither did he believe they could ever be made states—or that statehood would be best for them. More than any other governor, Roosevelt thought about the destiny of the two possessions and of the need for a policy toward a settlement of the issue.[63] And more than any other governor, he spoke out often, especially after his term as governor, advocating a specific solution—the dominion status. The present "commonwealth" status of Puerto Rico would have been what Theodore Roosevelt, Jr., wanted. He died in 1944, eight years before that status was accorded the island.

7 | Porto Rico Becomes Puerto Rico

When newspaper reports indicated that Theodore Roosevelt, Jr., was being given the governorship of the Philippine Islands, Antonio Barceló, leader of the Liberal Party (which he continued to call the Unionist Party), quickly tried to gain some political mileage from the question of Roosevelt's successor. In a telegram to President Hoover that looked suspiciously as though it was written primarily for home consumption, Barceló first indignantly rejected the right of any political group in Puerto Rico other than his to speak for the voters of the island. Then he said, "The issue is not as between an American or a Puerto Rican governor . . . it is as between the American or the Puerto Rican constitution and sovereignty." He concluded that the appointment of any one man would not solve the problem, which was the need for "a Puerto Rico that shall be for the Puerto Ricans."[1] Barceló's message did not make clear what President Hoover might do in this gubernatorial selection that would satisfy the Liberals, but it did make more obvious the fact that neither this nor other such choices were ever influenced by Puerto Rican wishes. James Rumsey Beverley, who had been the acting governor each time Roosevelt visited the United States, was certain to be the new governor, and on January 20, 1932, the War Department sent the president the formal recommendation for Beverley's appointment. There was not much change in Beverley's work, for he was presently serving as acting governor during Roosevelt's last absence.

James Beverley was young to assume the governorship, being then only thirty-six. He was a lawyer, and had served in the office of the attorney general in Puerto Rico since 1925 and as attorney general since May 1928. His policies and actions as governor have been considered merely continuations of those of Theodore Roosevelt,

Jr.[2] Although the basic similarity between Governors Roosevelt and Beverley was their concentration on the economic problems of Puerto Rico, Beverley did not have all of Roosevelt's advantages in carrying out a program of economic rehabilitation. He did not have the Roosevelt name and connections; nor did he have as much time in which to accomplish his programs. Beverley brought on himself the further handicap of ill will from many people in the United States by making public his beliefs about the need for birth control in Puerto Rico.

Ted Roosevelt had understood that one fundamental problem of the island was overpopulation. In a letter to Lawrence Richey, President Hoover's secretary, Roosevelt had said: "Our vital statistics will show up well. The death rate is down, infant mortality down, all diseases down. I am sorry to say the birthrate is up."[3] But Roosevelt did not publicize his view, and was reluctant to mention it at all. When Ernest Gruening asked him in a letter for his views on "birth control and Porto Rico's population problems," and suggested that the insular government combine birth control clinics with ordinary health clinics throughout the island, the governor did not answer immediately. When he did, he gave Gruening a rather cautious and fence-straddling response:

> As far as birth control goes, I, like every sane person, believe in it, but I believe birth control comes more from raising the standard of living and education of a community than simply through clinical work. In other words, if we are successful in raising the economic level of Porto Rico, we will have automatically birth control. The difficulty of our problem down here if we approach the matter directly is that the community is overwhelmingly Catholic, and that the storm of opposition would be such as to destroy all ability on our part to accomplish the other vitally necessary reforms and improvements, without attaining our ends on the clinics. We are, however, more advanced than certain of the States, for by law any doctor down here is allowed to give to anyone who asks it, full information on contraceptive measures. I don't have to say that

I would not wish to be quoted publicly on this matter at this time.[4]

Governor Beverley, on the other hand, was not hesitant to "approach the matter directly." In his inaugural address on January 30, 1932, he spoke several times of the need for Puerto Rico to stress the quality of its population, not the quantity. He told the Puerto Ricans, "Sooner or later the question of our excessive population must be faced."[5] Strangely enough, in the accounts of the inaugural speech of the new governor, no Puerto Rican newspaper made mention of Beverley's statements on the population. His statements made no impact in the United States for a short while either, and he continued to dwell on this problem. In a letter to the president the Texan explained: "The population question worries me exceedingly. During the last calendar year, our birth rate was 45.4 per thousand and our death rate 20.4. Both are entirely too high. . . . I approached this question very cautiously in my inaugural address in such a manner, I hope, as not to offend any one unduly."[6]

Unfortunately, some people were offended by Beverley's later allusions, however indirect, to birth control: these were American Catholics and Puerto Rican Nationalists. Catholics in the United States took the matter much more seriously than did the people on the island, even though Puerto Ricans were nearly all Catholics. Puerto Ricans viewed their religion in a low-key, undemanding way, and were not easily swayed for a person on the sole grounds that he was a good Catholic (as Governor Robert H. Gore, who succeeded Beverley, found out) or against him because he was not a Catholic or espoused something contrary to Catholic doctrine. This is not to say that Puerto Ricans followed Governor Beverley's suggestion and rushed to their physicians for advice on birth control, but merely that they could let Beverley speak his mind on the subject without bringing on a storm of protest.

Reaction in the United States was touched off by the governor's first annual report to the president, which appeared in September. In that printed report, Governor Beverley again called for birth control as one of the partial remedies needed immediately for Puerto

Rico's population problems. In what was otherwise a routine compendium of statistics, this appeal was sensational, at least sufficiently so to make it front-page news in some American newspapers.[7] Within days, the Rev. A. J. Willinger, Bishop of Ponce, Puerto Rico, spoke out against the governor's advocacy of birth control; and the National Catholic Alumni Federation—boasting three hundred thousand members in the United States—lodged formal protests with President Hoover and Secretary of War Patrick J. Hurley, demanding that Beverley publicly withdraw his statements regarding birth control and cease dealing with the topic.[8] Margaret Sanger of the National Committee on Federal Legislation for Birth Control, Elizabest Shafer of the Minnesota Birth Control League, and Blanche Ames of the Birth Control League of Massachusetts, all quickly spoke out in Beverley's defense.[9] In a few weeks the fuss blew over, for Franklin D. Roosevelt defeated Hoover for the presidency, and it was certain that Governor Beverley's administration of Puerto Rico would be terminated early in 1933.

The stir raised by the Nationalists in Puerto Rico came much sooner. The incident that touched it off was the public knowledge of a letter written by Dr. Cornelius P. Rhoads. Rhoads was one of several continental physicians who had been sent to work with the Presbyterian Hospital in San Juan by the Rockefeller Institute. He returned to the United States at the end of 1931 or in the first weeks of 1932. Late in January the Nationalist press on the island began to tell about a letter which Rhoads had written but had discarded in his Puerto Rican living quarters, and which a Nationalist servant had retrieved for his party's use. The letter was shown in a photo in *La Democracia* (the Unionist paper of Barceló) on January 27, along with a Spanish translation of the complete document; *El Mundo* reprinted the letter in both languages on February 13. The text of Rhoads's letter was a bombshell:

Dear Ferdie:

The more I think about the Larry Smith appointment the more disgusted I get. Have you heard any reason advanced for it? It certainly is odd that a man out with the entire Boston group, fired by Wallach, and as far as I know, absolutely devoid of any scientific reputation should be given the place. There is something wrong somewhere probably with our point of view.

The situation is settled in Boston. Parker and Nye are to run the laboratory together and either Kenneth or MacMahon to be assistant; the chief to stay on. As far as I can see, the chances of my getting a job in the next ten years are absolutely nil. One is certainly not encouraged to attempt scientific advances, when it is a handicap rather than an aid to advancement. I can get a damn fine job here and am tempted to take it. It would be ideal, except for the Porto Ricans. They are beyond doubt the dirtiest, laziest, most degenerate and thievish race of men ever inhabiting this sphere. It makes you sick to inhabit the same island with them. They are even lower than Italians. What the island needs is not public health work but a tidal wave or something to totally exterminate the population. It might then be livable. I have done my best to further the process of extermination by killing off 8 and transplanting cancer into several more. The latter has not resulted in any fatalities so far. . . . The matter of consideration for the patients' welfare plays no role here— in fact all physicians take delight in the abuse and torture of the unfortunate subjects.

Do let me know if you hear any more news.

Sincerely,
"Dusty"[10]

The Nationalists saw the Rhoads letter as proof that the U.S. government had a "policy to exterminate our people," by keeping wages in the sugar industry so low that workers would starve, selling Puerto Ricans food "unfit for human consumption and the source of serious disease," and having its governors emphasize emigration and birth control. The United States, said the Nationalists, had all but wiped out the American Indian and the Hawaiians with tuberculosis, starvation, and vaccination shots, but they did not believe even Americans would stoop so low as to inoculate people with cancer, until Dr. Rhoads admitted his part in the fiendish plot.[11] More thoughtful Puerto Ricans probably agreed with *La Democracia* that Rhoads was not a part of a conspiracy, but simply a homicidal "loco."[12]

Rhoads admitted he had written the letter (it was in longhand and could have been compared with his writing), but explained that it was only a form of personal recreation; he wrote fictitious letters expressing the anti–Puerto Rican sentiments of some continental residents he knew, intending to use the material someday in a novel. He offered to return to the island if that would help. Governor Beverley, in one of his first official acts, appointed an investigative team made up of Puerto Rican physicians. No cases of deaths in the hospital could be linked to the story in the Rhoads letter; nor were there reported any cases of cancer among patients with whom Dr. Rhoads had worked. Beverley summed up his own feelings by assessing Rhoads as "just a damned fool . . . a good doctor, but not very strong mentally on anything else."[13] But one effect of the Rhoads letter, as we have seen, was to call attention to the counsel of the continental governors regarding birth control and emigration (Governors Yager, Reily, Towner, Roosevelt, and Beverley, each had said or done something favoring the emigration of Puerto Rican laborers from the island). To many a suspicious mind in Puerto Rico, there could have been a monstrous genocidal plot.

It is no surprise that Governor Beverley achieved nothing in the way of government involvement in the question of birth control. But he was not much more successful in another area into which he put far more public effort—the attempt to have Congress apply to Puerto Rico certain laws, particularly those concerning economic improvement. The Reconstruction Finance Corporation Act, one of the main weapons of the Hoover administration against the depression, was the legislation Governor Beverley most desired to see enlarged to include Puerto Rico. The fact that Puerto Rico was not originally included the governor blamed on the resident commissioner from Puerto Rico: "Córdova went to sleep on the job in Washington, and we were not included in the Reconstruction Finance

Corporation Act."[14] Beverley urged President Hoover to help get the law changed to apply to Puerto Rico; the insular legislature petitioned Congress for it; and José Pesquera, Córdova Dávila's successor as resident commissioner, introduced a bill in the House which would extend the Reconstruction Finance Corporation benefits to Puerto Rico.[15] Peter Norbeck of South Dakota also introduced a bill for that purpose in the Senate, but both his and Pesquera's bills died in their respective committees on banking and currency.[16]

Congress gave Puerto Rico better treatment in regard to another law desired by the people of the island. The English version of the Treaty of Paris, signed with Spain in December 1898, had called the island "Porto Rico"; the final version (but not the first) of the Foraker Act repeated this error. From that time forward "Porto Rico" had been official, and even natives called it that when speaking to continental Americans. During Roosevelt's administration there were some efforts to get a bill through Congress changing the official spelling of the island's name to the correct "Puerto Rico," but they failed to get far. In May 1932 joint resolutions to effect this change were introduced in both the House of Representatives and the Senate. Surprisingly, even this innocuous bill ran into trouble. Representative Albert Johnson of Washington fought against using time debating such a "light-weight bill," the "absolute irreducible minimum in public legislation." His colleague William Stafford of Wisconsin opposed the bill on three grounds. First, he said, "Porto" was the accepted English name for the island, and any member of the House old enough to have been in school before 1898 would remember that it was so called in their geography books. Second, "Porto" was a perfectly good place name; the dictionary shows over a dozen locations in the world named "Porto" something. Third, the bill, if passed, would entail enormous expense, changing everything that read "Porto" to "Puerto."

To these arguments Representative Ralph Lozier of Missouri replied that "Porto" was not correct Spanish, no matter what the American geography books had called it; also, the many "Porto" places listed in the dictionary were Portuguese, Italian, British, or

Latin names, not Spanish. One of the resident commissioners from the Philippine Islands, Camilo Osias, responded to Johnson's argument that the bill was insignificant with the assurance that to approve this measure would be "investing in friendship." Oscar Keller of Minnesota applied the clinching argument when he told the House that to spell the name of the island "Porto" was like allowing someone to use "Naw York" or "Mulewaukee" for the geography of the United States—quite offensive. Finally Guinn Williams of Texas substituted a Senate joint resolution changing the spelling to "Puerto" for the similar House resolution he had presented at the beginning of debate, and it was passed.[17] Less than a week later President Hoover signed the bill.

The reluctance of Congress to pass legislation helping Puerto Rico was one of many things which made the governorship discouraging for Beverley. An even more disheartening situation was the lack of constructive legislation by the lawmaking body of Puerto Rico. As he often did when discouraged, Governor Beverley wrote to former governor Roosevelt:

> Our Legislature has been in session now something over forty days and has done just exactly nothing. They have passed so far seven piffling little measures, most of them to admit somebody to practice something or other or to give somebody some money. I have had to veto five of the seven. . . . I don't think that there is much possibility of getting anything this year unless it is a municipal bill. Wonder of wonders, Bolivar Pagan prepared a really decent municipal law to take effect at the beginning of next year. I . . . was afraid to praise it for fear they would never even introduce it.[18]

This was not unusual. In many years governors vetoed more bills than they signed, and the governors' messages to the legislatures frequently repeated requests for certain legislation year after year.

One aspect of Puerto Rican life which often plagued the work of governors was hurricanes. The island was hit by one in September 1931, and then another struck a year later. The amount of relief money that came to the island was never sufficient even to begin replacing the enormous crop losses each hurricane left. Relief came from the American Red Cross, from the United States Army, and, to a lesser extent, from congressional relief measures. Puerto Ricans in New York also formed a "Puerto Rico Relief Committee" to send aid to the island.[19] Just as President Hoover was often thought of as unfeeling in regard to victims of the Great Depression in the United States, so he was depicted regarding hurricane victims in Puerto Rico by the Spanish press in the United States. One pro–Franklin Roosevelt newspaper, *El Universal,* ran a headline that bluntly stated, "Hoover Refuses Help to Puerto Rico—The Demands of Governor Beverley for Aid Are Ignored."[20] This story was released only a month before the presidential election, and threatened to influence many Spanish-speaking voters against Hoover, so the New York Republicans in the Puerto Rican community appealed to the administration to publicize the ways in which aid was being sent to the stricken island.[21]

Elections were approaching in Puerto Rico too. The political shifts since the 1928 election left people in the United States uncertain where the political forces in Puerto Rico stood. The Bureau of Insular Affairs was alarmed at the reports it received of rampant sentiments for independence among Antonio Barceló's Liberals. Governor Beverley told the BIA that those rumors were not true, that between 50 and 70 percent of the members of the Liberal Party were not *independentistas* but *autonomistas*. Further, he assured the department, the reports of a great deal of proindependence political activity by teachers and police in Puerto Rico were equally false; neither teachers nor police in the island were permitted to engage in political activities beyond voting.[22]

Continental Americans were not the only ones unsure of the stand of Puerto Rican political alignments. It was difficult for the Puerto Ricans themselves to keep up with the political shifts. In the first eight or nine months of 1932, the Puerto Rican political spectrum was the closest it would ever be to a return to the situation between 1904 and 1924: there was the prostatehood Republican Union Party (formerly the Republican Party), representing the wealthy, conservative interests; the proautonomy, independence-hinting Liberal Party (formerly the Unionist Party), which attracted the young, activist politicians; and the Socialist Party of Santiago Iglesias, critical of the other two parties for their failure to deal with the economic problems of Puerto Rico.

The Republican Union Party, the belated coalition between those *Alianza* members who did not follow Antonio Barceló and their previous enemies, the Pure Republicans, was a shaky union. Recognizing this, Barceló's Liberals tried to split their rivals. The Republican Union feebly issued a statement of faith: "In our Party no one remembers the past. We are all Union-Republicans in the fullest sense, united by the ties of an absolute solidarity."[23]

Since 1924 the Socialists had been restrained by their participation in the *Coalición* with the Pure Republicans, but since that organization had broken up, they were again unfettered radicals. Never had Iglesias sounded more independent, more indignant, than in a statement to *El Mundo* in August 1932: "The Socialist Party has not changed and will not change." He condemned the "bourgeois politicians" of the other two parties for 250,000 children without schools, over 300,000 men without yearlong jobs, and a "500-acre" land law that had never been complied with by the corporations that held Puerto Rico in "slavery." The "bourgeois politicians," he said, talked tough before elections, but their passivity before the corporations once they were in office cast real doubt on their sincerity.[24]

But Santiago Iglesias had tasted the sweet fruits of political co-operation, and he again accepted the apple. In the November election his Socialist Party functioned in an "electoral arrangement" with the Republican Union Party. (See figure 1, page 77.) Together, they sent the Liberal Party—the largest *single* party—to the first defeat its members, former Unionist and *Alianza* men, had known since the Unionist Party had entered the political arena in 1904. This new *Coalición* of Socialists and Republican Unionists won thirty of the thirty-nine seats in the House of Representatives and fourteen of the nineteen in the Senate. Its candidate for resident commissioner, Santiago Iglesias, also won. Once more the Socialist Party had accepted a role in the political "establishment" of Puerto Rico, rather than being either a truly socialistic party or a nonpolitical labor union like the AF of L, with which it was affiliated. It remained within the *Coalición* as that political party continued to dominate insular politics throughout the 1930s, always in traditional, conservative ways. Puerto Rican economic problems were ultimately attacked, but not by the Socialist Party—it had frittered away its chances in exchange for the pottage of patronage.

The 1932 election pointed up the need for curtailing somehow the abuse being made of an electoral safeguard in Puerto Rican statutory law, the right of challenging the registration of a voter. This law had a good purpose, that of making one type of election fraud difficult, but Governor Beverley observed that it was being used as a weapon by each party. Such a challenge was made under legal oath. The person challenged could make a counter affidavit, and the question would then be settled by the Election Board (itself a political bone of contention) or, in some cases, by the insular courts. Most persons challenged eventually proved their right to registration and suffrage, but only at the cost of considerable time and money. It was a handy method of harassment of political opponents, and Beverley had seen the number challenged rise from 10,000 in the 1924 election, to nearly 30,000 in the election of 1928, and finally to the "ridiculous figure" of 72,000 challenges in 1932.[25] He realized that he would not be in office long enough to do anything about this abuse, but he left a warning that it could seriously endanger the electoral process in Puerto Rico if some future governor and the insular legislature did not bring it under control.

There was some talk about the possibility that the next governor of Puerto Rico would be a native, but in August 1933 President Franklin D. Roosevelt appointed Robert Hayes Gore of Florida. Gore, a businessman with no governmental experience and little knowledge of Puerto Rico, had long been a faithful and generous backer of the new president. Beverley, unlike all the governors who preceded him, remained in Puerto Rico, taking a position with a law firm in San Juan and doing better financially than when he was governor. But he wistfully told Ted Roosevelt, "In spite of everything, public service appeals to me."[26] His one and a half years as governor of Puerto Rico would indicate that this was so; like the man he followed, Beverley enjoyed trying to accomplish things and to bring about change for the better. James Beverley and Ted Roosevelt continued to correspond, sharing their disgust over the boorish "Americanization" ideas of Governor Gore, rivaling each other with groans about how the Democrats were ruining both the United States and Puerto Rico, and gossiping about the twists and turns of insular politics.[27]

The period of Governor Beverley's administration was indicative of Puerto Rico's future in two ways. First, two of the chief occurrences of his year in office were the Nationalist outcry against the Rhoads letter and his suggestions for birth control. The violent clashes between the Nationalists and the insular government in the 1933 to 1939 period were a heightened form of the outburst against the Rhoads letter. Second, the Roosevelt-Beverley era was a portent of things to come, perhaps, in the way those two governors ignored the political-status issue that had mesmerized earlier insular administrators, and concentrated their efforts upon the economic problems of Puerto Rico. In the same way a later party led by Luis Muñoz Marín, the Popular Democratic Party (*Partido Popular Democrático*), which was founded in 1938 and was dominant from the early 1940s until 1968, stressed economic problems. During Muñoz Marín's governorship (1949–64), pride of insular political achievement was less in the achieving of "commonwealth" status in 1952 than in "Operation Bootstrap," a self-help thrust toward a modern economy.

8 | The Policy of No Policy

Samuel McCune Lindsay, who had been the second commissioner of education under American civil rule in Puerto Rico, boasted in 1926 after a visit to the island: "The fears and croakings of the anti-imperialists in 1898 have been confounded."[1] Lindsay saw the period following the Jones Act as successful and full of progress for the Puerto Ricans. Imperialism, in spite of what some Puerto Ricans were saying, had been a good thing for the colonials.

It is true that some of the most vivid fears of the anti-imperialists had not come to pass: empire had not resulted in a constant repetition of the United States' war against the Filipino "insurgents"; empire had not ended democracy in the United States; American capital had not rushed madly into the overseas insular possessions and exploited them to the bone; and empire had not led to a flood of non-Caucasian immigrants into the United States from its far-flung colonies, to compete against American labor and "dilute" American blood.[2] The American overseas empire had proved to be different from the colonial empires of other modern nations.[3] But Lindsay's assurance that a colonial role under the United States had been a blessing for Puerto Rico deserves investigation. More particularly, the assumption held by many Americans that the Jones Act had ushered in a virtual golden age for Puerto Rico needs examination.

What was this period from 1917 to 1933 for Puerto Rico? In the light of the events covered in this study, it is plain that it was a period of continuity. For all the heat and flash of insular politics, these years were not marked by very important changes in the political or economic environments of Puerto Rico. Any such important changes would have had to emanate from the United States, and there were none.

Politically, Puerto Rico's state in 1933 was similar to where it had been in 1917: the important functions of government and statecraft were controlled by the United States. The governors and most other administrative officers were still non–Puerto Ricans, appointed by the president of the United States; and those colonial officials were as isolated as ever from the Puerto Rican people, political movements, and culture. Americans often erroneously thought of Puerto Rico as a territory similar to the earlier continental territories of the United States, for example, Wyoming, Arizona, and Oklahoma. But the United States Supreme Court had by the end of this period not altered the principle it had first laid down in the 1901 "insular cases" and later reaffirmed in the case of *Balzac* v. *People of Porto Rico* (1922): Puerto Rico was not under the Constitution, for it was neither foreign nor domestic.[4]

Nothing better illustrated this continued position as an "unincorporated" possession than the isolation of the colonial governors and other officials. The continentals who governed Puerto Rico had an independence from local political control wholly lacking in the positions of the governors and judges of the older continental territories. Among the differences between the governor-legislature relationships of the earlier continental territories and that still prevailing in 1933 in Puerto Rico was that the Puerto Rican legislature did not have the limited "power of the purse" which the continental territorial legislatures had held over the heads of their governors. In those territories the legislatures had voted supplementary salaries for their underpaid governors.[5] The governor of Puerto Rico, however, was not underpaid. During debate on the Jones bill there was some opinion expressed in Congress that the governor of the island was making enough money at the $8,000 per year set by the Foraker Act, and that to raise it to $10,000 would not be fair. The governors of Hawaii and Alaska at that time each received salaries of $7,000 per year, and neither one had a governor's mansion provided, as did the governor of Puerto Rico.[6] The $10,000 salary did become part of the Jones Act, and no governor in this period, at least, asked the insular legislature to grant him a supplementary amount or for Congress to raise his income.

The continental governors of Puerto Rico had far more independence from local politicians than any of the governors of the continental territories had secured from the people or interests of their areas. The governors of Puerto Rico were untouchable economically; they had no need to fear violence (until the 1930s), as had some of the continental territorial governors in the "wild West";[7] and they did not even have to worry about public opinion. Puerto Ricans might say or write what they pleased, but the governors knew that it was United States opinion which counted. As long as a governor kept in the good graces of a president, and preferably also of the Bureau of Insular Affairs, there was little likelihood that even the opposition of some members of Congress would put his job in jeopardy.

The Puerto Ricans who opposed a particular governor could do one thing—try to make his tenure in office so hectic that it might raise doubts within the mind of the president about the governor's administrative abilities. Fortunately for most of the Puerto Rican governors, their enemies were generally of the minority political parties, and these were less able to raise a furor that would be meaningful in the United States. For example, the mutual animosity between Governor Yager and Socialist leader Santiago Iglesias did no damage to Yager in Washington. Governors Post and Reily, however, made the mistake of incurring the wrath of the Unionists when they were by far the most powerful political group on the island.

The greatest difference between the governor-legislature relationships of the continental territories of the United States and those of Puerto Rico was that the civil governors over the island were—until 1946—not Puerto Ricans. Until 1885 it had been common for the continental United States territories to have governors from elsewhere, but the local hostility to this brought about from that date fewer and fewer nonresident appointments to the territorial governorships.[8] Senator William King of Utah recalled the ill feeling of people in the western territories against "carpetbag" governors as he discussed the charges against Governor Reily.[9] But at its worst, resentment against nonresidents appointed as governors of the continental territories could never have rested upon the solid foundation of fact available for Puerto Rican opposition to their governors: that the governors were all Anglo-Saxon Americans, unfamiliar with the language and culture of Puerto Rico. They could never be fully accepted, no matter how good a job they might do, no matter how much they might desire only the best for Puerto Rico, so long as they were not Puerto Ricans. Theodore Roosevelt, Jr., was aware of this problem even with lower-level positions. He wrote to Thomas E. Benner, a former president of the University of Puerto Rico, concerning some problems Benner's successor, Carlos Chardón, had been encountering:

> I am glad to say I think Chardón has worked out all his troubles excellently. He took back the expelled individuals after they had apologized. Oddly enough, I think he got a real backing from the community. You and I, because we love Porto Rico, can say that this would not have been the case had he been born on the continent,—even if he were the Archangel Gabriel.[10]

This estrangement of the Puerto Rican colonial officials from the people they governed was only one manifestation of the difference between the island and the former continental territories. Another was the difference between Puerto Rico's representation in Congress and that of those earlier continental territories. The resident commissioner from Puerto Rico had what seemed to be the same position as the territorial delegates to the House of Representatives had had in the years before 1912: he was popularly elected, and he could initiate bills and participate in debate but could not vote. But there the similarity ended. Earl Pomeroy has described how the continental territorial delegates had banded together in the House for their common interests, and how as the "Territorial Syndicate" their favor was wooed by members of Congress from the States.[11] These alliances did not happen for the resident commissioners from Puerto Rico. Almost never did they find common causes with the resident commissioners from the Philippine Islands, and there is no indication of any cooperation with the territorial delegates from Hawaii or Alaska. The basic reason for this isolation of the resident commissioners was that there were almost no similar interests among the representatives of these widely varied and scattered territories and possessions. What did Alaskans care about Puerto Rico's coffee crop, or Filipinos about whether or not the Reconstruction Finance Corporation was applicable to Puerto Rico? Unlike the continental territories, these four places all had different situations in regard to status—and their people knew it. Hawaii and Alaska, it was widely assumed, would someday become states in the Union, and the 1916 Jones Act had set the Philippines on the road to eventual independence. Puerto Rico fitted into neither category. And, at least to an equal extent as the Philippines—perhaps more—Puerto Rico had its own politics. The citizen of New Mexico Territory might well have been vitally interested in Populism, bimetallism, the single tax, the elections of 1896 and 1900, and the debate over empire which followed the Spanish-American War. It is quite unlikely that the citizen of Puerto Rico in the 1920s was similarly concerned about the Washington Naval Conference, the "Teapot Dome" scandal, European reparations payments to the United States, the Progressive movement of 1922–24, or even the stock-market crash of 1929. Also, unlike the delegates of the continental territories, the resident commissioners from Puerto Rico had not even "crumbs" of patronage to offer; that is, there is no indication that the advice of any of these men was sought or heeded by any president or governor in making insular appointments. Neither the Republican nor the Democratic Party sought to build a strong organization on the island: everyone knew that Puerto Rico was not headed for statehood soon, if ever. With all these facts in mind, congressmen of the time felt no need to curry the favor of Puerto Rico's resident commissioners.

Besides this continuation of a status which carried few of the advantages or possibilities of traditional territorial status, there were other ways in which the political situation of Puerto Rico had not altered appreciably by 1933. Insular politics were, in that year, just as personality centered and status oriented as in 1917, and party patronage was still the major quest of every political organization. Also, the political view from the United States was the same. The

Republican and Democratic platforms of presidential election years still largely ignored the island.[12] Presidential and congressional discussions relating to Puerto Rico still came about nearly entirely only when either there was a specific problem—hurricane relief, President Coolidge's response to the challenge of the "Lindbergh resolution" (see chapter 4), or Congress' move toward granting woman suffrage to the island as a result of a stir about it in the United States —or when a new governor needed to be selected. In other words, Puerto Rico presented a negative situation from time to time, never an opportunity for positive planning.

The Puerto Rican economy had not changed within this period any more than had its political ambiance. The tendency for the sugar lands of the island to be concentrated in a few hands had not slowed by 1933. There was not much more diversification of the insular economy at the end of this period than before, for all the efforts of Governor Roosevelt. Governor Beverley's few comments about a need for doing something about Puerto Rico's population growth had produced only animosity, not tangible results. Political leaders and bureaucratic officials who dealt with Puerto Rico, whether natives or continentals, still were seldom as interested in the economic problems of the island as its political vicissitudes. And the Great Depression had by 1933 only intensified the poverty Americans had noted in Puerto Rico since 1898; San Juan's "Hoovervilles" existed long before Herbert Hoover was president.

Thus, in both political and economic matters, the years from 1917 to 1933 were for Puerto Rico a time of drift, of few important changes. For a number of Puerto Ricans this lack of change produced increasing frustration. Obviously, the Nationalist Party's turn to violence and intimidation in the 1930s represented the frustration of a few Puerto Ricans. But disillusionment over the United States' failure to enact important reform legislation for the island, or even to announce a clear policy for Puerto Rico, was not confined to the Nationalists. Jorge Bird Arias, long known as a friend of the United States, wrote to President Hoover when the chief executive was visiting the island. Bird decried the anti-American statements made by some Puerto Ricans, but then told the president:

Nevertheless I sincerely and honestly believe that after 32 years of political association, and as citizens of the American Union that we are, we ought to know by this time whether or not we are to remain as an integral part of the nation or whether there is any possibility of our island ever becoming independent, though it might be under a protectorate.[13]

There is no evidence that Hoover answered Bird's letter.

The lack of significant transformation in Puerto Rico's political or economic relationships with the United States leads to an important question: Why? Why didn't the governors, the Bureau of Insular Affairs, the presidents of the United States, or the Congress set about during the 1920s to alter the colonial structure of either Puerto Rico's political system or the island's economy? After all, the changes that did come later in both facets of Puerto Rico's situation were born of ideas which were not new. Some of the economic measures used by the New Deal and the "Bootstrap" programs in Puerto Rico had been suggested during the 1920s or before; for example, there had been a number of requests for Congress to provide relief to the island by extending federal relief legislation to the island or by passing separate but similar programs for Puerto Rico.[14] And the resettlement of landless farm laborers on farms of their own, which was one part of the work of the Puerto Rico Reconstruction Administration during the time of the New Deal, had been proposed many years earlier.[15] In the same manner, suggestions and requests for an elective governor and a commonwealth status—both of which were accorded Puerto Rico after World War II—were presented to the men in charge of the island throughout this period.[16] Too, the action of Congress in providing for major changes in the status of the Philippine Islands with the Tydings-McDuffie Act (1934) was additional evidence that people in the U.S. government knew about such governmental forms as commonwealths, but were reluctant to apply any to Puerto Rico.

Why was this period one of a continued status quo? For presidents and members of Congress, part of the problem was a paucity of clear information about Puerto Rico's needs. The information upon which presidents and congressmen based their decisions about the island came from the governors and—more frequently—the Bureau of Insular Affairs. The governors were handicapped in their effectiveness as sources of information about Puerto Rico by their short tenures of office, their newness to the Spanish language and Latin culture, and their frequent immersion in political, rather than economic, questions.[17] Further, it is possible that the governors received most of their own information from the wealthy elite of the island and from non–Puerto Ricans. The reportage on Puerto Rico by the Bureau of Insular Affairs was warped somewhat by the fact that its officials were stationed in Washington, not on the island. The BIA itself relied heavily upon the governors for knowledge about the island.[18]

A second reason for the lack of change in Puerto Rico's political and economic patterns in the era between 1917 and 1933 was the influence of the Bureau of Insular Affairs. The BIA developed its own point of view toward Puerto Rican affairs, and was in a position to inculcate that viewpoint into actions and attitudes of presidents, congressmen, and governors.

The Bureau of Insular Affairs advised presidents in Puerto Rican matters. When President Harding planned a trip to the island in 1923, the BIA—through the secretary of war, its usual liaison with presidents—sent him a full explanation of U.S. "policy" toward Puerto Rico, with the implication that this information was to guide him in public statements while there.[19] In 1924 President Coolidge refused to speak out in favor of a bill for an elective governor for Puerto Rico until he received the endorsement of the bill from the War Department, and then he had that department write up a draft for his own public statement on it.[20] At the advice of the Bureau of Insular Affairs, Coolidge backed up Governor Towner's veto of a Puerto Rican legislative action.[21] Coolidge also followed the counsel of the War Department in not giving José Coll Cuchi an appointment and in refusing to send a photograph of himself to a suspicious-sounding "Porto Rican Brotherhood of America, Inc."[22]

The Bureau of Insular Affairs only advised presidents, usually through the secretaries of war, but there was nothing that subtle about its dealings with the governors of Puerto Rico. E. Mont. Reily rejected the guidance of the bureau, and paid a high price for it: the BIA abandoned him to his enemies in Puerto Rico and the United States.[23] The only other governor of this period to incur in any way the opposition of the BIA was Theodore Roosevelt, Jr., whose article on Puerto Rican economic misery published in the *New York Herald Tribune Sunday Magazine* brought from the bureau a quick demand for silence.[24] But Roosevelt generally had good relations with the BIA. He wrote his inaugural speech with its aid, and he rarely corresponded directly to the president (as Reily had done), but used the proper channels through the secretary of war and the chief of the Bureau of Insular Affairs. Governor Towner was a model colonial administrator, following the forms and advice of the BIA, for example, when he listened to General McIntyre's suggestion to ignore a New York-based "Porto Rican Bureau of Indentification."[25] The Bureau of Insular Affairs was not reluctant to issue advice that amounted to orders to the governors. One instance of this was when its chief, General Parker, wrote to Governor Beverley: "I assume that Albizu Campos' activities are being noted by you and that if, at any time, they transgress the limits set by the law, appropriate action will be taken."[26] As we saw in chapter 2, General McIntyre told Governor Yager what to do about German residents, German freighters, and other matters during the World War.[27]

The Bureau of Insular Affairs also involved itself in specific policies regarding Puerto Rico's economy. The day before Santiago Iglesias called on Secretary of War Weeks in January 1925, General McIntyre gave Weeks a memorandum on Iglesias. Among other things, the memorandum told Weeks that one remedy for the economic ills of Puerto Rico was the emigration of workers to Hawaii or elsewhere (an idea utterly repugnant to Iglesias).[28] In 1930 through the secretary of war, the BIA sent its advice to Senator Hiram Bingham, chairman of the Senate Committee on Territories and Insular Affairs, in regard to a bill which was then under debate. The bill was for the extension to Puerto Rico "upon the same terms and conditions as apply to the several States" certain federal laws relating to vocational education and rehabilitation, with a $120,000 federal appropriation. The War Department suggested that the bill be killed, because it would give other federal agencies outside of the War Department some authority over Puerto Rico, and it was the conviction of the War Department that any direct application of federal funds to Puerto Rico should be contained to temporary, emergency situations (such as after a hurricane).[29]

In the BIA's viewpoint about Puerto Rico's status, both statehood and independence were ruled out. General McIntyre wrote a memo in 1924 as advice to the Coolidge administration concerning a bill then before Congress which would have made the Puerto Rican governorship elective, in which he counseled: "It would seem to be wise to take advantage of this unanimity of opinion in Porto Rico, and thus prevent, if possible, the spasmodic talk, on the one hand, of independence, and, on the other hand, of an incorporated Territory and statehood—requests which could not be seriously considered."[30]

Over the years there were sporadic complaints against the Bureau of Insular Affairs and the War Department as the supervisory bodies for Puerto Rico. There was one resolution by the American Federation of Labor in 1925 that claimed that the "inefficiency of this Department to deal with this colonial possession" pointed up the need for the president to transfer Puerto Rican affairs to "a civic [civil?] department, preferably to the Department of the Interior."[31]

The very word "efficiency," however, was actually the strong point made by the BIA in arguing the case for its continued authority over the island. In 1927 General McIntyre listed for the Office of the Inspector General seven things that the Bureau of Insular Affairs had accomplished in its operations: It was the link between the federal government and the governments of Puerto Rico and the Philippine Islands, the "clearing office for all correspondence, as well as the repository and source of data on insular subjects." The BIA supervised the customs receivership of the Dominican Republic. It had custody of the civil records of the United States occupations of Cuba and Vera Cruz. It saw "to the protection of the interests" of the insular possessions and of the United States by making studies of trends of international affairs and questions of policy. The bureau purchased supplies for the governments of Puerto Rico and the Philippines. "Appointments of persons resident in the United States" were made "at the request of the insular governments, and their transportation arranged, as well as their passports." Finally, the BIA was storing statistics and other information on scientific, business, and immigration matters relating to the insular possessions.[32] A few years later, McIntyre, by then retired from duty, wrote an article for *Foreign Affairs,* the basic thesis of which was that "with regard to the unincorporated territories of the United States, it seems clear that . . . they can be most efficiently supervised by the War Department through the Bureau of Insular Affairs."[33]

The Bureau of Insular Affairs oversaw Puerto Rico at least efficiently enough to keep most of the people in Washington satisfied. If the viewpoints held by the BIA about Puerto Rico or the American overseas empire in general had been sufficiently at variance with the wishes of Congress or any president, it would not have had the influence it did. This brings out another major factor in the failure of the United States to effect changes toward a healthier economy or a greater measure of self-government for Puerto Rico during the period under study: apathy. The level of apathy in Washington in regard to Puerto Rico was very pronounced. An excellent example of that lack of interest in the island was the cursory attention given Puerto Rican laws and franchises by the presidential administrations.

The Foraker and Jones organic acts required that copies of all laws and resolutions passed by the insular legislature, and all franchises granted by it, be sent immediately for examination by appropriate members of the federal government. This was intended as a safeguard against foolish laws or corrupt franchises, but in practice it was less than efficient. As an example, on December 2, 1924, Secretary of War Weeks sent President Coolidge two copies of the laws and resolutions enacted and the sixteen franchises granted by a special session of the insular legislature. Three days later Coolidge sent the documents to Brigadier General Herbert M. Lord, director of the Bureau of the Budget. The next day Lord returned them to the president, noting, "I have no suggestions to make concerning them." Two days later Coolidge sent the laws and resolutions to Congress with his approval.[34] Neither General Lord nor President Coolidge had held the copies of the laws and franchises long enough to assess them properly. But how could they intelligently examine some laws and franchises with titles like, "An Ordinance granting to the Municipality of Adjuntas authority to take water from the brook 'Del Cura' for municipal water supply"? The casual rapidity with which the presidential administration approved these legislative actions was evidence not only of the difficulties inherent in having an overseas empire, but of the apathetic assumption that such little things did not matter and that, in any case, the colonial officials in San Juan and in the BIA would advise the administration correctly about whether the laws and franchises should be approved.

The question of control over Puerto Rico was yet another facet of the continued status quo for the island in this period. In part, the failure of Congress or the presidential administrations to implement changes for Puerto Rico rested upon the belief that the Puerto Ricans could not be entrusted with very much self-government. Under the Jones Act, the governors had the power to chop isolated sections out of any bills passed by the legislature, without vetoing the bills entirely. They were also able to frustrate legislation merely by not putting it into execution—as did Reily and Towner to some acts which they considered economically unwise. And as we have seen, Governor Towner on one occasion used his prerogative of asking President Coolidge to squelch a bill passed over his veto.

Even municipal government was controlled by the United States. First, the governor made many appointments to municipal governments. Second, there was only an island-wide police force, headed by a chief who was appointed by the governor. Third, municipal governments did not have complete control over the money brought in by taxes. Section two of the Jones Act included a clause stipulating that no money derived from special taxes in Puerto Rico could be spent in a manner different from that for which the funds had been collected without the approval of the president. The Jones Act did not explicitly apply this principle to the municipalities, but the island-wide municipal law of Puerto Rico stated that all limitations imposed upon the insular legislature by the Jones Act should, as far as possible, also apply to the municipal assemblies. And so, from time to time, letters came to the president of the United States via the BIA and War Department, and with their approval, asking him to affix his signature to an ordinance passed by some Puerto Rican municipality which would be an exception to this rule. Thus, for example, the president would authorize the municipal assembly of Fajardo to use the surplus from a special tax to paint the lampposts in the town plaza, or the city fathers of Bayamón to spend a special tax surplus of $9.42 in any way they saw fit.[35] The role of the United States toward Puerto Rico, as most Americans saw it, was that of a tutor.[36]

The United States' dominant role over Puerto Rico was not considered proper simply because the island was a possession, a spoil of war. It was right primarily because the Puerto Ricans were not Anglo-Saxons. And only Anglo-Saxons could understand or properly exercise a republican form of government; the "natives" would have to learn by having Anglo-Saxons run their government for them. Racial factors were often referred to when the question of Puerto Rican capacity for self-government was raised.[37] A former judge on the island, Peter Hamilton, wrote to Secretary of War Weeks in 1922: "These people are not Anglo-Saxons. They are excitable and in the past few months are getting wilder on politics than I have ever seen them. . . . You can only realize it by going to a foreign quarter of N.Y. or Boston—then add that there is no counterbalancing American quarter."[38]

One aspect of this racism was another of the factors involved in the lack of change initiated by the United States for Puerto Rico during this period. That was the fact that very few non–Puerto Ricans, whether on the island or not, considered the Puerto Rican culture. Very few colonial officials even tried seriously to learn

Spanish. As we have noted, when the question arose of allowing the island to have again its proper name of Puerto Rico rather than Porto Rico, many members of Congress thought the whole issue only an occasion of hilarity. And even at the end of this period, Governor Gore shocked Former Governor Ted Roosevelt when the two men met by "talking the entire time about Americanizing Puerto Rico," which Roosevelt described as having "for its basic thesis the general thought that everything in America is better than anything, including the language, of the Spanish-American countries."[39]

A final reason for the static nature of Puerto Rico in these years was that most of the U.S. officials who dealt with the island thought that the Puerto Rican concern about the status of their island was insincere. They believed that the statements about a desire for more self-government were not based upon fact, because Puerto Rico already had enough autonomy, and therefore that any Puerto Rican expressing such wishes was merely engaging in self-serving rhetoric. As Secretary of War Weeks lectured one Puerto Rican, the United States had often told the islanders what Puerto Rico's official status was and to what it would lead.[40] Besides that, why should Puerto Ricans constantly ask for self-government when the Jones Act had conferred it upon them? President Harding snippily confided to his secretary of war that "if self government in Porto Rico means a constant opposition on the part of the Senate there . . . I would ask for a change in the organic law."[41]

One important point in all this was the way American political figures and Puerto Ricans differed in their definition of Puerto Rican self-government. President Harding was not unique in believing that the islanders had self-government; H. P. Krippene flatly stated in 1922 that "Porto Rico today practically enjoys home rule," and Henry Kittredge Norton wrote three years later that the United States allowed Puerto Rico more self-government than it did Haiti, Santo Domingo, or Cuba.[42] (This may have been so, but it did not mean that Puerto Rico had self-government.) Home rule and self-government were terms that meant in this context a government with some of the officials popularly chosen by the "natives." It did not mean, as President Coolidge defined it to a Latin American audience in 1928, that "it is better for the people to make their own mistakes than to have someone else make their mistakes for them."[43] The reason for this was simple—as Adolf A. Berle, Jr., concisely phrased it in 1921, "Porto Ricans do not run Porto Rico as well as Americans do."[44]

This was precisely the crux of the issue. Puerto Rican politicians understood that the desire for more self-government did not necessarily mean what United States political figures usually termed it: anti-Americanism. Instead, said Antonio Barceló, what the cry for autonomy meant was "the high sentiment of dignity of a people that prefers its own disaster—if it is that which might come—in its own hands, to remaining forever a slave."[45]

There is no way to prove that Barceló or other Puerto Ricans did not feel about status as they said they did, so we must assume that they sincerely desired more self-government and some major economic changes. The United States did not make such changes between 1917 and 1933. Was this some sort of evil plot on the part of the United States? The apathy, the ignorance, and the philosophical and political beliefs that were factors in this lack of change would indicate that there was no plot or concerted effort to exploit or hurt Puerto Rico. Rather, there was a total lack of any real policy or plan for the island—benevolent or malevolent. Former Governor Theodore Roosevelt, Jr., wrote in 1937 that he could not "conceive of the United States having a consistent, long-range colonial policy."[46] The story of the relationship between Puerto Rico and the United States for the first decade and a half of the Jones Act was one of a policy of no policy. Perhaps, as Whitney Perkins has suggested, by formulating no stated policy for empire, the people of the United States could successfully deny to themselves that their nation was an imperial power.[47]

Notes

Bibliography

Index

Notes

PREFACE

1. William Appleman Williams, *The Contours of American History* (Chicago, 1966), and *The Tragedy of American Diplomacy* (New York, 1962); Gordon K. Lewis, "The Rise of the American Mediterranean," *Studies on the Left,* 2 (1961), 42–58.
2. This argument is brought out in Truman R. Clark, " 'Educating the Natives in Self-Government': Puerto Rico and the United States, 1900–1933," *Pacific Historical Review,* XLII (May 1973), 220–33.

CHAPTER 1. FROM SPANISH TO UNITED STATES CITIZENSHIP

1. Lidio Cruz Monclova, *Luis Muñoz Rivera: diez años de su vida política* (San Juan, 1959), p. 674. Puerto Ricans (and many "continental" Americans) have used this brief autonomous government as proof that Puerto Rico had been granted more self-government under Spain than was given by the Foraker Act or the Jones Act. They overlook the fact that under the autonomous decree or constitution of 1897 the Spanish governor-general for Puerto Rico was still able to rule the island as a virtual dictator. On the other hand, an equally fallacious argument in regard to the autonomous government under Spain is that since it accomplished nothing, it proved either that Spain had actually not given the islanders any home rule at all, or that Puerto Ricans were incapable of self-government. The autonomous government provided by the constitution of 1897 really did not have time for a fair trial.
2. *Documents on the Constitutional History of Puerto Rico* (Washington, D.C., n.d.), p. 55.
3. See Ramón Medina Ramírez, *El Movimiento Libertador en la Historia de Puerto Rico,* 2nd ed. (San Juan, P.R., 1964), I, 29–30; Kal Wagenheim, *Puerto Rico: A Profile* (New York, 1970), pp. 63–64; Manuel Maldonado-Denis, *Puerto Rico: A Socio-Historic Interpretation* (New York, 1972), pp. 60–62; Morton J. Golding, *A Short History of Puerto Rico* (New York, 1973), pp. 97–98.

4. For an analysis of the period of military government, see Edward J. Berbusse, *The United States in Puerto Rico, 1898–1900* (Chapel Hill, N.C., 1966).

5. See Thomas A. Bailey, "Was the Election of 1900 a Mandate on Imperialism?," *Mississippi Valley Historical Review*, XXIV (June 1937), 43–52.

6. Lyman Jay Gould, *La Ley Foraker: raíces de la política colonial de los Estados Unidos* (San Juan, 1969).

7. This commission was composed of General Robert P. Kennedy, Major C. W. Watkins, and Judge Henry G. Curtis. The investigation by this "Insular Commission" was not so thorough or impartial as that by Carroll a year earlier. The Carroll report has been quoted frequently over the years, but the report of the "Insular Commission" is almost forgotten.

8. The title cited here for Payne's bill, in which the spelling "Puerto" Rico is used, was the heading for H.R. 8245 as it was discussed in the House of Representatives. By the time it came to the floor of the Senate, however, the title had changed to: "A bill temporarily to provide revenues and a civil government for Porto Rico, and for other purposes." (See page 25.) The wording—and the scope of the bill—had been changed in Senator Foraker's committee. U.S., Congress, House and Senate, *Congressional Record* (hereafter cited as *Cong. Record*), 56th Cong., 1st sess., 1900, pp. 2421, 3698. For Sereno Payne's statement attributing authorship of the Foraker Act to Elihu Root, see *ibid.*, 61st Cong., 2nd sess., 1910, p. 8183.

9. Earl S. Pomeroy, *The Territories and the United States, 1861–1890* (Seattle, 1969), p. 4.

10. Joseph Benson Foraker, *Notes of a Busy Life* (Cincinnati, 1916) II, 84.

11. A textbook written for Puerto Rican students says, incorrectly, that the tariff levied by the Foraker Act was a *15 percent* duty, which would be quite different from 15 percent of the Dingley Tariff rates. (This same book attributes the Carroll report not to Henry Carroll, but to Lewis Carroll.) See José Luis Vivas, *Historia de Puerto Rico* (New York, 1962), p. 195.

12. *Documents on the Constitutional History of Puerto Rico*, pp. 70–71.

13. Henry G. Curtis, "The Status of Puerto Rico," *Forum*, XXVIII (December 1899), 408.

14. *Cong. Record*, 61st Cong., 2nd sess., 1910, p. 7619.

15. Quoted in Bolívar Pagán, *Historia de los partidos políticos Puertorriqueños, 1898–1956* (San Juan, 1959), I, 173.

16. "Denunciaba las aspiraciones de status político de Estado o Independencia, como mentiras convencionales que dividían a los trabajadores y que distraían al pueblo de urgentes necesidades económicas y sociales" (*ibid.*, I, 171). ("He always denounced the yearnings for a political status of Statehood or Independence as traditional lies which only served to divide the

workers and to distract the people from their urgent economic and social problems.")

17. See "President Gompers in Porto Rico," *American Federationist,* XI (April 1904), 293–306; and Samuel Gompers, "Porto Rico: Her Present Condition and Fears for the Future," *ibid.,* XXI (May 1914), 377–89.

18. Garrison to Felix Frankfurter, n.d., Lindley M. Garrison Papers, Folder 76, Firestone Library, Princeton University, Princeton, N.J.

19. William Willoughby, "The Problem of Political Education in Porto Rico," *Proceedings: Twenty-Seventh Lake Mohonk Conference of Friends of the Indian and Other Dependent Peoples* (Lake Mohonk, N.Y., 1909), p. 167.

20. U.S., War Department, *Report of the Governor of Porto Rico to the Secretary of War: 1909* (Washington, D.C., 1910), p. 6; *ibid., 1913,* p. 29.

21. *Ibid., 1913,* p. 36.

22. U.S., War Department, *Second Annual Report of the Governor of Porto Rico to the President of the United States* (Washington, D.C., 1902), p. 57.

23. James D. Richardson, ed., *A Compilation of the Messages and Papers of the Presidents,* 20 vols. (New York, 1897–1927), XV, 7386–87.

24. For a fuller account of the appropriations crisis, see Truman R. Clark, "President Taft and the Puerto Rican Appropriation Crisis of 1909," *The Americas,* XXVI (October 1969), 152–70.

25. Earl S. Pomeroy, "The American Colonial Office," *Mississippi Valley Historical Review,* XXIX (March 1944), 521–32.

26. *Cong. Record,* 64th Cong., 2nd sess., 1917, p. 3009.

27. *Ibid.,* 64th Cong., 1st sess., 1916, Appendix, p. 1036.

28. "Education in Porto Rico," *Proceedings: Twenty-Second Lake Mohonk Conference* (1904), pp. 90–91.

29. Willoughby, *Proceedings: Twenty-Seventh Lake Mohonk Conference* (1909), p. 162.

30. Quoted in Arturo Morales Carrión, *The Loneliness of Luis Muñoz Rivera* (Washington, D.C., 1965).

31. Elting E. Morison and John M. Blum, eds., *The Letters of Theodore Roosevelt,* 8 vols. (Cambridge, Mass., 1951), V. 501.

32. *Cong. Record,* 64th Cong., 2nd sess., 1917, p. 2250.

33. *Ibid.,* p. 3009.

34. "Citizenship and Self-Government for Porto Ricans," *Proceedings: Twenty-Sixth Lake Mohonk Conference* (1908), p. 144.

35. Elihu Root to Dr. Lyman Abbott, December 24, 1908, quoted in Philip C. Jessup, *Elihu Root,* 2 vols. (New York, 1938), I, 378.

36. "Porto Rico—Its Present and Future," *Proceedings: Twenty-Seventh Lake Mohonk Conference* (1909), p. 152.

37. Martín Travieso, "Citizenship and Self-Government for Porto Ricans,"

Proceedings: Twenty-Sixth Lake Mohonk Conference (1908), p. 144. See also Article IX of the Treaty of Paris in *Documents on the Constitutional History of Puerto Rico,* p. 51.

38. Richardson, *Messages and Papers of the Presidents,* XV, 7300.

39. Roosevelt to Federico Degetau, 1901, quoted in Angel M. Mergal, *Federico Degetau: un orientador de su pueblo* (New York, 1944), p. 177.

40. Richardson, *Messages and Papers of the Presidents,* XV, 7801.

41. *New York Times,* November 14, 1913, p. 10.

42. Arthur D. Gayer, Paul T. Homan, and Earle K. James, *The Sugar Economy of Puerto Rico* (New York, 1938), p. 21.

43. *Cong. Record,* 64th Cong., 1st sess., 1916, p. 7488.

44. Samuel Gompers, *Seventy Years of Life and Labor: An Autobiography,* 2 vols. (New York, 1925), I, 546.

45. Yager to Wilson, March 29, 1916, Arthur Yager Papers, residence of Mrs. Diana Yager Eskew, Louisville, Ky.

46. Taft to McIntyre, August 10, 1909, William Howard Taft Papers, Manuscript Division, Library of Congress, Presidential Series 8, Letterbook 6, p. 232.

47. The Olmsted bill provided for a complex system of progressively making the Puerto Rican Senate completely elective over a period of thirty-six years.

48. It was more realistic because a sugar plantation, besides needing some of its land left fallow, required a considerable number of acres set aside for grazing areas for the oxen used in sugar production. *Cong. Record,* 61st Cong., 2nd sess., 1910, p. 6872.

49. *Ibid.,* pp. 7223, 7231.

50. *Ibid.,* p. 7623.

51. Root to Lyman Abbott, December 24, 1908, quoted in Jessup, *Elihu Root,* I, 378.

52. In 1900 the Democrats had called the Foraker Act "a bold and open violation of the nation's organic law and flagrant breach of the national good faith. It imposes upon the people of Porto Rico a government without their consent and taxation without representation." They further claimed that they were for "home rule" and a "territorial form of government" for Puerto Rico. Kirk H. Porter and Donald B. Johnson, eds., *National Party Platforms, 1840–1960* (Urbana, Ill., 1961), pp. 112, 115, 133, 150.

53. Jones was chairman of the House Committee on Insular Affairs, and Shafroth headed the Senate Committee on Pacific Islands and Porto Rico.

54. Yager to Jones, June 10, 1914, Yager Papers.

55. Wilson to Jones, June 25, 1914, Woodrow Wilson Papers, Manuscript Division, Library of Congress, Series 3, Letterbook 14, p. 298.

56. Muñoz Rivera to Yager, July 10, 1914, Yager Papers.

57. Williams to Wilson, August 17, 1914, and Wilson to Williams, August 21, 1914, Wilson Papers, Series 4, Casefile 47.

58. *New York Times,* December 6, 1916, p. 1.

59. Muñoz Rivera's own newspaper made this connection in no uncertain terms during the months after passage of the Jones Act. See *La Democracia* (San Juan), any issue in April or June 1917. For a discussion of Muñoz Rivera's role in the new organic law, see Frank O. Gatell, "The Art of the Possible: Luis Muñoz Rivera and the Puerto Rican Jones Bill," *The Americas,* XVII (July 1960), 1–20.

60. *New York Times,* December 9, 1916, p. 10; *Cong. Record,* 64th Cong., 2nd sess., 1917, p. 2251.

61. The Danish West Indies looked important too, and its purchase at this time was, like the Jones Act, part of American war preparation.

62. *Cong. Record,* 64th Cong., 1st sess., 1916, p. 7487.

63. Under the Foraker Act, five representatives to the House of Delegates were elected from each of seven areas, and the party that won a district got all five seats; this is one reason why the House of Delegates was so often solidly of one party or the other.

64. For the 1913–14 fiscal year, taxes on liquors provided $1,230,584.52 of the total receipts of the insular government, which were $4,742,229.74. U.S., War Department, *Report of the Governor: 1914,* p. 36.

65. *Cong. Record,* 64th Cong., 2nd sess., 1917, p. 3073.

66. Yager to Wilson, March 29, 1916, Yager Papers.

67. Wilson to Yager, April 5, 1916, Wilson Papers, Series 3, Letterbook 28, p. 364.

68. *New York Times,* March 3, 1917, p. 8.

69. Root to Mrs. H. Fairfield Osborn, December 24, 1917, quoted in Jessup, *Elihu Root,* I, 379.

70. For example, President Wilson wrote to Governor Yager on April 1 that he was pleased that "the last legal barrier between Americans and Porto Ricans has been removed. . . . The people of Porto Rico have now the name, privileges and responsibilities of all other citizens of the United States" (Wilson Papers, Series 3, Letterbook 39, p. 311).

71. Hamilton to Yager, June 27, 1917, Bureau of Insular Affairs Files, File 20819–38–A, War Department Records, National Archives.

72. McIntyre to Yager, July 6, 1917, *ibid.,* File 20819–38.

73. U.S., War Department, *Report of the Governor: 1918,* p. 577. The specific question of the Tapia and Muratti cases was the right to indictment by a grand jury; in June 1919, the Puerto Rican legislature passed a law granting this right.

74. For example, see the resolution by the Puerto Rican Senate in 1919, asking for the Federal Farm Loan Act and the Smith-Hughes Vocational

Education Act to be applied to Puerto Rico. *Cong. Record,* 66th Cong., 1st sess., 1919, p. 3918.

75. *Ibid.,* 64th Cong., 1st sess., 1916, p. 7472.

76. U.S., War Department, *Report of the Governor: 1917,* p. 1.

77. *Actas de la Cámara de Delegados,* Octava Asamblea, Tercera Sesión, (February 12–April 12, 1917), typewritten manuscript in Tarea 58–A–3, Archivo General, San Juan.

78. Pagán, *Historia de los partidos políticos,* I, 180.

79. Declaration of Union Party, May 6, 1917, BIA Files, File 719–50–A.

80. U.S., Congress, Senate, *Reorganization of the Army: Hearings Before The Committee on Military Affairs* (Washington, D.C., 1920), p. 25.

81. Declaration of Union Party, May 6, 1917, BIA Files, File 719–50–A.

82. Pagán, *Historia de los partidos políticos,* I, 182–83.

83. For example, see Córdova Dávila's speech in *Cong. Record,* 65th Cong., 2nd sess., 1918, p. 9288.

84. Yager to General Charles C. Walcutt, Jr., of the BIA, September 24, 1918, BIA Files, File 858–38.

85. Yager to Walcutt, January 28, 1919, and October 3, 1919, *ibid.,* Files 26429–55 and 26429–67.

86. Yager to McIntyre, August 1, 1917, *ibid.,* File 1028–50.

87. *Ibid.*

88. U.S., War Department, *Report of the Governor: 1918,* p. 576.

89. Pagán, *Historia de los partidos políticos,* I, 185.

90. Examples of American-style political innovations are the use of such words (in Spanish) as "second reading," "joint resolution," "Committee of the Whole," "table a bill," and the general wording of legislative bills, e.g., "An act, to establish a food commission regulating and investigating prices, and for other purposes" (*Actas de la Cámara,* Tarea 58–A–3, Archivo General, San Juan). For an excellent discussion of the acquisition by Puerto Ricans of American political styles and values, see Henry Wells, *The Modernization of Puerto Rico: A Political Study of Changing Values and Institutions* (Cambridge, Mass., 1969).

CHAPTER 2. PROHIBITION, WAR, AND WOMAN SUFFRAGE

1. Gordon K. Lewis, *Puerto Rico: Freedom and Power in the Caribbean* (New York, 1963), p. 105.

2. U.S., Congress, House and Senate, *Congressional Record,* 64th Cong., 1st sess., 1916, pp. 2859, 4167, 4821, 6266.

3. Bolívar Pagán, *Historia de los partidos políticos Puertorriqueños, 1898–1956,* 2 vols. (San Juan, 1959), I, 186.

4. In my interview with the daughter of Governor Yager, Mrs. Diana Yager Eskew, on May 21, 1967, I was told that the governor chose the election symbols, and that after prohibition had won, he happily commented to his family, "The coconut did it." If this is true, I cannot explain why Yager helped to bring about the victory for prohibition; he was not a "teetotaler," and he had opposed the Gronna prohibition amendment to the Jones bill on the grounds that it might endanger passage of the bill, that it would strain Puerto Rican relations with the United States, and that it would seriously diminish insular governmental revenues. I can only guess that Yager might have been displaying an upper-class attitude that liquor, being bad for the lower classes, should be withheld from them for their own good. In any case, whatever his efforts for prohibition may have been, other factors were far more significant in bringing about the surprising election result.

5. See *La Democracia* (San Juan), March 22, 24, 27, and 30, 1917. Included in these issues are accounts of prohibition meetings in Juncos, Guayama, Lares, Toa Alta, Yauco, San Juan, and Bayamón, as well as a long letter of resignation by J. Ruiz Soler as vice-president and manager of the San Juan Anti-Prohibition Committee.

6. See the small advertisements, "El Prohibicionismo en Acción (Diálogo)," by the Martini and Rossi Company, in *La Democracia,* March 20, 1917, and many other dates.

7. U.S., War Department, *Report of the Governor of Porto Rico to the Secretary of War: 1918* (Washington, D.C., 1919), pp. 25, 570.

8. Wilson to Yager, April 2, 1918, Woodrow Wilson Papers, Manuscript Division, Library of Congress, Series 3, Letterbook 49, p. 175.

9. U.S., Congress, *Statutes at Large,* vol. 42, pt. 2, 67th Cong., 2nd sess., 1922, p. 993.

10. Memorandum by J. A. Hull, acting judge advocate general, December 15, 1922, BIA Files, File 468–58, War Department Records, National Archives.

11. Yager to McIntyre, March 27, 1917, *ibid.,* File 1175–38.

12. U.S., War Department, *Report of the Governor: 1918*, p. 25.

13. *Ibid., 1923*, p. 78.

14. *Ibid., 1919*, p. 357.

15. *Ibid., 1923*, p. 39.

16. *New York Times,* July 19, 1921, p. 21.

17. Report from John T. Barrett, federal prohibition director for the island, to Lincoln C. Andrews, assistant secretary of the treasury, May 4, 1925, BIA Files, File 468–64–A.

18. *Ibid.*

19. *Inaugural Address of Hon. E. Mont. Reily, Governor of Porto Rico* (San Juan, 1921), p. 13.

20. Telegram, Edward J. Berwind of Berwind White Coal Mining Company to Secretary of War John W. Weeks, October 11, 1922; cablegram, Lee, president of San Juan Chamber of Commerce, to BIA, October 17, 1922; Reily to Weeks, October 25, 1922, BIA Files, Files 468–52, 468–54, 468–57.

21. In the 1918–19 fiscal year, a total of 2,431 vessels entered and cleared Puerto Rican ports; in 1921–22 the figure was 2,592; and in 1928–29 it had risen to 3,084. U.S., War Department *Report of the Governor: 1919*, p. 504; *ibid., 1922*, p. 38; *ibid., 1929*, p. 63.

22. These letters from such atypical Puerto Rican groups as congregations of Baptist, Methodist, Presbyterian, United Brethren, Disciples of Christ, and Congregational churches in Puerto Rico are in the BIA Files, File 19916–14.

23. Yager to McIntyre, March 27, 1917, *ibid.*, File 1175–38.

24. McIntyre to Yager, April 5, 1917, *ibid.*

25. Cable from Barceló to Wilson, May 11, 1917, *ibid.*, File 719–48.

26. Emilio J. Pasarell, "Porto Rico in the War," *Review of Reviews,* LVIII (September 1918), 286.

27. Earl Parker Hanson, *Transformation: The Story of Modern Puerto Rico* (New York, 1955), p. 83.

28. Pasarell, "Porto Rico in the War," p. 286.

29. *Message of the Governor of Porto Rico to the Ninth Legislature* (San Juan, 1918).

30. U.S., War Department, *Report of the Governor: 1919,* p. 501.

31. *New York Times,* June 9, 1918, section VI, p. 6.

32. Report of the Food Commission, in U.S., *Report of the Governor: 1918,* p. 677.

33. Victor S. Clark et al., *Porto Rico and Its Problems* (Washington, D.C., 1930), p. 489.

34. *Cong. Record,* 65th Cong., 2nd sess., 1918, p. 7597.

35. *New York Times,* June 7, 1918, p. 1.

36. Henry Wells, *The Modernization of Puerto Rico: A Political Study of Changing Values and Institutions* (Cambridge, Mass., 1969), pp. 24–25.

37. Mrs. Milagros Benet de Mewton to McIntyre, June 10, 1921, BIA Files, File 27260–10.

38. Telegram, Mrs. Benet de Mewton to Coolidge, January 22, 1924, *ibid.*, File 3377–380.

39. "We are organizing the island, founding the local committees" (Angela Negrón Muñoz, vice-president of the Puerto Rican Association of Suffragettes, to Sra. Ana Roqué de Duprey, September 2, 1926, Ana Roqué de Duprey Manuscripts, Colección Puertorriqueña, University of Puerto Rico, Río Piedras).

40. "We are trying to collect signatures on some rolls of paper like film rolls, which is the way Beatriz has told me they did it in the United States" (*ibid.*).

41. Mrs. Benet de Mewton to McIntyre, May 5, 1921, BIA Files, File 27260–9.

42. Mrs. Isabel Andreu de Aguilar to Mrs. Ana Roqué de Duprey, February 12, 1931, Roqué de Duprey Mss.

43. *Ibid.*

44. Mrs. Andreu de Aguilar to Mrs. Roqué de Duprey, January 14, 1932, *ibid.*

45. For a good account of the United States' woman suffrage movement, see Eleanor Flexner, *Century of Struggle: The Woman's Rights Movement* (Cambridge, Mass., 1959).

46. Pablo Morales Cabrera, "Electoral Rights for the Woman," *La Correspondencia de Puerto Rico* (San Juan), August 17, 1917, p. 1.

47. Luis Ortíz Lebrón in *La Democracia,* August 22, 1917, p. 2. On June 16, 1919, a bill for woman suffrage was defeated in the Puerto Rican Senate. One Senator, Félix Santoni, explained that he believed the time was not right for that reform, for "a better preparation of the environment is necessary so that the vote of the woman can produce beneficient results in our political and social progress" (*Actas del Senado de Puerto Rico, 1918–1920* [San Juan, 1920], p. 792).

48. General McIntyre said this was what he had heard, and hoped the women would refute it. McIntyre to Mrs. Benet de Mewton, May 19, 1921, BIA Files, File 27260–9.

49. For example, see the open letter, "From My Trench," from Mrs. Cruz de Marta, in *La Correspondencia,* August 20, 1917, p. 1. Also, letter from Mrs. Benet de Mewton to McIntyre, May 5, 1921, BIA Files, File 27260–9.

50. María Romero to Barceló, March 21, 1919, in *Actas del Senado, 1918–1920,* p. 231.

51. *El Mundo* (San Juan), July 13, 1923, p. 2.

52. Memorandum, McIntyre to E. H. Crowder, judge advocate general, September 7, 1920, BIA Files, File 27260–1. Crowder to McIntyre, November 11, 1920, *ibid.,* File 27260–4.

53. Mrs. Ida Husted Harper to Secretary of State Bainbridge Colby, January 6, 1921, *ibid.,* File 27260–6–A. McIntyre to Mrs. Harper, February 14, 1921, *ibid.,* File 27260–6.

54. Pan-American Association of Women of Puerto Rico and Suffragist Social League of Puerto Rico, memorial to President Calvin Coolidge, October 14, 1927, Calvin Coolidge Papers, File 400ZB, Series 1, Manuscript Division, Library of Congress.

55. *Ibid.*

56. McIntyre to Mrs. Benet de Mewton, May 19, 1921, BIA Files, File 27260–9.

57. *Cong. Record,* 70th Cong., 1st sess., 1928, p. 4058.

58. *Ibid.*, 70th Cong., 2nd sess., 1929, pp. 3191–92.

59. *Message of the Governor of Porto Rico to the Twelfth Legislature* (San Juan, 1929), p. 7.

60. Angela Negrón Muñoz, secretary of the Insular Association of Voting Women, to Mrs. Roqué de Duprey, May 10, 1929, Roqué de Duprey Mss.

61. Card of Introduction, Republican Party Commission to Washington, n.d., Herbert Hoover Papers, File OF 400–PR, Herbert Hoover Presidential Library, West Branch, Iowa.

62. Ana Roqué de Duprey, "Mensaje a la mujer Puertorriqueña" [Message to the Puerto Rican women], *Nosotras*, 1, no. 4 (February 1932), 1. See also Barceló to Mrs. Roqué de Duprey, September 24, 1931, Roqué de Duprey Mss.

63. Barceló told her, "You know Doña Ana that I was the first one who presented valiently in the Senate the law giving the vote to the woman," but said that he had allowed young Senator García Méndez to introduce a similar bill which Barceló helped become law, so that the young legislator could have a political triumph to help his career. December 6, 1932, *ibid.*

64. U.S., War Department, *Report of the Governor: 1929*, p. 84. *Ibid., 1933*, p. 14. *Ibid., 1925*, p. 93.

65. These names come out better in Spanish: *"América," "Justicia," "Igualdad,"* and *"Libertad."*

CHAPTER 3. "100% AMERICANISM" COMES TO PUERTO RICO

1. In 1913 separationist José de Diego had led a move in the Unionist Party to adopt the one-star flag as the banner of the party. This flag had been constructed originally in 1895 by a revolutionary group in New York City, the "Puerto Rican Section of the Cuban Revolutionary Party," and was similar to the Cuban flag, but with the colors inverted. Cayetano Coll y Toste, ed., *Boletín histórico de Puerto Rico* (San Juan, 1922), IX, 267–68.

2. As an example, Federal Judge Peter J. Hamilton wrote a long tirade against the use of the lone-star flag and independence oratory by the Unionists, advising General McIntyre, "It seems to me the local government [Yager] has been rather blind to the signs of the times" (Hamilton to McIntyre, November 27, 1920, BIA Files, War Department Records, National Archives, "P" File, Peter J. Hamilton.

3. Yager to McIntyre, December 23, 1920, *ibid.*, File 1294–18.

4. Yager to Harding, March 29, 1921, Warren G. Harding Papers, Box 252, Ohio State Historical Society, Columbus, Ohio.

5. "I have reported to the Secretary [of War] orally and in writing that nothing in Porto Rico called for a change and that, owing to the session of

the Legislature to be followed by the end of the fiscal year, an early change was clearly not desirable" (McIntyre to Yager, March 10, 1921, BIA Files, File 3234–After 119).

6. Concurrent Resolution of February 28, 1921, Harding Papers, Box 252.

7. Harding to Yager, April 9, 1921, *ibid.*

8. *New York Times*, May 7, 1921, p. 10.

9. Francis Russell, in his *The Shadow of Blooming Grove: Warren G. Harding in His Times* (New York, 1968), says—erroneously, I believe—that Reily was a "newspaperman" (p. 313). He also calls Reily "young," and he was at the time (1919) fifty-three years old.

10. *New York Times,* May 7, 1921, p. 10.

11. Harding to Reily, August 23, 1919, E. Mont. Reily Papers, Manuscript Division, New York Public Library, New York City.

12. Letterhead on letter from Reily to George Christian, June 22, 1921, Harding Papers, Box 252.

13. Reily to Harding, September 21, 1921, Reily Papers.

14. Miller to McIntyre, May 11, 1921, BIA Files, File 19101-112.

15. McIntyre to Miller, May 17, 1921, *ibid.*

16. Reily to Christian, June 22, 1921, Harding Papers, Box 252.

17. Harding to Reily, June 27, 1921, *ibid.*

18. Weeks to Reily, June 30, 1921, BIA Files, "P" File, E. Mont. Reily.

19. *La Democracia* (San Juan), July 19, 1921, p. 4; U.S., Congress, House and Senate, *Congressional Record,* 67th Cong., 2nd sess., 1922, pp. 3302, 5030.

20. *La Correspondencia de Puerto Rico* (San Juan), July 19, 1921, p. 1.

21. *La Democracia,* July 19, 1921, p. 4.

22. This and all later references to the actual marked draft of Reily's speech are from the Reily Papers.

23. The speech contains several other minor changes and deletions by the blue pencil. The only other significant one was Reily's mention of Puerto Rican coffee. In his original draft the governor said that he would "like to see and hope to see, at no distant day, a bounty or subsidy on your coffee that will make the growing of the same more profitable," and proceeded to use a paragraph to give the details of the bounty he would seek. The Harding administration was not about to be committed to so controversial a promise as a subsidy on Puerto Rican coffee with one glib statement by Governor Reily. The whole paragraph was marked out and Reily's comment on coffee reduced to an innocuous hope that he would "like to see, and somehow help to make, the growing of coffee here more profitable."

24. E. Mont. Reily continued to use this plural phraseology as late as 1929, for in that year he wrote to newly appointed Governor Theodore

Roosevelt, Jr., that he was sure Roosevelt would "know how to work out a real American spirit in the Islands" (Reily to Roosevelt, September 12, 1929, Theodore Roosevelt, Jr., Papers, Box 29, Manuscript Division, Library of Congress). The only other American in public life to use this unique wording was President Harding. Among examples of this were his statement to Reily's auditor that "I confess myself not a little distressed by the situation in Porto Rican Islands" and his suggestion to Attorney General Harry Daugherty that "we ought to name a new Attorney General for the Islands of Porto Rico" (Harding to William L. Kessinger, May 24, 1922; Harding to Harry Daugherty, September 25, 1922, Harding Papers, Box 253). It should be noted that Governor Reily had been told that the plural "islands" was not correct. Just before Reily embarked for Puerto Rico, he left a copy of the inaugural address with McIntyre. On July 22, 1921, McIntyre sent a hurried note to Reily in care of the New York steamship line by which the governor was to go to Puerto Rico. In it McIntyre warned Reily: "I notice that you refer to 'these islands.' . . . It is usual to refer to Porto Rico as a single island, though it has near it several smaller islands" (BIA Files, "P" Files, E. Mont. Reily).

25. *El Tiempo,* July 30, 1921, p. 2.

26. *Ibid.,* August 1, 1921, p. 1.

27. *El Mundo* (San Juan), August 1, 1921, p. 1.

28. *La Democracia,* August 1, 1921, p. 1.

29. *La Correspondencia*, August 1, 1921, p. 1; August 2, 1921, p. 1.

30. Cablegram, Barceló to McIntyre, August 18, 1921, Harding Papers, Box 252.

31. *Ibid.*

32. Harding to Reily, August 20, 1921, *ibid.*

33. Reily to Harding, August 31, 1921, Reily Papers.

34. *Ibid.*

35. Copy of Resolution, August 13, 1921, Harding Papers, Box 252.

36. Todd to Harding, August 2, 1921, September 27, 1921, and March 1, 1922, *ibid.*

37. Reily to Harding, November 15, 1921, Reily Papers. In 1922 Governor Reily recommended Sweet for appointment as attorney general of Puerto Rico. (Reily to Harding, August 16, 1922, Reily Papers.) Harding, at the advice of the War Department, told Reily this would not be a wise move.

38. Reily to Harding, September 28, 1921, Reily Papers.

39. Harding to Reily, October 5, 1921, Harding Papers, Box 252.

40. *La Democracia,* October 29, 1921, p. 4.

41. Adolf A. Berle, Jr., "Porto Rican Independence," *The Survey,* XLVI (September 24, 1921), 704.

42. As a comparison, Governor Horace Mann Towner seldom wrote to

President Coolidge, more often communicating with him through one of his private secretaries. On December 24, 1924, Governor Towner apologized to the president's secretary, C. Bascom Slemp, for having been so long (several months) between letters to either Coolidge or Slemp: "I have not bothered you during your rush season, because I did not need to do so" (Calvin Coolidge Papers, File 400ZB, Series 1, Manuscript Division, Library of Congress). On one occasion, Governor Theodore Roosevelt, Jr., apologized to President Hoover: "This is a very long letter, and I am ashamed to be guilty of imposing it on you." The letter was five pages long, about an average size for Reily's many epistles to President Harding. (Roosevelt to Hoover, December 6, 1929, Herbert Hoover Papers, OF 400–PR, Herbert Hoover Presidential Library, West Branch, Iowa.)

43. Reily to Harding, October 19, 1921, Reily Papers.

44. Reily to Harding, March 22, 1922, *ibid.*

45. Harding to Reily, January 23, 1922, and Reily to Harding, March 23, 1922, Reily Papers.

46. Reily to McIntyre, July 22, 1922, BIA Files, File 24234–31.

47. Confidential memorandum, McIntyre to Weeks, January 13, 1922, *ibid.,* File 975–After 316.

48. Reily to Christian, January 19, 1922, Harding Papers, Box 252.

49. Harding to Weeks, April 5, 1922, *ibid.*

50. Reily to Harding, September 21, 1921, Reily Papers.

51. This may have been untrue. On December 31, 1921, Reily wrote to General McIntyre to say that he would be tardy in going back to Puerto Rico. In that letter Reily listed the number of appointments to be settled in Kansas City at thirty. (BIA Files, "P" File, Reily.) But in a telegram to George Christian on January 12, 1922, the governor made the figure forty. Also, in the earlier letter the governor said he was hurrying to Clovis, New Mexico, to see a seriously ill sister. In this message to Christian he said he had "been delayed here [Kansas City] by illness," implying a *personal* illness. (Harding Papers, Box 252.)

52. Reily to Harding, November 15, 1922, Reily Papers.

53. Reily to Harding, December 6, 1922, *ibid.*

54. Governor Reily told President Harding he was going to do this in a letter of February 22, 1922, and then boasted of having done it in a second letter, March 1, 1922. (Reily Papers.)

55. Weeks to Harding, August 25, 1922, Harding Papers, Box 253.

56. *El Mundo,* October 24, 1921, p. 1.

57. Reily to Harding, November 9, 1921, Reily Papers.

58. *Cong. Record,* 67th Cong., 2nd sess., 1922, p. 5026.

59. *El Mundo,* October 24, 1921, p. 1.

60. One example is *La Democracia,* October 29, 1921, p. 4.

61. *El Mundo,* July 6, 1922, p. 1; *Cong. Record,* 67th Cong., 2nd sess., 1922, p. 3303.

62. *El Mundo,* July 6, 1922, p. 1.

63. Weeks to Reily, December 29, 1921, Harding Papers, Box 252.

64. Reily to Harding, October 26, 1921, Reily Papers.

65. Reily to Harding, April 6, 1922, *ibid.*

66. Reily to Harding, September 28, 1922, *ibid.*

67. Reily to Harding, April 19, 1922, and May 3, 1922, *ibid.*

68. *New York Times,* November 21, 1921, p. 5.

69. " 'I Accuse'—in Porto Rico," *The Nation,* CXV, (September 6, 1922), 236.

70. Reily to Harding, May 18, 1922, Reily Papers.

71. Travieso to Harding, December 27, 1922, Harding Papers, Box 703.

72. Reily to Harding, May 10, 1922, Reily Papers.

73. Reily to Harding, October 19, 1922, *ibid.*

74. *Cong. Record,* 67th Cong., 2nd sess., 1921, pp. 36, 84.

75. Reily to Harding, December 17, 1921, Reily Papers.

76. *Cong. Record,* 67th Cong., 2nd sess., 1921, p. 607.

77. Córdova Dávila to Harding, December 23, 1921, Harding Papers, Box 252.

78. Weeks to Harding, December 29, 1921, *ibid.*

79. Harding to Weeks, January 2, 1922, *ibid.*

80. *Cong. Record,* 67th Cong., 2nd sess., 1922, p. 745.

81. Reily to McIntyre, February 8, 1922; McIntyre to Reily, February 16, 1922, BIA Files, File 26429–124.

82. *The Times* (San Juan), February 11, 1922, p. 5.

83. Reily to Harding, August 31, 1921, Reily Papers. Also, *New York Times,* November 21, 1921, p. 1. Reily to Harding, May 10, 1922, and February 22, 1922, Reily Papers.

84. Berle, "Porto Rican Independence," p. 704. Bolívar Pagán, the Socialist historian, says it was Santiago Iglesias who gave Reily this nickname. In view of the fact that it was a nickname of ridicule, and noting the closeness of Iglesias to the Reily administration, this is quite doubtful. Bolívar Pagán, *Historia de los partidos políticos Puertorriqueños, 1898–1956* (San Juan, 1959), I, 205.

85. Luis Muñoz Marín, "A 'Ninety-Eight Percent American' in Porto Rico," *The New Republic,* XXIX, (January 4, 1922), 152.

86. Christian to Manuel Diez de Andino, October 31, 1921, Harding Papers, Box 252.

87. Pagán, *Historia de los partidos políticos,* I, 196. See also Yager to Harding, March 29, 1921, Harding Papers, Box 252.

88. For an example of Iglesias' backing of Reily, see telegram, Iglesias and José Tous Soto, president of the Republican Party, to Harding, November 13, 1922, Harding Papers, Box 253. The War Department helped to arrange for remission of tuition for Santiago Iglesias, Jr., at Pennsylvania State College in 1921-22 and 1922-23. (McIntyre to Dr. John M. Thomas, president of Pennsylvania State College, May 3, 1922; Thomas to McIntyre, May 8, 1922, BIA Files, "P" File, Santiago Iglesias.) For typical accusations that Reily consorted with Communists (Iglesias), see interview with Alfonso Lastra Charriez, speaker of the House in Puerto Rico, in *New York Journal of Commerce and Commercial Bulletin*, November 4, 1921, p. 1.

89. *New York Times*, April 8, 1922, p. 1, and April 11, 1922, p. 3.

90. Reily to Harding, April 8, 1922, Reily Papers.

91. *New York Times,* April 13, 1922, p. 8, and April 14, 1922, p. 19.

92. Towner to Harding, April 11, 1922, Harding Papers, Box 252.

93. *New York Times,* April 15, 1922, p. 5.

94. Reily to Harding, April 19, 1922, Reily Papers.

95. *Ibid.*

96. *New York Times*, June 1, 1922, p. 2, and June 4, 1922, p. 12.

97. Reily to Harding, June 8, 1922, Reily Papers. Travieso to Christian, July 18, 1922; Harding to Travieso, July 24, 1922, Harding Papers, Box 253.

98. Harding to Reily, August 2, 1922, Reily Papers.

99. Harding to Harry Daugherty, September 25, 1922, Harding Papers, Box 253.

100. Reily to Harding, November 29, 1922, Reily Papers.

101. McCormick to Weeks, July 28, 1921, BIA Files, "P" File, Reily.

102. *New York Times,* November 24, 1921, p. 18, and November 26, 1921, p. 8.

103. Weeks to Harding, November 12, 1921, Harding Papers, Box 252.

104. Weeks to Reily, December 29, 1921, *ibid.*

105. Harding to Reily, March 22, 1922, Reily Papers.

106 Harding to Kessinger, May 24, 1922, Harding Papers, Box 253. Harding to Towner, August 31, 1922, Harding Papers, Box 703.

107. Reily to Harding, March 8, 1922, Reily Papers. (See also Harding to Reily, February 16, 1922, and Reily to Harding, March 1, 1922, Reily Papers; *Cong. Record,* 67th Cong., 2nd sess., 1922, pp. 3301, 3372, 3479, 3583, 4044; and Philip P. Campbell to Harding, March 21, 1922, Harding Papers, Box 252.)

108. Resolution of Puerto Rican Senate, sent to President Harding, February 25, 1922, Harding Papers, Box 252.

109. *La Correspondencia,* November 24, 1921, p. 1.

110. *New York Times,* November 26, 1921, p. 8, and April 3, 1922, p. 1.

(The latter reference is to a first-page story on Reily's imminent resignation; the next day, in a small note at the bottom of page 17, the paper printed Reily's refutation of the rumor.)

111. Reily to Harding, September 28, 1921, March 8, 1922, October 19, 1922, and November 22, 1922, Reily Papers.

112. Harding to Reily, April 13, 1922, June 2, 1922, and September 5, 1922, *ibid.*

113. Harding to Towner, April 13, 1922, Harding Papers, Box 252.

114. Harding to Weeks, September 5, 1922, *ibid.*, Box 253.

115. W. W. Boyd to Senator Frank Willis, June 18, 1922; Mandel Sener to Harding, September 15, 1922; Felix Agnus to Harding, January 13, 1923; Harding to J. W. Fordney, February 19, 1923; Harding to Senator J. S. Frelinghuysen, February 24, 1923, *ibid.*

116. Cummins to Harding, January 13, 1923; Harding to Cummins, January 15, 1923, *ibid.*

117. Reily to Harding, October 25, 1922, Reily Papers.

118. Inghram D. Hook to Roosevelt, September 14, 1929, Roosevelt Papers, Box 29.

119. Reily to Harding, February 14, 1923, Reily Papers.

120. Towner to Weeks, June 16, 1923, BIA Files, File 719–65.

121. Reily to Sanders, April 14, 1927, Coolidge Papers, File 400ZB, Series 1.

122. Reily to Roosevelt, September 12, 1929, and September 30, 1929, Roosevelt Papers, Box 29.

123. See Robert K. Murray, "Harding on History," *The Journal of American History,* LIII (March 1967), 781–84.

CHAPTER 4. THE KALEIDOSCOPE OF PUERTO RICAN POLITICS, 1923–1929

1. Roosevelt to Colonel Lafayette B. Gleason, October 20, 1930, Theodore Roosevelt, Jr., Papers, Box 29, Manuscript Division, Library of Congress.

2. Roosevelt to Dr. Hubert C. Herring, December 5, 1931, *ibid.*

3. Albert S. Osborn to Miguel Guerra Mondragón, speaker of Puerto Rican House of Representatives, February 17, 1923, E. Mont. Reily Manuscripts, Colección Puertorriqueña, University of Puerto Rico, Río Piedras.

4. Frank H. Rogers, secretary to Governor Reily, to George Christian, secretary to President Harding, March 21, 1923, Warren G. Harding Papers, Box 253 Ohio State Historical Society, Columbus, Ohio.

5. Tous Soto to Harding, February 17, 1923, BIA Files, File 50-with 81, National Archives.

6. Yager to McIntyre, December 23, 1920, *ibid.*, File 1294–18.
7. Roberto H. Todd to Harding, May 16, 1923, Harding Papers, Box 253.
8. Harding to Towner, June 12 and June 20, 1923, *ibid.*
9. Towner to C. Bascom Slemp, September 6, 1923, Calvin Coolidge Papers, File 400ZB, Series 1, Manuscript Division, Library of Congress.
10. Slemp to Towner, September 27, 1923; Slemp to Todd, September 27, 1923, *ibid.*
11. Secretary of War John W. Weeks to Coolidge, December 5, 1923, *ibid.*
12. Towner to Slemp, February 17, 1924, *ibid.*
13. Towner to Coolidge, May 20, 1925, *ibid.*
14. Yager to McIntyre, March 29, 1921, Harding Papers, Box 252.
15. Gompers to Iglesias, March 14, 1917, Samuel Gompers Papers, Manuscript Division, Library of Congress, Letterbooks, vol. 231, p. 545.
16. Philip Taft, *Organized Labor in American History* (New York, 1964), pp. 237–42.
17. One of the major historical controversies in modern Puerto Rican history is the question of credit for the concept of the "Free Associated State" status presently occupied by Puerto Rico. Bolívar Pagán, in *Historia de los partidos políticos Puertorriqueños, 1898–1956* (San Juan, 1959), I, 190, says that Iglesias spoke out for autonomous status similar to that of Canada and Australia within the British Empire in 1919. Arturo Morales Carrión, however, traces the idea back to Henry L. Stimson, secretary of war under President Taft, in his testimony before a congressional committee in 1912. (Arturo Morales Carrión, "The Historical Roots and Political Significance of Puerto Rico," in A. Curtis Wilgus, ed., *The Caribbean: British, Dutch, French, United States* [Gainesville, Fla., 1963], p. 147.) But Barceló, the pragmatic Unionist chief, claimed to be its author, and most secondary sources attribute it to him: "You know that I am the author of the solution of 'Free Associated State'" (Barceló to Ana Roqué de Duprey, September 24, 1931, Ana Roqué de Duprey Manuscripts, Colección Puertorriqueña, University of Puerto Rico, Río Piedras).
18. Memorandum of McIntyre on interviews with Puerto Rican political figures during his visit to Puerto Rico, October 29, 1920, BIA Files, File 1175–53.
19. Mary Weld Coates, "What's the Matter in Porto Rico?" *Current History,* XVI (April 1922), 108–14. Among other things, she stated that anti-American sentiment, "though not universal, is the most potent influence on the island" (p. 109).
20. U.S., Congress, House and Senate, *Congressional Record*, 67th Cong., 2nd sess., 1922, p. 1431.
21. Reily to McIntyre, February 8, 1922, BIA Files, File 26429–124.

22. Cayetano Coll y Toste, ed., *Boletín histórico de Puerto Rico* (San Juan), IX, 361. See also Pagán, *Historia de los partidos políticos*, I, 212.

Roosevelt to Lawrence Richey, secretary to the President, August 26, 1931, Herbert Hoover Papers, OF 400–PR, Herbert Hoover Presidential Library, West Branch, Iowa.

23. Albizu Campos to McIntyre, May 11, 1918; R. Siaca Pacheco, executive secretary of Puerto Rico, to McIntyre, October 23, 1918, BIA Files, "P" File of Pedro Albizu Campos.

24. *Ibid.;* McIntyre to Albizu Campos, June 6, 1918, *ibid.*

25. Earl Parker Hanson, *Transformation: The Story of Modern Puerto Rico* (New York, 1955), p. 83.

26. Roberto F. Rexach Benítez, *Pedro Albizu Campos: leyenda y realidad* (San Juan, 1961), p. 14.

27. Coates, "What's the Matter in Porto Rico?," p. 110.

28. Letter to editors, Ralph George Gatell, February 27, 1921, *New York Times,* Section VII, p. 3. This was in protest against a short article by Louis S. Delaplaine, Jr., on p. 13, of the February 23, 1921, issue.

29. One of Albizu Campos' speeches is recorded in *El Mundo* (San Juan), January 31, 1923, p. 10; another was published by him in a pamphlet called *La Resolución Conjunta No. 2* (Ponce, P.R., 1923). See also Rexach, *Pedro Albizu Campos,* p. 16.

30. Rexach, *Pedro Albizu Campos,* p. 15; Frost to the Bureau of Insular Affairs, August 20, 1927, BIA Files, "P" File, Pedro Albizu Campos.

31. Rexach, *Pedro Albizu Campos,* p. 15.

32. *Ibid.*

33. Memorandum, McIntyre to secretary of war, October 12, 1927, BIA Files, "P" File, Pedro Albizu Campos.

34. "Anti-American Sentiment found here by McFadden more than justified by nullification of General Miles' promises of freedom, instead of which we suffer under a regime of colonial servitude and exploitation without precedent. Real inner aspiration of the people of Porto Rico is immediate and absolute independence" (cablegram, Federico Acosta Velarde, president of the Nationalist Party, to Coolidge, April 18, 1927, *ibid.,* File 26429–209).

35. Handbill in *ibid.,* "P" File of Pedro Albizu Campos.

36. Rexach, *Pedro Albizu Campos,* p. 6.

37. It is interesting to compare the account of the bloody 1930s and the trials of Albizu Campos and other Nationalists which followed the violence in Ramón Medina Ramírez, *El movimiento libertador en la historia de Puerto Rico,* 2 vols. (San Juan, 1964), with that of Thomas G. Mathews, *Puerto Rican Politics and the New Deal* (Gainesville, Fla., 1960). Mathews's book is a scholarly treatment which tries for a minimum of biases. Medina Ramírez has written a rabidly anti-U.S. justification of the Nationalists. Worse, he does

not bother with such details as factual evidence, citations of references, or adequate separation of his conclusions from historical events.

38. U.S., War Department *Report of the Governor of Porto Rico to the Secretary of War: 1929*, pp. 83–84; *ibid., 1933*, p. 14.

39. Petition, August 27, 1919, BIA Files, File 858–46.

40. Copy of joint resolution of Puerto Rican legislature, July 24, 1923, Coolidge Papers, File 400ZB, Series 1.

41. Statement of delegation to President Coolidge and Congress, January 23, 1924, *ibid.*

42. Coolidge to "Mr. Speaker" (Miguel Guerra Mondragón), January 23, 1924, *ibid.*

43. Sewall to Coolidge, February 2, 1924, *ibid.*

44. *Cong. Record,* 68th Cong., 1st sess., 1924, pp. 861–62, 1589–90, 1908, 4119; *House of Representatives Report No. 291,* March 13, 1924 (Washington, D.C., 1924).

45. *Cong. Record,* 68th Cong., 1st sess., 1924, p. 2167; *ibid.,* pp. 8599–8600.

46. Weeks to Coolidge, May 26, 1924, Coolidge Papers, File 400ZB, Series 1.

47. Slemp to Weeks, June 3, 1924, *ibid.*

48. Weeks to Slemp, June 5, 1924, *ibid.*

49. The *Congressional Record* reported that this bill was given to the Committee on Indian Affairs. I believe this is an error in the *Record*. The speaker of the house, Frederick H. Gillett of Massachusetts, indicated to Secretary of War Weeks that he was in favor of the bill, and it is unlikely that he would have placed it in an entirely wrong committee. Weeks to Coolidge, May 26, 1924, Coolidge Papers, File 400ZB, Series 1. (See *Cong. Record,* 68th Cong., 1st sess., 1924, p. 11212, for statement that S. 2448 was assigned to the Committee on Indian Affairs.)

50. For petitions see *Cong. Record,* 70th Cong., 1st sess., 1928, pp. 2939, 4058; for elective governor bills, see *ibid.,* pp. 1911, 4950, and *ibid.,* 71st Cong., 1st sess., 1929, p. 29. Congressman La Guardia, later a colorful mayor of New York, was quite sympathetic toward the ideals of Puerto Rican autonomy; see ch. 5 for more of his activities in behalf of Puerto Rico.

51. In 1926 Governor Towner wrote to General McIntyre of the BIA: "Regarding the elective Governor, that of course, is entirely within the discretion of the President. Personally, as you know, I favor the legislation and I think it would be a good thing to do from the political and administrative standpoint. But the President's desire will of course govern, and if he thinks it should not be brought up at this session, we should not attempt to press the matter" (November 26, 1926, BIA Files, File 942–142).

52. Todd to Wells, November 25, 1924; Odlin to Wilfley, January 2, 1925;

Barrett to Representative Charles L. Underhill, November 26, 1924, Coolidge Papers, File 400ZB, Series 1.

53. Good to Sanders, April 4, 1925, *ibid.*

54. Towner to Coolidge, April 23, 1925, *ibid.*

55. Ashford to General M. W. Ireland, April 23, 1925, *ibid.*

56. Neidlinger to Clark, April 9, 1926, *ibid.*

57. Clark to Neidlinger, April 10, 1926, *ibid.*

58. Sra. Ricarda L. de Ramos, a member of the Territorial Committee of the Constitutional Historical Party (*Republicanos Puros*), sent a number of news clippings from the English-language San Juan *Times* to Mrs. Calvin Coolidge, November 12, 1924. See also Todd to Slemp, November 26, 1924. Both in Coolidge Papers, File 400ZB, Series 1.

59. Henry Wells, *The Modernization of Puerto Rico: A Political Study of Changing Values and Institutions* (Cambridge, Mass., 1959), p. 106.

60. Coll Cuchi would probably have gotten the interview with the president except for a letter from Roberto Todd to C. Bascom Slemp, in which Todd told the purpose of Coll Cuchi's mission. Coll Cuchi quickly disavowed any intention of pursuing such a project, but it was obvious that he had no better purpose in his proposed visit with the president than to complain about the election. At the advice of the War Department, he was brushed off with the excuse that the president was too busy to see him, and was asked if he would like to see the secretary of war instead. At this point Coll Cuchi dropped the matter. See Slemp to Coll Cuchi, January 3, 1925; Coll Cuchi to Slemp, January 7, 1925; Weeks to Slemp, January 8, 1925; and Slemp to Coll Cuchi, January 9, 1925, Coolidge Papers, File 400ZB, Series 1.

61. Copy of cablegram in McIntyre to Towner, February 12, 1925, BIA Files, File 1028–101.

62. Towner and Coats to McIntyre, February 14, 1925, *ibid.*, File 1028–102.

63. Winslow to Stearns, January 27, 1925, Coolidge Papers, File 400ZB, Series 1.

64. Seusall to Coolidge, May 6, 1925, BIA Files, File 1175–66.

65. Reily to Coolidge, May 12, 1925, Coolidge Papers, File 400ZB, Series 1.

66. Sanders to Towner, May 5, 1925, *ibid.*

67. Towner to Sanders, May 13, 1925, *ibid.* The federal prohibition director for Puerto Rico, John T. Barrett, who strongly backed Governor Towner, was also opposed to Coats. Barrett told Congressman Charles L. Underhill that Coats was "primarily responsible for all the trouble and bother I have experienced in Porto Rico." He further remarked that Coats had confided to him that he was opposed to prohibition and liked to drink—"and judging from his actions since he has been in Porto Rico, he has not missed many chances" (November 26, 1924, *ibid.*).

68. Text of the cablegram in letter from Weeks to Coolidge, December 27, 1924, *ibid.*

69. Report on agriculture, Chardón to Towner, June 5, 1925; Mitchell to Coolidge, February 12, 1925, *ibid.*

70. General McIntyre sent the following cablegram to Governor Towner on May 6, 1925: "STRICTLY CONFIDENTIAL. After his call on the President Mr. Good assured Mrs. Towner that President stated unequivocally that he had no thought of making a change in the Governorship. This is for your personal information and not for publication" (BIA Files, "P" File, Horace M. Towner).

71. Rosaly to McIntyre, January 4, 1927, *ibid.,* File 28317–1.

72. On July 23, 1923, in a handwritten letter (for security), Governor Towner told General McIntyre that Odlin "acts very queerly. His statements on and off the bench are most shocking and are bringing the court into suspicion and worse" (*ibid.,* "P" File, Horace M. Towner).

73. Memorandum, McIntyre to Davis, October 9, 1925, *ibid.,* "P" File, Ira K. Wells.

74. Stone to Sanders, January 12, 1926, Coolidge Papers, File 400ZB, Series 1.

75. Wells to Stone, January 7, 1926, *ibid.*

76. Coolidge to E. J. Henning, acting secretary of labor, December 2, 1924, *ibid.*

77. Nichols to Coolidge, March 18, 1926, *ibid.*

78. Reily to Sanders, April 14, 1927, *ibid.*

79. For examples of these defenses see Towner to Coolidge, "Private and Confidential," February 23, 1927; Towner to Coolidge, January 20, 1928, *ibid.*

80. Towner to Coolidge, December 24, 1924, *ibid.* While sending the president a copy of his annual report, he boasted a bit of the progress made in Puerto Rico, and then said, "But I will not call your attention particularly to matters which you can notice on looking over the report (*ibid.*).

81. Winthrop to Coolidge, April 28, 1925, *ibid.*

82. Henry Kittredge Norton, "The Ethics of Imperialism," *The World's Work,* LI (January 1926), 327.

83. Caroline Dawes Appleton, "Porto Rico: A Study in Colonial Courtesies," *The American Review of Reviews,* LXXII (September 1925), 301–07; editorial in same issue, p. 239.

84. Félix Córdova Dávila to Coolidge, May 4, 1925, Coolidge Papers, File 400ZB, Series 1.

85. Iglesias quoted in *El Mundo* (San Juan), May 11, 1929, p. 3.

86. For an example of Iglesias' appeals for an investigation of Puerto Rico, see Iglesias to Secretary of War Davis, March 27, 1926, BIA Files, "P" File, Santiago Iglesias.

87. Davis to Sanders, December 3, 1925, Coolidge Papers, File 400ZB, Series 1.

88. Memorandum, McIntyre to Davis, January 6, 1925, BIA Files, File 25118–486.

89. Towner to Sanders, August 4, 1925 ("Private and Confidential"), Coolidge Papers, File 400ZB, Series 1.

90. Copy of memorial passed by Puerto Rican legislature, April 28, 1927, *ibid.*

91. For a good example of Taft's outlook, see his speech during the appropriations crisis of 1909 in James D. Richardson, ed., *A Compilation of the Messages and Papers of the Presidents* (New York, 1897–1917), XV, 7386–87. For a similar view concerning Taft's attitude toward the Philippine Islands, see Teodoro A. Agoncillo, *A Short History of the Philippines* (New York, 1969), p. 165.

92. Towner to Coolidge, October 14, 1925, Coolidge Papers, File 400ZB, Series 1.

93. Sanders to Davis, October 27, 1925, *ibid.*

94. "Resolución Concurrente," BIA Files, File 26429–214–B.

95. Cable, Barceló and Tous Soto to Coolidge, January 19, 1928, *ibid.*, File 26429–212.

96. (Italics mine.) Coolidge to Towner, February 28, 1928, Coolidge Papers, File 400ZB, Series 1. Just as President Taft had done in the 1909 appropriations crisis, President Coolidge blamed this difficulty on too much freedom for the Puerto Ricans for the amount of knowledge they had in how to use it.

97. All of these letters but that of Dr. Goyco were dated March 16, 1928; his was written on March 19. All are addressed to President Coolidge, and all are in Coolidge Papers, File 400ZB, Series 1.

98. Lastra Charriez to Coolidge, March 21, 1928, *ibid.*

99. *Cong. Record,* 70th Cong., 1st sess., 1928, pp. 6325–35.

CHAPTER 5. THE INSULAR ECONOMY, 1917–1933

1. Memorandum, BIA to secretary of war, February 4, 1921, BIA Files, File 119–129, National Archives.

2. Secretary of War Dwight Davis to Everett Sanders, secretary to the president, December 12, 1925, Calvin Coolidge Papers, File 400ZB, Series 1, Manuscript Division, Library of Congress.

3. Arthur D. Gayer, Paul T. Homan, and Earle K. James, *The Sugar Economy of Puerto Rico* (New York, 1938), p. 33.

4. U.S. War Department *Report of the Governor of Porto Rico to the Secretary of War: 1929*, p. 22.

5. Chardón to Towner, June 5, 1925, Coolidge Papers, File 400 ZB, Series 1.

6. *Ibid.* See also report by chief of BIA, October 1920, in which McIntyre calls the profits accruing to Puerto Rican sugar growers "excessive." BIA Files, File 26845–20. Also, Roosevelt to General F. LeJ. Parker of the BIA, in which Roosevelt urges continued high sugar tariff on the grounds that without it many of the smaller sugar mills would go into foreign hands— mostly into those of the four large foreign-owned sugar corporations operating in Puerto Rico. Roosevelt to Parker, January 17, 1930, Herbert Hoover Papers, OF 400–PR, Herbert Hoover Presidential Library, West Branch, Iowa.

7. Gayer et al., *Sugar Economy*, p. 21.

8. Victor S. Clark et al., *Porto Rico and Its Problems* (Washington, D.C., 1930), p. 606.

9. *Ibid.*, p. 488.

10. U.S., Congress, House and Senate, *Congressional Record*, 65th Cong., 3rd sess., 1918, p. 599.

11. *Ibid.*, 67th Cong., 1st sess., 1921, p. 169.

12. *Ibid.*, 70th Cong., 1st sess., 1928, pp. 5756, 9575, 10584; *ibid.*, 71st Cong., 1st sess., 1929, p. 3609.

13. Chardón to Towner, June 5, 1925, Coolidge Papers, File 400ZB, Series 1.

14. Clark et al., *Porto Rico and Its Problems*, pp. 606, 404.

15. Padín to Roosevelt, September 26, 1931, Theodore Roosevelt, Jr., Papers, Box 29, Manuscript Division, Library of Congress.

16. This included both fresh and canned fruits. Clark et al., *Porto Rico and Its Problems*, p. 404.

17. Chardón to Towner, June 5, 1925, Coolidge Papers, File 400ZB, Series 1.

18. Luis Muñoz Marín, "Porto Rico: The American Colony," *The Nation*, CXX (April 8, 1925), 379.

19. Clark et al., *Porto Rico and Its Problems*, p. 409.

20. Officers of Tobacco Strippers' Union #15330 of Caguas, P.R., to Gompers, June 24, 1919, Samuel Gompers Papers, Manuscript Division, Library of Congress, Volume 256, p. 655.

21. *Cong. Record*, 56th Cong., 1st sess., 1900, Appendix, p. 233.

22. C. H. Forbes-Lindsay, *America's Insular Possessions*, 2 vols., (Philadelphia, 1906), I, 159–60.

23. Gayer et al., *Sugar Economy*, p. 24.

24. Memorandum by McIntyre on large landholdings in Puerto Rico, October 20, 1927, BIA Files, File 94–70.

25. Roosevelt to Chardón, April 16, 1934, Roosevelt Papers, Box 30. Roosevelt to Bailey Diffie, November 30, 1931, *ibid.,* Box 29.

26. Towner to Parker, September 17, 1929, BIA Files, File 723–153.

27. Memorandum by McIntyre, October 20, 1927, *ibid.,* File 94–70.

28. *Report of the Governor of Porto Rico: 1918*, pp. 101-06.

29. One of the many instances when Hartzell gave advice on Puerto Rico is recorded in a letter he sent to Horace M. Towner just before Towner went to Puerto Rico as governor, February 13, 1923. Box 253, Harding Papers. That he achieved a place in prominent circles is shown by the letter of introduction that Governor Towner sent with Hartzell ("a leading attorney in Porto Rico . . . represents several large sugar centrales and other corporations") when Hartzell went to Washington to tell President Coolidge about the relief problems of Puerto Rico. Towner to Coolidge, September 19, 1928, File 400ZB, Series 1, Coolidge Papers.

30. Coolidge to Cutter, February 16, 1926; Everett Sanders (secretary of Coolidge) to Secretary of War Davis, February 16, 1926; Davis to Coolidge, February 25, 1926, *Ibid.*

31. U.S., War Department, *Report of the Governor: 1918,* p. 579.

32. *Ibid.,* pp. 580–81.

33. P. J. Rosaly to McIntyre, January 4, 1927, BIA Files, File 28317–1.

34. See Guy M. Winslow to Frank Stearns of Boston, January 27, 1925, "Memo in re Government of Porto Rico," Coolidge Papers, File 400ZB, Series 1. (Towner is "not acquainted with Spanish," and Huyke is the man "best qualified" on the island for governor.) Also Leslie A. MacLeod, the auditor of Puerto Rico, wrote to Governor Roosevelt in 1931 that the attacks of one Dr. Lopez against Roosevelt were inspired by "Guánica Central and other island interests . . . behind him in a move to reduce taxes." MacLeod to Roosevelt, October 10, 1931, Roosevelt Papers, Box 29.

35. Towner to Coolidge, February 23, 1927, and January 20, 1928, Coolidge Papers, File 400ZB, Series 1.

36. U.S., War Department, *Report of the Governor: 1929,* p. 11.

37. *Ibid.,* p. 3.

38. *Ibid.,* p. 4. Summary of radio message, Towner to secretary of war, September 18, 1928, Coolidge Papers, File 400ZB, Series 1. Telegram, United Puerto Rico Republican Club of New York City to Hoover, October 7, 1932, Hoover Papers, OF 400–PR.

39. James L. Fieser to Coolidge, October 25, 1928, Coolidge Papers, File 400ZB, Series 1.

40. Whitney T. Perkins, *Denial of Empire: The United States and Its Dependencies* (Leyden, Netherlands, 1962), p. 133. See also U.S., War Department, *Report of the Governor: 1929,* pp. 1–2.

41. *Status of Puerto Rico: Report of the United States–Puerto Rico Commission on the Status of Puerto Rico* (Washington, D.C., 1966), p. 149.

42. The reason why Russia and the United States achieved economic development even with high annual rates of population increase was that they both were "rapidly expanding the area under cultivation," something not possible for Puerto Rico. W. W. Rostow, *The Stages of Economic Growth: A Non-Communist Manifesto* (Cambridge, 1964), p. 141.

43. One could assume, I believe, that the housing situation in the urban communities would have been no better than that reported for a rural area, and might well have been worse. Clark et al., *Porto Rico and Its Problems,* p. 20.

44. See Beverley to Hoover, February 3, 1932, Hoover Papers, OF 400–PR.

45. This figure allowed for the winnings distributed among Puerto Ricans. Mrs. Theodore Roosevelt, Jr., assumed that three million dollars of lottery tickets were sold to Puerto Ricans each year. Mrs. Theodore Roosevelt, Jr., *Day Before Yesterday* (Garden City, N.Y., 1959), p. 236. The Brookings Institution survey reckoned the amount at only $1,285,000 annually, and guessed that about $285,000 in prize money came back to the island, leaving an outgo of a million dollars a year. Clark et al., *Porto Rico and Its Problems*, pp. 594-95. The Roosevelts wanted to permit Puerto Rico to have its own lottery, but they knew the United States would never stand for such an "'immoral" manner of help for the insular economy. Today, because Puerto Rico enjoys home rule, the visitor is well aware of lottery tickets for sale by street vendors.

46. Clark, *Porto Rico and Its Problems,* pp. 594–95.

47. Towner to Parker, September 9, 1929, BIA Files, File 28468–13.

48. *Ibid.*

49. *Primer informe de la comisión legislativa para investigar el malestar y desasosiego industrial y agrícola y que origina el desempleo en Puerto Rico* (San Juan, 1930), p. 61.

50. Clark et al., *Porto Rico and Its Problems,* p. 404.

51. Ex-Governor Roosevelt wrote to Ex-Governor Beverley that "now that prohibition has gone [tourism] may be more possible, as Cuba will be less of a lode-stone" (September 14, 1933, Roosevelt Papers, Box 48).

52. F. H. Newell to Roosevelt, August 10, 1931, *ibid.,* Box 29.

53. For example, in the 1916–17 fiscal year, Puerto Rico imported over 152 million pounds of rice, at a total value of six million dollars; in the 1917–18 fiscal year, 136 pounds of rice were imported, at a total value of nine and a half million dollars. For the same fiscal years, Puerto Rico imported 43,253 less barrels of wheat flour, yet paid a total of $805,594 more for them. There were 57,396 less bushels of beans and dried peas imported into Puerto Rico in 1917–18 than in 1916–17, but the total price was $2,780 more in the later year. "Report of the Food Commission," in U.S., War Department, *Report of the Governor: 1918,* pp. 704–13.

54. Report by McIntyre on fact-finding trip to Puerto Rico, October, 1920, BIA Files, File 26845–20.

55. Clark et al., *Porto Rico and Its Problems*, p. 409.

56. U.S., War Department, *Report of the Governor: 1924*, p. 63.

57. Iglesias to Coolidge, November 17, 1923, Coolidge Papers, File 400ZB, Series 1.

58. U.S., War Department, *Report of the Governor: 1923*, p. 30.

59. "Uncle Sam's Stepchild," *The Survey*, XLV (October 9, 1920), p. 63.

60. Tomasa V. Colón, president, and María Guevarez, secretary of Tobacco Strippers' Union #15330, Caguas, P.R., to Gompers, June 24, 1919, Gompers Papers, Volume 256, p. 655.

61. U.S., War Department, *Report of the Governor: 1923*, p. 30.

62. The women who wrote the letter cited in note 60, above, for example, complained that no one represented them in the weighing of tobacco.

63. U.S., War Department, *Report of the Governor: 1920*, p. 5.

64. *Ibid.*, p. 45.

65. Gompers to Wilson, November 18, 1920, BIA Files, File 975–293.

66. Eduardo Soto Modesto, president of Agricultural Union #16704 in Salinas, P.R., to Gompers, n.d. (but in early March 1920), Samuel Gompers Papers, Volume 263, p. 469.

67. Iglesias to Hoover, secretary of commerce, March 29, 1926, Hoover Papers, Porto Rico, Official File, Commerce Papers.

68. William George Whittaker, "The Santiago Iglesias Case, 1901–1902: Origins of American Trade Union Involvement in Puerto Rico," *The Americas*, XXIV (April 1968), 378–93.

69. Ramón A. Martínez in *Justicia* (San Juan), July 14, 1924, p. 2.

70. *Cong. Record*, 68th Cong., 2nd sess., 1925, p. 5596.

71. Robert W. Anderson, *Party Politics in Puerto Rico* (Stanford, 1965), p. 34.

72. Iglesias to the secretary of war, March 27, 1926, BIA Files, "P" File, Iglesias. (Iglesias, originally from Spain, came to Puerto Rico in the 1890s.)

73. Teofilo Maldonado, *Hombres de primera plana* (San Juan, 1958), p. 145.

74. Gompers to Wilson, November 18, 1920, BIA Files, File 975–293.

75. Yager to McIntyre, March 27, 1917, *ibid.*, File 1175–38.

76. Memorandum for secretary of war, January 6, 1925, *ibid.*, File 25118–486.

77. McIntyre to Dr. John M. Thomas, May 3, 1922; Thomas to McIntyre, May 8, 1922; Iglesias to Parker, May 26, 1933, *ibid.*, "P" File, Iglesias.

78. *Ibid.*, "P" File, Iglesias. There is no way to be sure of some of this, because the intimation was that Iglesias could set for himself a high salary as general organizer of the AF of L. This was possible partly because he

handled both the dues sent by Puerto Ricans to the organization in the United States and the money that came to Puerto Rican local unions from the United States. It would have been easy for Iglesias to have lived very affluently on union money, but there is no proof either way.

79. Henry S. Ortega to Secretary of War George Dern, April 10, 1933; memorandum from Parker to Martyn, secretary to Dern, April 18, 1933, *ibid.*, "P" File, Iglesias.

80. Yager to McIntyre, May 21, 1918; McIntyre to Yager, May 31, 1918, *ibid.*, File 975–180.

81. Gompers to Wilson, November 18, 1920, *ibid.*, File 975–293. At the time of one strike in 1918, Yager told General McIntyre, "I have instructed the police and advised the *alcaldes* [mayors], in view of war conditions and in view of the plan suggested by the United States Department of Labor for avoiding a strike, to discourage all those meetings tending to disorder and having for their object the creation of a strike and the stopping of the sugar industry" (Yager to McIntyre, February 19, 1918, *ibid.*, File 975–152).

82. See Roosevelt to Iglesias, November 23, 1931, Roosevelt Papers, Box 29. Also Iglesias to Hoover, December 21, 1929, Hoover Papers, OF 400–PR.

83. Clark et al., *Porto Rico and Its Problems,* p. 51. *Justicia,* July 14, 1925, p. 2.

84. *Justicia,* August 28, 1915, p. 2.

85. See for example the letter from the women officers of the Tobacco Box Decorators' Union No. 15367 of San Juan to Gompers, January 14, 1919, Gompers Papers, Volume 253, p. 317.

86. *Justicia,* July 28, 1924, p. 2.

87. U.S., War Department, *Report of the Governor: 1920,* p. 1; *ibid., 1923,* p. 20.

88. José E. Benedicto, acting governor of Puerto Rico, to General Charles C. Walcutt, acting chief of the BIA, January 28, 1920, BIA Files, File 975–262.

89. Report by McIntyre, October, 1920, BIA Files, File 26845–20. The Brookings report of 1929 agreed with McIntyre, saying that labor unrest was responsible for the decision of one of the largest tobacco companies to move its main factory to the continental United States. See Clark et al., *Porto Rico and Its Problems,* p. 51.

90. For example, *Justicia* reported that a lawyer named R. López Landrón was paid $96.20 for his services "in defense of the persecuted" in Juncos, Hunacao, Ponce, and Vieques. *Justicia,* August 28, 1915, p. 2.

91. *El Tiempo* (San Juan), March 3, 1923, p. 2.

92. *The Times* (San Juan), February 5, 1919, p. 5.

93. McIntyre to Yager, April 5, 1917, BIA Files, File 1175–38.

94. "May I also call your attention to the fact that the people of many

Latin-American countries regard the course which our Republic institutes in Porto Rico as a test of the idealism and the sincerity of our nation. Whatever is done in Porto Rico will affect the attitude of Pan-American countries toward our Republic" (Gompers to Wilson, March 14, 1917, Gompers Papers, Volume 231, p. 535). See also Gompers to Wilson, May 6, 1918, *ibid.*, Volume 246, p. 892.

95. R. Lee Guard, secretary to Gompers, to Santiago Iglesias, December 22, 1916, *ibid.*, Volume 228, p. 369. Gompers to Secretary of Labor W. B. Wilson, February 27, 1918, *ibid.*, Volume 244, p. 127. Gompers to President Wilson, July 30, 1918, *ibid.*, Volume 249, p. 349. Gompers to Coolidge, November 17, 1923, Coolidge Papers, File 400ZB, Series 1. Gompers to A. Mitchell Palmer, Alien Property custodian, March 26, 1918, Gompers Papers, Volume 245, p. 266.

96. Gompers to Iglesias, March 14, 1917, *ibid.*, Volume 231, p. 545.

97. Gompers to Iglesias, December 17, 1918, *ibid.*, Volume 252, p. 168.

98. See as examples Gompers to Iglesias, February 23, 1917, *ibid.*, Volume 230, p. 668, and Gompers to Iglesias, February 4, 1919, *ibid.*, Volume 253, p. 423.

99. An example is Gompers to Valentín Rochi, president of Agricultural Workers Local No. 16054 of Ponce, May 3, 1920, *ibid.*, Volume 266, p. 635.

100. Gompers to J. C. Camancho, president of Pier Clerks' Union No. 17001 of San Juan, July 16, 1920, *ibid.*, Volume 268, p. 524.

101. Gompers to Iglesias, May 11, 1918, *ibid.*, Volume 247, p. 42.

102. Yager to McIntyre, March 27, 1917, BIA Files, File 1175–38.

103. *Cong. Record,* 68th Cong., 2nd sess., 1925, pp. 1320–21. (Representative Louis W. Fairfield had Córdova Dávila's article reprinted in the *Congressional Record.*)

104. For examples see *ibid.*, 65th Cong., 3rd sess., 1919, p. 1501; 67th Cong., 4th sess., 1923, p. 2213; 68th Cong., 2nd sess., 1925, pp. 1122, 1360.

105. One example is Iglesias to Coolidge, November 17, 1923, Coolidge Papers, File 400ZB, Series 1.

106. Memorandum, McIntyre to secretary of war, January 6, 1925, BIA Files, File 25118–486.

107. Yager to McIntyre, April 30, 1917, *ibid.*, File 1175–39. Yager to McIntyre, February 19, 1918, *ibid.*, File 975–152. See also Gompers to Iglesias, November 20, 1919, Gompers Papers, Volume 259, p. 1025.

108. Benedicto to Walcutt, Janury 28, 1920; Secretary of War Newton Baker to Gompers, February 6, 1920; BIA to Benedicto, February 7, 1920; memorandum by Walcutt, "Strike of sugar laborers in Porto Rico," February 6, 1920, BIA Files, File 975–262.

109. Joseph Marcus, *Labor Conditions in Porto Rico* (Washington, D.C., 1919).

110. This was the English title of the report, as it was printed in both languages. The official title is *Primer informe de la comisión legislativa para investigar el malestar y desasosiego industrial y agrícola y que origina el desempleo en Puerto Rico* (San Juan, 1930).

111. *Ibid.*, p. 8.

112. *Ibid.*, pp. 32–37.

113. Clark et al., *Porto Rico and Its Problems,* pp. 517–18. U.S., War Department, *Report of the Governors: 1921*, p. 38. *El Mundo* (San Juan), October 20, 1921, p. 1.

114. Memorandum, Ethelbert Stewart, commissioner of labor statistics, to secretary of labor, March 30, 1931, Hoover Papers, OF 400–PR.

115. For a naive and vicious statement on this, see the article by Albizu Campos in *El Mundo,* March 31, 1933, pp. 1–6.

116. *El Mundo,* February 5, 1925, pp. 1, 5. Also Green, president of the AF of L, to Coolidge, December 5, 1925, Coolidge Papers, File 400ZB, Series 1.

117. Samuel McCune Lindsay, "Porto Rico Revisited: Contrasts of Twenty-Five Years," *The American Review of Reviews,* LXXIII (May 1926), 514. Clark et al., *Porto Rico and Its Problems,* p. 519.

118. When Barceló, in a public speech, boasted that only about 7 percent of the Puerto Rican population was illiterate, Iglesias stood up and denied it. *El Tiempo,* March 3, 1923, p. 2. The illiteracy of the island was actually much higher than Barceló's figure, for even in 1933 the rate was approximately 41.4 percent. U.S., War Department, *Report of the Governor: 1933*, p. 13.

119. See Juan José Osuna, *A History of Education in Puerto Rico,* 2nd ed. (Río Piedras, 1949), p. 282. The extent of "Americanization" as an educational policy and the methods used toward that end are dealt with in Aída Negrón de Montilla, *Americanization in Puerto Rico and the Public-School System, 1900–1930* (Río Piedras, 1971).

120. See for example, U.S., War Department, *Report of the Governor: 1920,* p. 35. In the 1928–29 fiscal year, the municipal governments added $1,625,785.16 to the amount spent on education in Puerto Rico. *Ibid., 1929,* p. 48.

121. The fact that the great mass of pupils in Puerto Rico was, throughout this period, in the first six grades is significant, indicating a high rate of dropout before even seventh grade. In the 1919–20 school year, there were 167,334 pupils in the elementary schools of the island, only 8,764 in grades seven through nine, and 1,973 in high school. In the 1929–30 school year, grade-school enrollment had increased to 204,698, but junior high only to 17,070 and high school to 4,782. Even though there were great percentage increases in the secondary grades, the small gains in actual numbers show that the dropout trend had not been reversed. (*Status of Puerto Rico: Report of the United*

States–Puerto Rico Commission on the Status of Puerto Rico [Washington, D.C., 1966], p. 152.)

122. See Roosevelt to Walter Newton, Secretary of the president, March 24, 1930, Hoover Papers, OF 400–PR.

CHAPTER 6. "THE HILLBILLY IN THE GOVERNOR'S MANSION"

1. Concurrent Resolution of Legislature of Porto Rico, sent to Hoover, March 1, 1929, Herbert Hoover Papers, OF 400–PR, Herbert Hoover Presidential Library, West Branch, Iowa.

2. Barceló to Butler, February 15, 1929, *ibid.*

3. Lawrence Richey, secretary to President Hoover, to Secretary of War James W. Good, May 15, 1929; Santiago Iglesias to Hoover, May 15, 1929, *ibid.*

4. In a handwritten letter to the president, one Ralph J. Simons of Pittsburgh, Pa., wrote on March 24, 1929: "I note in the Press that Theodore Rosevelt [*sic*] is being advocated for appointment to Governor General of the Phillipines [*sic*] and I most respectfully ask you to ignore such an appointment. We certainly have had enough of the Rosevelts" (BIA Files, "P" File, Theodore Roosevelt, Jr., National Archives). See also Frank L. Gift of San Francisco, writing in support of Roosevelt as governor-general of the Philippines, to Hoover, May 1, 1929, *ibid.* W. J. Cooke of Boston sent Hoover a clipping from the Worcester, Massachusetts *Telegram*, which said in part: "The report now is that Colonel Theodore Roosevelt is to be made governor of Porto Rico. . . . The governorship . . . ought to go to a gentleman who is fluent in Spanish, who understands the Latin temperament. . . . Nothing in Colonel Roosevelt's record indicates his special equipment in these lines. He is his father's son with his father's name and his father's craving to be ever conspicuous, but without his father's gifts for conspicuous accomplishment. However, his candidacy is strongly backed by strong men" (Cooke to Hoover, May 15, 1929, Hoover Papers, OF 400–PR).

5. Memo of telephone call to president's office from Bingham, April 19, 1929, *ibid.*

6. Lawrence Richey, secretary of the president, to Hoover, May 10, 1929; Córdova Dávila to Hoover, May 10, 1929, *ibid.*

7. Cable, José Tous Soto, speaker of the house, to Hoover, May 11, 1929; telegram, Pedro J. Biaggi to Hoover, May 10, 1929; cable José L. Pesquera, president of the Porto Rico Farmers' Association, to Hoover, May 11, 1929, *ibid.*

8. "President would like you to accept appointment as Governor Porto

Rico Stop Some very important economic problems to be solved Stop The President much interested in proper solution, and personally hope you can accept" (cable, Newton to Roosevelt, May 16, 1929, *ibid*.).

9. Entry for May 20, 1929, in diary of Theodore Roosevelt, Jr., Theodore Roosevelt, Jr., Papers, Box 2, Manuscript Division, Library of Congress. The flair for self-dramatization which was so famous in his father is evident in this passage, as well as throughout the papers of Theodore Roosevelt, Jr. Also in his father's image was the hunting trip itself, with its combination of sport, international derring-do, and rather popularized natural science. More will be said later of the way in which Roosevelt followed in his father's style of life.

10. Cable, Henry S. Waterman, U.S. consul in Saigon, to Walter Newton, May 27, 1929, Hoover Papers, OF 400–PR.

11. Mrs. Theodore Roosevelt, Jr., *Day Before Yesterday* (Garden City, N.Y., 1959), pp. 209 and 225.

12. General F. LeJ. Parker to Roosevelt, September 19, 1929, BIA Files, "P" File, Theodore Roosevelt, Jr.

13. Memorandum on inaugural address, Parker to Roosevelt, September 26, 1929; H. F. Arthur Schoenfeld, secretary general of Commission of Inquiry and Conciliation, Bolivia and Paraguay, to Parker, September 26, 1929 (enclosing Spanish draft of Roosevelt's speech), *ibid*. Mrs. Roosevelt said of her husband's inaugural speech: "After reading the first paragraph in English, instead of having an interpreter read it over in Spanish he did it himself. When he began, 'Señores y Señoras,' there came a great 'A-a-a-a-ah!' from the crowd, then a burst of applause and cheers" (*Day Before Yesterday*, p. 227).

14. Bingham to Hoover, August 15, 1929, Hoover Papers OF 400-PR.

15. Roosevelt to Walter Newton, secretary to the president, November 16, 1929, *ibid*.

16. Roosevelt to Newton, November 20, 1929; Etienne Totti to Richey, December 2, 1929; Hoover to Roosevelt, November 29, 1929, *ibid*.

17. Juan José Osuna, *A History of Education in Puerto Rico*, 2nd ed. (Río Piedras, 1949), pp. 282 ff. Thomas G. Mathews, in his *Puerto Rican Politics and the New Deal* (Gainesville, Fla., 1960), tells about the squeeze play put on Padín during the 1930s.

18. Roosevelt to Hoover, December 6, 1929, Hoover Papers, OF 400–PR.

19. Roosevelt to Colonel Lafayette B. Gleason, October 20, 1930, Roosevelt Papers, Box 29.

20. *Ibid*. and Roosevelt to Newton, October 24, 1930, Hoover Papers, OF 400–PR.

21. Roosevelt to Beverley, September 15, 1932, Roosevelt Papers, Box 48.

22. Roosevelt to Beverley, July 5, 1934, *ibid*.

23. Iglesias to Hoover, December 21, 1929, Hoover Papers, OF 400-PR.

24. On federal funds, see Roosevelt to Newton, March 23, 1930, and March 24, 1930, *ibid.* On the Agricultural Marketing Act, see Roosevelt to Newton, October 13, 1929, *ibid.* On the commercial adviser in New York, see the many cables between Roosevelt and H. P. MacGowan, in BIA Files, File 28636. For Roosevelt's view on the tariff, see Roosevelt to Parker, January 17, 1930, Hoover Papers, OF 400–PR. On the Puerto Rican Department of Labor, see Roosevelt to Newton, February 17, 1931, *ibid.* On tax collection, see Roosevelt to Seth W. Richardson, February 27, 1931, Roosevelt Papers, Box 29. Relative to the need for a more diversified economy, Roosevelt told José Padín on September 29, 1931, that "we think that our crops have a world significance, whereas, every product we have on the island could be permanently withdrawn from the world markets and none of them would be affected" (*ibid.*). Mrs. Roosevelt tells of the embroidery industry in *Day Before Yesterday*, pp. 238–40. See her book, p. 233, for much on the school lunch program; also Roosevelt to Dr. F. H. Newell, August 17, 1931, Roosevelt Papers, Box 29. About Roosevelt's speeches to universities, etc., see Roosevelt to Hoover, April 22, 1930, Hoover Papers, OF 400–PR. The comment about not telling the bitter truth about Puerto Rico was in a letter from Roosevelt to Bailey Diffie, November 30, 1931, Roosevelt Papers, Box 29.

25. Don Marquis to Roosevelt, September 19, 1930, *ibid.*

26. Roosevelt to Rice, January 30, 1931, *ibid.* This golf course, certainly one of the most unique and scenic in the world, does not exist today.

27. Mrs. Roosevelt, *Day Before Yesterday,* p. 237.

28. Roosevelt to Walter F. Brown, postmaster general, May 2, 1931, Roosevelt Papers, Box 29.

29. Roosevelt to Ernest Gruening, April 30, 1931; Roosevelt to Dean Ezra Pound, July 25, 1931, *ibid.*

30. Richey to Roosevelt, May 7, 1931, Hoover Papers, OF 400–PR.

31. Theodore Roosevelt, Jr., *Colonial Policies of the United States* (Garden City, N.Y., 1937), p. 100.

32. Mrs. Roosevelt, *Day Before Yesterday,* p. 248.

33. *Ibid.,* p. 230. Roosevelt's belief that learning Spanish was important is revealed in the suggestion made to General Douglas MacArthur, chief of staff, that officers assigned to the Sixty-fifth Regiment (the old "Porto Rican Regiment") "be reasonable [*sic*] facile in Spanish" (Roosevelt to MacArthur, January 17, 1931, Roosevelt Papers, Box 29).

34. Dr. Sara W. Brown of Howard University told Roosevelt of receiving a letter from the mother of a student at Howard. Dr. Brown wrote, "She states that you are winning the hearts of all the Porto Ricans by talking to them in their own language and by coming to their little towns" (Brown to Roosevelt, January 2, 1930, *ibid*). Also, Luis N. Jimenez wrote to Colonel Franklin D'Olier, vice-president of Prudential Insurance, on March 20, 1930, praising Roosevelt's speech-making in Spanish: "I can say in truth that there

was not any part of his address that I did not understand clearly. The few times that he mispronounced badly a word he repeated it to make himself understood" (*ibid.*).

35. Roosevelt to Gruening, March 29, 1931, *ibid.*

36. Financial statement of Theodore Roosevelt, Jr., for 1930, *ibid.*

37. Roosevelt to Getulio Echeandía, August 19, 1935, Roosevelt Papers, Box 30. See Mrs. Roosevelt, *Day Before Yesterday*, p. 230. The *jíbaro* is the Puerto Rican rural native, much like the "hillbilly" of Kentucky and West Virginia in respect to the attitudes that city folk hold toward them, and also in the fact that they represent a purer racial and linguistic strain, dating back to the original settlers, than do the more conglomerate urban people.

38. Roosevelt to Hoover, December 6, 1929, Hoover Papers, OF 400–PR.

39. Roosevelt to Newton, November 17, 1930, *ibid.*

40. Roosevelt, *Colonial Policies*, p. 118.

41. Roosevelt to H. V. Kaltenborn, April 21, 1930, Roosevelt Papers, Box 29.

42. *La Prensa*, June 14, 1931. A clipping of this editorial was sent to Roosevelt by Robert Woods Bliss of the United States Embassy in Argentina and is in Roosevelt Papers, Box 29.

43. Roosevelt to Gruening, March 29, 1931, *ibid.* Gruening was not equally pleased with Hoover's speech in Puerto Rico. He was disappointed that Hoover offered the islanders nothing but "what is offered the people of continental United States," and quoted a friend's comment on this: "Hoover's going to do for the Porto Ricans all he has done for the United States? 'Eaven 'elp the Porto Ricans! That may mean some appropriations for hogs, but nothing for children" (*ibid.*).

44. Fred B. Smith to Hoover, March 31, 1931, Hoover Papers, OF 400–PR.

45. Nelson B. Layman to Roosevelt, April 6, 1931; Walter F. Lineburger to Roosevelt, April 7, 1931, Roosevelt Papers, Box 29.

46. Roosevelt to Layman, April 14, 1931, *ibid.*

47. Henry Wells, *The Modernization of Puerto Rico* (Cambridge, Mass., 1969), p. 106.

48. Barceló to Sra. Ana Roqué de Duprey, September 24, 1931, Ana Roqué de Duprey Manuscripts, Colección Puertorriqueña, University of Puerto Rico, Río Piedras.

49. There are convenient summaries of the political changes of this period in Bolívar Pagán, *Historia de los partidos políticos Puertorriqueños, 1898–1956*, 2 vols. (San Juan, 1959); Wells, *Modernization of Puerto Rico;* and Robert J. Hunter, "Historical Survey of the Puerto Rico Status Question, 1898–1965," in *Status of Puerto Rico: Selected Background Studies* (Washington, D.C., 1966).

50. Roosevelt to Hoover, December 6, 1929, Hoover Papers, OF 400–PR.

51. Todd lost his office as mayor because San Juan changed to a commission form of city government, and Governor Roosevelt strongly backed the bill which effected the change. Incidentally, one interesting development which grew out of this was the first admission by Todd, who had been servile toward Governor E. Mont. Reily, that Reily had misused public funds. Todd to Roosevelt, October 1, 1931, Roosevelt Papers, Box 29.

52. Crockett to Roosevelt, October 7, 1931, *ibid.*

53. Roosevelt to James R. Beverley, March 6, 1932, *ibid.*, Box 48.

54. Gruening to Roosevelt, October 27, 1931, *ibid.*, Box 29.

55. Roosevelt to Gruening, November 6, 1931, *ibid.* Roosevelt to Beverley, January 11, 1932, *ibid.*, Box 48.

56. Roosevelt to Beverley, June 20, 1932, *ibid.*

57. To Governor Beverley, Roosevelt wrote from the Philippines on July 24, 1932, "Believe it or not,—the local leaders here are interested in policies and talk them to the exclusion of *nombriamentos* [patronage]!" (*ibid.*).

58. Roosevelt to Beverley, October 4, 1932, *ibid.*

59. Roosevelt to Beverley, September 9, 1933, *ibid.*

60. Roosevelt to Beverley, October 20, 1933, *ibid.*

61. See the discussion of the value of *dignidad* by John P. Gillin, "Some Signposts for Policy," in *Social Change in Latin America Today,* ed. Richard N. Adams et al. (New York, 1960), pp. 29–33.

62. Roosevelt did lose some luster with Puerto Ricans in 1936, however, when he made a critical statement to the press, calling Puerto Rico a liability, not an asset, to the United States, and suggesting that the Tydings bill—which would have committed the United States to follow the result of a referendum in Puerto Rico over independence—was not a bad idea. See Germánico S. Belaval to Roosevelt, April 27, 1936, Roosevelt Papers, Box 30. Also Roosevelt to Belaval, June 24, 1936, *ibid.* Also Roosevelt to Beverley, May 4, 1936, *ibid.*, Box 48.

63. Roosevelt told Ernest Gruening in a letter of November 6, 1931, that the next time they got together, he wanted to talk about "the United States' ultimate policy" regarding Puerto Rico: "The present form of administration cannot, of course, be permanent, and though I believe what we are doing now is a necessary step towards anything that may come, I think that at least those in authority in Washington should begin to think more in terms of the future and shape their course accordingly" (*ibid.*, Box 29). Throughout his book *Colonial Policies of the United States,* Roosevelt argues for dominion status for Puerto Rico (and the Philippine Islands).

CHAPTER 7. PORTO RICO BECOMES PUERTO RICO

1. Barceló to Hoover, January 13, 1932, Herbert Hoover Papers, OF 400–PR, Herbert Hoover Presidential Library, West Branch, Iowa.

2. Whitney T. Perkins, *Denial of Empire: The United States and Its Dependencies* (Leyden, Netherlands, 1962), p. 135.

3. Roosevelt to Richey, August 11, 1931, Hoover Papers, OF 400–PR.

4. Gruening to Roosevelt, March 17, 1931; Gruening to Roosevelt, March 26, 1931; Roosevelt to Gruening, March 29, 1931, Theodore Roosevelt, Jr., Papers, Box 29, Manuscript Division, Library of Congress.

5. *Inaugural Address of Governor James R. Beverley* (San Juan, 1932), pp. 5, 8.

6. Beverley to Hoover, February 3, 1932, Hoover Papers, OF 400–PR.

7. "Puerto Rico Report Urges Birth Control," *New York Times,* September 26, 1932, p. 1.

8. *Ibid.*, September 27, 1932, p. 13, and October 7, 1932, p. 6.

9. *Ibid.*, October 9, 1932, p. 9. Elizabeth H. Shafer, president of Minnesota Birth Control League, to President Hoover, October 8, 1932; telegram, Blanche Ames, president of Birth Control League of Massachusetts, to Hoover, October 11, 1932, Hoover Papers, OF 400–PR.

10. *El Mundo* (San Juan), February 13, 1932, p. 18.

11. English translation of letter, January 24, 1932, from José Lameiro, secretary to the president of the Nationalist Party (Pedro Albizu Campos), to Dr. Rafael Bernabé, president of the Medical Association of Puerto Rico, BIA Files, File 20750–53, National Archives.

12. *La Democracia* (San Juan), January 27, 1932, p. 1.

13. Beverley to Roosevelt, March 23, 1932, Roosevelt Papers, Box 29.

14. *Ibid.*

15. Beverley to Hoover, May 9, 1932, Hoover Papers, OF 400–PR. Concurrent resolution of Puerto Rican legislature read before U.S. Senate, May 17, 1932, *Congressional Record*, 72nd Cong., 1st sess., 1932, pp. 9966, 10380.

16. *Ibid.*, p. 10249.

17. *Ibid.*, pp. 10022–32. This is the only occasion I have found in which the resident commissioners from Puerto Rico and the Philippine Islands publicly took part in any legislative activities for the other. See chapter 8 for a comment on this lack of cooperation.

18. Beverley to Roosevelt, March 23, 1932, Roosevelt Papers, Box 29.

19. *El Universal* (New York City), October 8, 1932, p. 1.

20. *Ibid.*

21. Telegram, United Puerto Rico Republican Club of New York City to Hoover, October 7, 1932, Hoover Papers, OF 400–PR.

22. Beverley to General Parker, chief of BIA, April 18, 1932, BIA Files, File 26429–with 203.

23. *El País* (San Juan, P.R.), September 2, 1932, p. 2.

24. *El Mundo,* August 10, 1932, p. 2.

25. U.S., War Department, *Report of the Governor of Puerto Rico to the Secretary of War: 1933*, pp. 14–15.

26. Beverley to Roosevelt, August 30, 1933, Roosevelt Papers, Box 48.

27. Beverley to Roosevelt, October 30, 1933; Roosevelt to Beverley, November 3, 1933; Beverley to Roosevelt, January 3, 1934; Beverley to Roosevelt, January 20, 1934; Roosevelt to Beverley, July 5, 1934; Roosevelt to Beverley, May 4, 1936; Beverley to Roosevelt, January 3, 1939; Beverley to Roosevelt, September 16, 1939, *ibid.*

CHAPTER 8. THE POLICY OF NO POLICY

1. Samuel McCune Lindsay, "Porto Rico Revisited: Contrasts of Twenty-Five Years," *The American Review of Reviews,* XLIII (May 1926), p. 511.

2. For these patterns of anti-imperialist thought, see Fred H. Harrington, "The Anti-Imperialist Movement in the United States, 1898–1900," *Mississippi Valley Historical Review,* XXII (September 1935), pp. 211–30.

3. Robin Winks, "American and European Imperialism Compared," in *American Imperialism in 1898,* ed. Richard H. Miller (New York, 1970), pp. 179–90.

4. See the majority opinion of the Court, written by Chief Justice William Howard Taft, in *United States Reports, Supreme Court* (Boston, New York, and Washington, D.C., 1876–), vol. 258, 300–14.

5. Jack Ericson Eblen, *The First and Second United States Empires: Governors and Territorial Government, 1784–1912* (Pittsburgh, 1968), pp. 189–90.

6. U.S., Congress, Senate and House, *Congressional Record,* 64th Cong., 2nd sess., 1917, pp. 2264, 3011, 3071–72.

7. Eblen, *First and Second United States Empires,* p. 190.

8. *Ibid.,* p. 275.

9. *Cong. Record,* 67th Cong., 2nd sess., 1921, p. 607.

10. Roosevelt to Benner, November 16, 1931, Theodore Roosevelt, Jr., Papers, Box 29 Manuscript Division, Library of Congress.

11. Earl S. Pomeroy, *The Territories and the United States, 1861–1890* (Seattle, 1969), pp. 81–82.

12. In 1932 the Democratic platform included the statement, "Independence for the Philippines; ultimate statehood for Porto Rico." Four years later, that same party had not one word about Puerto Rico, directly or indirectly, in its campaign platform. The Republicans offered better things—at least more immediately attainable—for Puerto Rico in 1932: "Puerto Rico being a part of the United States and its inhabitants American citizens, we believe that they are entitled to a good-faith recognition of the spirit and purposes of their organic act. We, therefore, favor the inclusion of the island

in all legislative and administrative measures enacted or adopted by Congress or otherwise for the economic benefit of their fellow-citizens of the mainland. We also believe that, in so far as possible, all officials appointed to administer the affairs of the island government should be qualified by at least five years of bona-fide residence therein." In 1936 the Republicans did the same thing as their opponents, leaving Puerto Rico completely out of their platform. Kirk H. Porter and Donald Bruce Johnson, eds., *National Party Platforms, 1840–1960,* 2nd ed. (Urbana, Ill., 1961), pp. 332, 349.

13. Bird Arias to Hoover, March 23, 1931, Hoover Papers, OF 400–PR.

14. William Green to Hoover, January 29, 1932; memorandum, Beverley to Hoover, May 9, 1932, *ibid.*

15. George Cabot Ward, "The Rural Population of Porto Rico," *Proceedings: Twenty-Sixth Lake Mohonk Conference of Friends of the Indian and Other Dependent Peoples* (Lake Mohonk, N.Y., 1908), p. 151; U.S., War Department, *Report of the Governor of Porto Rico to the Secretary of War: 1914,* p. 46; *ibid., 1929,* p. 43; Roosevelt to Walter Newton, March 24, 1930, Hoover Papers, OF 400–PR.

16. For example, the Puerto Rican commission which came to the United States in 1923 sought a clarification of the island's status, an elective governor, and legislative autonomy for Puerto Rico. Also, Resident Commissioner Córdova Dávila introduced bills for one or more of these reforms on numerous occasions in the 1920s. See *Cong. Record,* 68th Cong., 1st sess., 1923, p. 345; *ibid.,* 70th Cong., 1st sess., 1928, p. 1911. Party leaders Barceló and Tous Soto sent cables to the U.S. Senate in 1928 asking for an elective governor and the right to draft a constitution. *Ibid.,* 70th Cong., 1st sess., 1928, p. 2939.

17. This preoccupation of the governors with the status question was not entirely their fault; insular politics was so completely centered upon that and other purely partisan political concerns that the governors had little choice.

18. For example, see General F. LeJ. Parker's request for Governor Beverley to send him a list of necessary legislation for Puerto Rico which Congress might someday enact if the Puerto Rican legislature continued to fail to do so. Thus, Parker's knowledge of "the facts" and "appropriate recommendations" was based upon Beverley's perception of them. Parker to Beverley, July 28, 1932, BIA Files, File 19101–181.

19. Weeks to Harding, July 5, 1923, *ibid.,* File 1175–63.

20. Weeks to Coolidge, May 26, 1924; Weeks to Slemp, June 5, 1924, Coolidge Papers, Manuscript Division, Library of Congress, File 400ZB, Series 1. The War Department (which in insular matters meant the BIA) gave its endorsement to this bill only with the addition that it take effect not in 1928 but in 1932. In spite of Senator King's statement, "The Secretary of War may make his findings and may make his statements to the committee . . . but I

do not think that in legislation of this character his opinion ought to be controlling or that his recommendation should be of the peremptory character which this seems to be," the 1932 suggestion was tacked on. *Cong. Record*, 68th Cong., 1st sess., 1924, p. 8601.

21. Everett Sanders to Secretary of War Dwight F. Davis, October 27, 1925, Coolidge Papers, File 400ZB, Series 1.

22. Weeks to C. Bascom Slemp, January 8, 1925; Davis to Sanders, March 1, 1928; Sanders to Antonio Gonzalez, March 3, 1928, *ibid.*

23. In a memo to the general who followed him as head of the BIA, McIntyre set forth a policy of backing governors against their critics, except for any governor "who does not value the support of the War Department or . . . disregards the advice of the Department" (McIntyre to Parker, May 4, 1931, BIA Files, File 858–71).

24. Mrs. Theodore Roosevelt, Jr., *Day Before Yesterday* (Garden City, N.Y., 1959), p. 231.

25. McIntyre to Towner, April 10, 1928, BIA Files, File 28401–2.

26. Parker to Beverley, July 20, 1932, *ibid.*, "P" File.

27. McIntyre to Yager, April 5, 1917, *ibid.*, File 1175–38.

28. Memorandum, McIntyre to secretary of war, January 6, 1925, *ibid.*, File 25118–486.

29. Patrick J. Hurley, secretary of war, to Senator Hiram Bingham, December 18, 1930, *ibid.*, File 3377–555.

30. Memo by McIntyre, March 28, 1924, *ibid.*, File DTIP 9–6–68.

31. William Green to Coolidge, December 5, 1925, with text of resolution passed by American Federation of Labor convention, October 6, 1925, Coolidge Papers, File 400ZB, Series 1. See also the suggestion by Senator John Sharp Williams to President Wilson that "it is about time we were recognizing the fact that Porto Rico ought not to be governed by the War Department as if there were still a military occupation of it" (Williams to Wilson, August 17, 1914, Woodrow Wilson Papers, Series 4, Casefile 47, Manuscript Division, Library of Congress).

32. Memorandum, McIntyre to Colonel Thorne Strayer, Office of the Inspector General, July 6, 1927, BIA Files, File 119–165.

33. Major General Frank McIntyre, "American Territorial Administration," *Foreign Affairs*, X (January 1932), 300.

34. Weeks to Coolidge, December 2, 1924; Slemp to General Lord, December 5, 1924; Lord to Slemp, December 6, 1924; letter of transmittal, Coolidge to Congress, December 8, 1924, Coolidge Papers, File 400ZB, Series 1.

35. Acting Secretary of War Payne to Hoover, June 1, 1931; Secretary of War Hurley to Hoover, July 21, 1931, Hoover Papers, OF 400–PR.

36. President Coolidge stated in 1924 that the United States was "a trustee

for the welfare of the people" of Puerto Rico, with the duty of "assist[ing] them in developing a stable form of self-government" (Coolidge to Miguel Guerra Mondragón, speaker of the Puerto Rican House of Representatives, January 23, 1924, Coolidge Papers, File 400ZB, Series 1).

37. For example, during a discussion in the House of Representatives over a further grant of self-government for Puerto Rico, Milton H. Welling of Utah asked the resident commissioner from the island "how many white people there are living in Porto Rico today" (*Cong. Record,* 65th Cong., 3rd sess., 1919, p. 3211).

38. Hamilton to Weeks, April 12, 1922, BIA Files, File 26429–141.

39. Roosevelt to Charles R. Hartzell, October 6, 1933, Roosevelt Papers, Box 30.

40. "It does not seem that the questions which you ask could be more clearly answered by words now than they have been in the past by each American Administration and by the actual acts of the several administrations and of the several Congresses which have legislated on Porto Rican questions.

"In some form each administration has announced that the connection between Porto Rico and the United States is regarded as permanent; and each administration has announced that it was the desire not to make any promise which would hamper the wise handling of the relations between Porto Rico and the United States in future, but that it desired to go as far as, under existing conditions, wisdom and prudence dictated in constituting Porto Rico a self-governing community under the sovereignty of the United States" (Weeks to Pedro Capo-Rodriguez, January 14, 1922, printed in *The Times* [San Juan], February 11, 1922, p. 5). Actually, Weeks' rebuttal to Capo-Rodriguez is a masterpiece of double-talk and half-truths.

41. Harding to Weeks, April 3, 1922, Warren G. Harding Papers, Box 252, Ohio State Historical Society, Columbus, Ohio.

42. H. P. Krippene, "Porto Rico's Playful Politics," *Current History: A Monthly Magazine of the New York Times,* XV (January 1922), 615; Henry Kittredge Norton, "American Imperialism in the Indies," *The World's Work,* LI (December 1925), 216.

43. *Cong. Record,* 70th Cong., 1st sess., 1928, p. 6334.

44. Adolf A. Berle, Jr., "Porto Rican Independence," *The Survey,* XLVI (September 24, 1921), 704.

45. Barceló to Ana Roqué de Duprey, September 24, 1931, Ana Roqué de Duprey Manuscripts, Colección Puertorriqueña, University of Puerto Rico, Río Piedras.

46. Theodore Roosevelt, *Colonial Policies of the United States* (Garden City, N.Y., 1937), p. 195.

47. Whitney T. Perkins, *Denial of Empire: The United States and Its Dependencies* (Leyden, Netherlands, 1962), pp. 341–43.

Bibliography

BIBLIOGRAPHICAL AIDS

Bird, Augusto, ed. *Bibliografía Puertorriqueña de fuentes para investigaciones sociales, 1930–1945.* 2 vols. Río Piedras: Universidad de Puerto Rico, 1946–47.

Evidently an attempt to extend Pedreira's work (see below) fifteen years, but not as well indexed. These volumes are small for the ground they supposedly cover; they include no annotations or descriptions of the entries. Works mentioned include books, articles, and pamphlets. Headings in volume 1 include "Natural History," "Anthropology and Ethnology," and "Health." Volume 2 contains "Social Economy," "Political and Administrative History," "Cultural Organization," and "History of Puerto Rico."

Geigel y Zenon, José, and Morales Ferrer, Abelardo, eds. *Bibliografía Puertorriqueña.* Barcelona: Editorial Araluce, 1934.

Even though this book was written in the 1890s, it was only published in 1934. The 453 pages of entries cover less than eight hundred books, all of them published between 1807 and 1892. It does list books written by non–Puerto Ricans and published abroad. There are descriptions of each book, ranging from one line to several pages, but these are often merely colorful subjective narrative.

Pedreira, Antonio S., ed. *Bibliografía Puertorriqueña, 1493–1930.* Monografías de la Universidad de Puerto Rico, Serie A, Estudios Hispanicos, número 1. Madrid: Editorial Hernando, 1932.

This is the most complete bibliography on Puerto Rico to 1930. It has 655 pages of entries, with generally fifteen to twenty entries per page. References are arranged alphabetically by author or by title if no author is indicated. It includes books, articles, and pamphlets in Spanish, English, German, French, Dutch, Latin, and perhaps other languages. The titles not in Spanish are not translated. There is no real description of each entry, but often there are subtitles or other brief explanations. Alphabetical lists are within sections: "General Information," "Natural History," "Health," "Social Economy," "Political and Administrative History," "Cultural Organization," "History of Puerto Rico," "Literary History," and "Miscellaneous." In the back there are alphabetical indexes of authors and topics. The references in English frequently have errors in spelling, date, or exact wording of a title.

Velazquez, Gonzalo, ed. *Anuario bibliográfico Puertorriqueño*. San Juan, 1950–.

These are bibliographical supplements intended to bring the works of Pedreira and Bird up to the present time. Unfortunately, they have not always come out annually, and sometimes are published as much as six years after the previous volume. They are small, with no annotations for entries. Entries include only books, pamphlets, and relevant periodicals —no listings of articles. The only indexing is a mixture of topics, authors, and titles of periodicals. In the back of each volume is a list of publishers, printers, and booksellers in Puerto Rico.

PRIMARY SOURCES

Unpublished Manuscripts

For the scholar who wants to save time by having a good idea of which files he will use when he gets to an archive, the Library of Congress has published indexes to many of the collections in its Manuscript Division, including the papers of Woodrow Wilson, Theodore Roosevelt, William Howard Taft, and Calvin Coolidge. The Instituto de Cultura Puertorriqueña has published two books to aid research in Puerto Rico. Lino Gómez Canedo, comp., *Los archivos históricos de Puerto Rico* (San Juan, 1964) is a guide to the municipal archives of the island (not unlike Philip M. Hamer, ed., *A Guide to Archives and Manuscripts in the United States* [New Haven, Conn.: Yale University Press, 1961]). Unfortunately, it lists civil and ecclesiastical records only for pre-1898 Puerto Rican history, possibly because that is all the depositories described contain. *Guía al Archivo General de Puerto Rico* (San Juan, 1964) describes the various materials in the Archivo General deposited up to the book's publication. It is indispensable for doing research in the Archivo General.

Antonio R. Barceló Manuscripts. Colección Puertorriqueña, University of Puerto Rico, Río Piedras.

Bureau of Insular Affairs Files. War Department Records, National Archives.

Calvin Coolidge Papers. Manuscript Division, Library of Congress.
Lindley M. Garrison Papers. Firestone Library, Princeton University, Princeton, N.J.
Samuel Gompers Papers. Manuscript Division, Library of Congress.
Warren G. Harding Papers. Ohio State Historical Society, Columbus, Ohio.
Herbert Hoover Papers. Herbert Hoover Presidential Library, West Branch, Iowa.
E. Mont. Reily Manuscripts. Colección Puertorriqueña, University of Puerto Rico, Río Piedras.
E. Mont. Reily Papers. Manuscripts and Archives Division, New York Public Library (Astor, Lenox and Tilden Foundation), New York City.
Ana Roqué de Duprey Manuscripts. Colección Puertorriqueña, University of Puerto Rico, Río Piedras.
Theodore Roosevelt, Jr., Papers. Manuscript Division, Library of Congress.
William Howard Taft Papers. Manuscript Division, Library of Congress.
Tareas 58–A–3, 58–F, Government Documents. Archivo General, San Juan.
Woodrow Wilson Papers. Manuscript Division, Library of Congress.
Arthur Yager Papers. Residence of Diana Yager Eskew, Louisville, Ky.

Newspapers

El Mundo (San Juan). 1921–1938.
El País (San Juan). 1932.
El Tiempo and *The Times* (San Juan). 1919–1923.
El Universal (New York City). 1932.
Journal of Commerce and Commercial Bulletin (New York City). 1921.
Justicia (San Juan). 1915, 1924, 1925 (scattered issues).
Kansas City Star. 1921.
La Correspondencia de Puerto Rico (San Juan). 1909–1929.
La Democracia (San Juan). 1909–1932.
New York Times. 1913–1932.

Published Documents and Collections

Actas de la Cámara de Representantes de Puerto Rico, 1929. San Juan, 1929.
Actas del Senado de Puerto Rico, 1918–1920. San Juan, 1920.
Documents on the Constitutional History of Puerto Rico. Washington, D.C.: Office of Puerto Rico, n.d.
Inaugural Address of Governor James R. Beverley. San Juan, 1932.
Inaugural Address of Hon. E. Mont. Reily, Governor of Porto Rico. San Juan, 1921.
Message of the Governor of Porto Rico to the Ninth Legislature. San Juan, 1918.

Message of the Governor of Porto Rico to the Twelfth Legislature. San Juan, 1929.

Morison, Elting E., and Blum, John M., eds. *The Letters of Theodore Roosevelt.* 8 vols. Cambridge, Mass.: Harvard University Press, 1951.

Porter, Kirk H., and Johnson, Donald B., eds. *National Party Platforms, 1840–1960.* Urbana, Ill.: University of Illinois Press, 1961.

Primer informe de la comisión legislativa para investigar el malestar y desasosiego industrial y agrícola y que origina el desempleo en Puerto Rico. San Juan, 1930.

Proceedings: Lake Mohonk Conference of Friends of the Indian and Other Dependent Peoples. Twenty-second through thirty-fourth conferences. Lake Mohonk, N.Y., 1904–1916.

Richardson, James D., ed. *A Compilation of the Messages and Papers of the Presidents.* 20 vols. New York: Bureau of National Literature, Inc., 1897–1917.

U.S., Congress, Senate. *Reorganization of the Army: Hearings Before the Committee on Military Affairs.* Washington, D.C., 1920.

U.S., Congress, Senate and House. *Congressional Record.* 55th–72nd Cong., 1899–1932.

U.S., War Department. *Report of the Governor of Porto Rico to the Secretary of War.* 1909–1933. (Sometimes as vol. III of the *Annual Report* of the War Department.)

U.S., War Department. *Second Annual Report of the Governor of Porto Rico to the President of the United States through the Secretary of War.* Washington, D.C., 1902.

Books and Pamphlets

Albizu Campos, Pedro. *La Resolución Conjunta No. 2.* Ponce, P.R., 1923.

Foraker, Joseph Benson. *Notes of a Busy Life.* 2 vols. 2nd ed. Cincinnati: Stewart and Kidd Co., 1916.

Forbes-Lindsay, C. H. *America's Insular Possessions.* 2 vols. Philadelphia: John C. Winston Co., 1906.

Gompers, Samuel. *Seventy Years of Life and Labor: An Autobiography.* 2 vols. New York: E. P. Dutton and Co., 1925.

Roosevelt, Mrs. Theodore, Jr. *Day Before Yesterday: The Reminiscences of Mrs. Theodore Roosevelt, Jr.* Garden City, N.Y.: Doubleday, 1959.

Roosevelt, Theodore. *Colonial Policies of the United States.* Garden City, N.Y.: Doubleday, Doran and Co., 1937.

Articles

Allen, Charles H. "How Civil Government Was Established in Porto Rico." *North American Review,* CLXXIV (February 1902), 159–68.

Appleton, Caroline Dawes. "Porto Rico: A Study in Colonial Courtesies." *The American Review of Reviews,* LXXII (September 1925), 301–07.

Berle, Adolf A., Jr. "Porto Rican Independence." *The Survey,* XLVI (September 24, 1921), 704.

Coates, Mary Weld. "Puerto Rico's Independence Slogan." *Current History: A Monthly Magazine of the New York Times,* XVI (July 1922), 651–52.

———. "What's the Matter in Porto Rico?" *Current History: A Monthly Magazine of the New York Times,* XVI (April 1922), 108–14.

Coll Cuchi, Cayetano. "American Rule in Porto Rico." *The Living Age,* CCCXIV (July 29, 1922), 262–66.

Curtis, Henry G. "The Status of Porto Rico." *Forum,* XXVIII (December 1899), 403–10.

Gompers, Samuel. "Porto Rico: Her Present Condition and Fears for the Future." *American Federationist,* XXI (May 1914), 377–89.

" 'I Accuse'—in Porto Rico." *The Nation,* CXV (September 6, 1922), 236–37.

Iglesias, Santiago. "Strike of Agricultural Laborers in Porto Rico." *American Federationist,* XII (June 1905), 380.

Krippene, H. P. "Porto Rico's Playful Politics." *Current History: A Monthly Magazine of the New York Times,* XV (January 1922), 610–15.

Lindsay, Samuel McCune. "Porto Rico Revisited: Contrasts of Twenty-Five Years." *The American Review of Reviews,* LXXIII (May 1926), 511–14.

McIntyre, Major General Frank. "American Territorial Administration." *Foreign Affairs,* X (January 1932), 293–303.

Muñoz Marín, Luis. "A 'Ninety-Eight Percent American' in Porto Rico." *The New Republic,* XXIX (January 4, 1922), 151–53.

———. "Porto Rico: The American Colony." *The Nation,* CXX (April 8, 1925), 379–82.

Norton, Henry Kittredge. "American Imperialism in the Indies." *The World's Work,* LI (December 1925), 210–18.

———. "The Ethics of Imperialism." *The World's Work,* LI (January 1926), 321–28.

Pasarell, Emilio J. "Porto Rico in the War." *Review of Reviews,* LVIII (September 1918), 286–87.

Post, Regis H. "What's Wrong in Porto Rico?" *The World's Work,* XLIII (January 1922), 261–67.

"President Gompers in Porto Rico." *American Federationist,* XI (April 1904), 293–306.

Reed, Mary. "Politics and Porto Rico." *The Nation,* CXIV (February 1, 1922), 131–32.

Roqué de Duprey, Ana. "Mensaje a la mujer Puertorriqueña." *Nosotras,* Año 1, Num. 4 (February 1932), 1.

St. John, Charles W. "What's the Matter in Porto Rico?" *Current History: A Monthly Magazine of the New York Times,* XVI (July 1922), 650–51.

"Self-Government in Porto Rico." *The World's Work,* XLIII (March 1922), 463–64.

"Uncle Sam's Stepchild." *The Survey,* XLV (October 9, 1920), 63–64.

Warner, Arthur. "The Pot and the Kettle in Porto Rico." *The Nation,* CXVI (January 31, 1923), 117–18.

Other Primary Source

Interview with Diana Yager Eskew in her home in Louisville, Ky., May 20–21, 1967.

SECONDARY SOURCES

Books and Pamphlets

Adams, Richard N., et al. *Social Change in Latin America Today.* New York: Vintage Press, 1960.

Agoncillo, Theodore A. *A Short History of the Philippines.* New York: New American Library, 1969.

Anderson, Robert W. *Party Politics in Puerto Rico.* Stanford, Ca.: Stanford University Press, 1965.

Beisner, Robert L. *Twelve Against Empire: The Anti-Imperialists, 1898–1900.* New York: McGraw-Hill, 1968.

Berbusse, Edward J. *The United States in Puerto Rico, 1898–1900.* Chapel Hill, N.C.: University of North Carolina Press, 1966.

Clark, Victor S., et al. *Porto Rico and Its Problems.* Washington, D.C.: Brookings Institution, 1930.

Coll y Toste, Cayetano, ed. *Boletín histórico de Puerto Rico.* Vol. IX. San Juan, 1922.

Cruz Monclova, Lidio. *Luis Muñoz Rivera: diez años de su vida política.* San Juan: Instituto de Cultura Puertorriqueña, 1959.

Diffie, Bailey W. and Justine W. *Porto Rico: A Broken Pledge.* New York: Vanguard Press, 1931.

Eblen, Jack Ericson. *The First and Second United States Empires: Governors and Territorial Government, 1784–1912.* Pittsburgh: University of Pittsburgh Press, 1968.

Flexner, Eleanor. *Century of Struggle: The Woman's Rights Movement in the United States.* New York: Atheneum, 1968.

Gayer, Arthur D.; Homan, Paul T.; and James, Earle K. *The Sugar Economy of Puerto Rico.* New York: Columbia University Press, 1938.

Golding, Morton J. *A Short History of Puerto Rico.* New York: New American Library, 1973.

Gould, Lyman Jay. *La Ley Foraker: raíces de la política colonial de los Estados Unidos.* San Juan: Editorial Universidad de Puerto Rico, 1969.

Hanson, Earl Parker. *Transformation: The Story of Modern Puerto Rico.* New York: Simon and Schuster, 1955.

Hunter, Robert J. "Historical Survey of the Puerto Rico Status Question, 1898–1965." In *Status of Puerto Rico: Selected Background Studies.* Washington, D.C.: Government Printing Office, 1966.

Jessup, Philip C. *Elihu Root.* 2 vols. New York: Dodd, Mead, 1938.

Lewis, Gordon K. *Puerto Rico: Freedom and Power in the Caribbean.* New York: Monthly Review Press, 1963.

Maldonado, Teófilo. *Hombres de primera plana.* San Juan: Editorial Campos, 1958.

Maldonado-Denis, Manuel. *Puerto Rico: A Socio-Historic Interpretation.* New York: Vintage Press, 1972.

Marcus, Joseph. *Labor Conditions in Porto Rico.* Washington, D.C.: Government Printing Office, 1919.

Mathews, Thomas G. *Puerto Rican Politics and the New Deal.* Gainesville, Fla.: University of Florida Press, 1960.

Medina Ramírez, Ramón. *El movimiento libertador en la historia de Puerto Rico.* 3 vols. San Juan: Imprenta Nacional, 1964.

Mergal, Angel M. *Federico Degetau: un orientador de su pueblo.* New York: Hispanic Institute, 1944.

Morales Carrión, Arturo. *The Loneliness of Luis Muñoz Rivera.* Washington, D.C.: Office of the Commonwealth of Puerto Rico, 1965.

Negrón de Montilla, Aída. *Americanization in Puerto Rico and the Public-School System, 1900–1930.* Río Piedras: Editorial Edil, 1971.

Osuna, Juan José. *A History of Education in Puerto Rico.* 2nd ed. Río Piedras: Editorial de la Universidad de Puerto Rico, 1949.

Pagán, Bolívar. *Historia de los partidos políticos Puertorriqueños, 1898–1956.* 2 vols. San Juan: Librería Campos, 1959.

Perkins, Whitney T. *Denial of Empire: The United States and Its Dependencies.* Leyden, Netherlands: Sythoff, 1962.

Pomeroy, Earl S. *The Territories and the United States, 1861–1890.* Seattle, Wash.: University of Washington Press, 1969.

Rexach Benítez, Roberto F. *Pedro Albizu Campos: leyenda y realidad.* San Juan: Editorial Coqui, 1961.

Rostow, W. W. *The Stages of Economic Growth: A Non-Communist Manifesto.* London: Cambridge University Press, 1964.

Russell, Francis. *The Shadow of Blooming Grove: Warren G. Harding in His Times.* New York: McGraw-Hill, 1968.

Status of Puerto Rico: Report of the United States–Puerto Rico Commission on the Status of Puerto Rico. Washington, D.C.: Government Printing Office, 1966.

Taft, Philip. *Organized Labor in American History.* New York: 1964.

Vivas, José Luis. *Historia de Puerto Rico.* New York: Las Americas Publishing Co., 1962.

Wagenheim, Kal. *Puerto Rico: A Profile.* New York: Praeger, 1970.

Wells, Henry. *The Modernization of Puerto Rico: A Political Study of Changing Values and Institutions.* Cambridge, Mass.: Harvard University Press, 1969.

Wilgus, A. Curtis, ed. *The Caribbean: British, Dutch, French, United States.* Gainesville, Fla.: University of Florida Press, 1963.

Winks, Robin. "American and European Imperialism Compared." In *American Imperialism in 1898.* Edited by Richard H. Miller. New York: Wiley, 1970.

Articles

Bailey, Thomas A. "Was the Election of 1900 a Mandate on Imperialism?" *Mississippi Valley Historical Review,* XXIV (June 1937), 43–52.

Clark, Truman R. " 'Educating the Natives in Self-Government': Puerto Rico and the United States, 1900–1933." *Pacific Historical Review,* XLII (May 1973), 220–33.

———. "Governor E. Mont. Reily's Inaugural Speech." *Caribbean Studies,* XI (January 1972), 106–08.

———. "President Taft and the Puerto Rican Appropriation Crisis of 1909." *The Americas: A Quarterly Review of Inter-American Cultural History,* XXVI (October 1969), 152–70.

Gatell, Frank Otto. "The Art of the Possible: Luis Muñoz Rivera and the Puerto Rican Jones Bill." *The Americas: A Quarterly Review of Inter-American Cultural History,* XVII (July 1960), 1–20.

———. "Independence Rejected: Puerto Rico and the Tydings Bill of 1936." *Hispanic American Historical Review,* XXXVIII (February 1958), 25–44.

Harrington, Fred H. "The Anti-Imperialist Movement in the United States, 1898–1900." *Mississippi Valley Historical Review,* XXII (September 1935), 211–30.

Lewis, Gordon K. "The Rise of the American Mediterranean." *Studies on the Left,* 2 (1961), 42–58.

Murray, Robert K. "Harding on History." *The Journal of American History,* LIII (March 1967), 781–84.

Pomeroy, Earl S. "The American Colonial Office." *Mississippi Valley Historical Review,* XXIX (March 1944), 521–32.

Whittaker, William George. "The Santiago Iglesias Case, 1901–1902: Origins of American Trade Union Involvement in Puerto Rico." *The Americas: A Quarterly Review of Inter-American Cultural History,* XXIV (April 1968), 378–93.

Index

Agriculture. *See Centrales;* Crops; Food; Sugar; Tobacco

Aguirre Central, 111. *See also Centrales*

Albizu Campos, Pedro: life of, 84–87; and emigration of Puerto Ricans, 131; mentioned, 145, 169. *See also* Nationalists

Alegría, José S.: joins Liberal Party, 145; mentioned, 84

Alianza: formation of, 80–82; dislike of Coolidge, 104; against replacement of Towner, 133; split, 144; mentioned, 91-101 *passim,* 137, 143, 158. *See also* Republican Union Party, Union Party

Allen, Governor Charles H.: on appointments by governors, 11–12; life of, 18; and "Lindbergh resolution," 102; mentioned, 8

Alliance Party. *See Alianza*

American Federation of Labor: policy about politics, 81; and Free Federation of Labor, 121; and Iglesias' conviction, 121; and strikes in Puerto Rico, 127; sends investigators, 129; complaints against, 170; mentioned, 123, 125, 126, 159. *See also* Free Federation of Laborers; Gompers, Samuel

"Americanism," 53, 66, 72. *See also* Americanization

Americanization: and education, 131, 136; goal of Governor Reily, 132; Governor Roosevelt's opposition to, 141; goal of Governor Gore, 160, 174; mentioned, 47, 66, 74

American Review of Reviews, The: praised Governor Towner, 99

Ames, Blanche, 152

Anglo-Saxon, 100, 164, 173

Anti-Americanism, 122, 175

Anti-imperialists, 161

Appointments: governors' powers of, 11, 21; by Governor Reily, 50, 60, 63–66, 68; presidential, 97, 165

Appropriation crisis, 11–12

Ashford, Dr. Bailey K.: denies ill health of Towner, 92; mentioned, 91

Assassinations, 3, 87

Autonomist Party, 3

Autonomy: in Foraker Act, 9; arguments against increase of, 13; views of Ana Roqué de Duprey, 45; in Jones Act, 162–66 *passim,* 172–73; views of U.S. officials about amount of, 174–75; mentioned, 100–03 *passim,* 131, 132. *See also* Status issue

Baker, Secretary of War Newton D.: opposes transfer of Puerto Rico from War Department, 27–28; mentioned, 25

Balzac v. *People of Porto Rico,* 162

Barceló, Antonio R.: and illegal stills in Puerto Rico, 34; and Unionists, 36, 144; and Food Commission, 38; and woman suffrage, 45; and *Estado Libre Asociado,* 82–83, 144; on 1923 commission, 88; coauthor of "Lindbergh resolution," 101; and literacy rate, 131; against replacement of Towner,